BRITISH CULT CINEM

THE HAMMER Vampire

Hemlock Books
England

PICTURE CREDITS: *Richard Klemensen, Wayne Kinsey, Denis Meikle, Gary Parfitt, John Hamilton, Doug Murray, Horror Connection, Universal Studios, Columbia Pictures, Magnet Releasing, 518 Media, WB Television Network, Warner Bros. Pictures, Vivendi Entertainment and Hammer Film Productions Limited. Any omissions will be corrected in future editions.*

Visit our website:
www.hemlockbooks.co.uk

First published in 2010 by
Hemlock Books Limited,
The Bristol Office,
2 Southfield Road,
Westbury-on-Trym,
Bristol
BS9 3BH

A CIP catalogue record for this book is available from the British Library.

ISBN 978-0-9557774-2-4

Design by Hemlock Books Limited.

Printed and bound in Great Britain by

CPI Antony Rowe, Chippenham and Eastbourne

BRITISH CULT CINEMA: THE HAMMER VAMPIRE

Bruce G Hallenbeck

Editorial Associate:
Denis Meikle

Acknowledgements

A great many people and institutions deserve my most profound thanks for their assistance in completing this book. In no particular order, I am extremely grateful to: Richard E Klemensen, for his amazing array of Hammer-related photographs and other material, The New York State Library, for providing me with all the research material that anyone could ask for, Wayne Kinsey, the late James Bernard, Walter L Gay, Ted Newsom, Isobel Black, Edward De Souza, Jennifer Daniel, Anthony Hinds, Veronica Carlson, the late Michael Ripper, the late Ralph Bates, Linda Hayden, Ingrid Pitt, Madeline Smith, the late Tudor Gates, the late Harry Robertson, the late Pippa Steele, Suzanna Leigh, Damien Thomas, Caroline Munro, the late Michael Carreras, Derek Whitehurst and Adrienne Corri. Last but not least, a very special thanks to my publisher and fearless editor, Denis Meikle, whose knowledge of the subject, editorial talent and skill at tracking down photographs are as impressive as his graphic design. I'm reminded of a dialogue exchange in *Dracula—Prince of Darkness*:, when Ludwig asks Father Sandor for his opinion of a newly-completed folio: 'Is it exquisite or merely magnificent?' 'Exquisite,' Sandor replies. Exquisite, Denis. Thank you so much for all your fine work.

CONTENTS

To my Aunt Barbara, for always being there;
and, as always, to Rosa, for being.

In all the darkest pages of the malign supernatural there is no more terrible tradition than that of the Vampire, a pariah even among demons. Foul are his ravages; gruesome and seemingly barbaric are the ancient and approved methods by which folk must rid themselves of this hideous pest. Even today in certain quarters of the world, in remoter districts of Europe itself, Transylvania, Slavonia, the isles and mountains of Greece, the peasant will take the law into his own hands and utterly destroy the carrion who—as it is yet firmly believed—at night will issue from his unhallowed grave to spread the infection of vampirism throughout the countryside.

—Montague Summers, *The Vampire: His Kith and Kin* (1928)

FOREWORD
by
Jimmy Sangster

(screenwriter of Hammer's *Dracula* and *The Brides of Dracula*)

Dracula was the second Gothic horror script I wrote for Hammer. *The Curse of Frankenstein* was the first and, I suppose, the one that launched the whole Gothic horror business. Both of them were written and made over 50 years ago.

Never having been exposed to earlier Dracula movies, I was starting from scratch. I read Bram Stoker's novel, loved every page, but realised right away there was too much material in it to cut down to 80 minutes, which was the maximum screen-time I was allowed. So, I went to work with a blue pencil. To this day, I hope I didn't ruin the story.

Subsequently I did a few more Gothics, both for Hammer and for other companies. Then I decided enough was enough.. no more Gothics. So I changed course and wrote 'psycho'-type movies, a couple of 'tits and swords' and a bunch of other stuff.

But, looking back, it was the Gothic horrors that gave me the most satisfaction and I'm pleased and proud that they are still around, giving pleasure to people who weren't even born when they were made.

And enjoy the book. I did.

Introduction

I have been haunted since I was five years old.

It was at that tender age that my sainted grandmother and my older cousin Russell took me to see *Dracula* (US title: *Horror of Dracula*) at the Valatie Theatre in my hometown of Valatie, New York. Film fans in Great Britain might be shocked to learn that, in 1958, when they had to be sixteen to see a horror film, we in the US had no such restrictions. I am not sure what that says about our cultural differences, but there it is.

Mind you, I was already a veteran of the Universal classics, even at age five. They had debuted on American television in November of 1957 under the umbrella title of *Shock Theatre*. I had seen James Whale's 1931 *Frankenstein* and Tod Browning's 1931 *Dracula* and had loved them both. Surely seeing Dracula on the big screen, whether or not he was played by Bela Lugosi, would simply be more of the same?

And so it was, on a fine August afternoon, that I was exposed to the horror of *Dracula*, in blazing Eastman colour. To say that it stayed with me is a gross understatement; it did indeed haunt me for years to come, its images burned into my young, developing brain. Through the eyes of a child, I seemed to interpret those images in a very dreamlike, irrational way.

For example: the opening shot of the stone eagle behind the credits impressed me at the time as overwhelming, as though the eagle were somehow moving of its own accord. Of course, it is the camera that is actually moving in the shot, but I did not realise that until I saw the film for a second time, aged twelve.

Then there was the opening of the film proper, with the coach arriving near the castle amidst beautiful autumn foliage. Autumn has always been my favourite time of year, but this was the first occasion on which I had seen it represented on the big screen. Bear in mind that most American films in those days were shot in southern California, where there are no distinct seasons to speak of.

Of course, the castle and the count within it both appeared to be quite different from what I had experienced in the Lugosi film, even at that age. I am sure I had no idea at the time as to who the actor was, but it seemed to me as though his hair was blue. That was a side-effect of Jack Asher's brilliant and moody lighting but, again, these childhood impressions remained with me over the years.

Needless to say, the film's climax was unforgettable. But to my five-year-old sense of logic, it was as though the 'good guy' caused Dracula to turn to ash by holding up candles. Any kind of light would destroy a vampire, right?

However, the scene that really haunted me, and does to this day, was the one that involved the newly-minted vampire, Lucy (Carol Marsh), and the little girl, Tania (Janina Faye). Again, my child's mind tended to fill the blanks in what I could not understand. Was Lucy sitting in a tree waiting for the little girl, or did she merely push aside a tree branch? And then she smiled, exposing those long, canine teeth. It was not a smile; it was a grin—a bit like those I had seen on the death's heads in Disney's classic 1929 cartoon, *The Skeleton Dance*, when it was broadcast on television a couple of years before. There was something extraordinarily frightening about that expression. I could not get it out of my mind.

(I do recall seeing at least one little boy run screaming from the theatre into the sunlight of that long-ago afternoon. But not me. I was enthralled, enchanted; yet it was not the gore or the dramatic action that impressed me that day. It was Lucy. It was that grin.)

Ultimately, that was what Hammer brought to the vampire film: that grin.. both sensual and terrifying—especially from the female of the species. Whereas Universal's vampire films had concentrated on the count and paid scant attention to his female victims once they became vampires, Hammer's did the opposite. Many, many frames of film were devoted to the activities of his full-bodied 'brides', who epitomised both sex and death. As we shall see, Hammer brought out the sexual element inherent in the vampire of literature, whether it be by Bram Stoker or Joseph Sheridan Le Fanu, and forever put to rest the idea of a florid, fangless vampire in a tuxedo, transforming the count into an attractive, autocratic seducer—'The terrifying lover who died yet lived!' screamed the poster—and turning his brides into predatory, wanton women of the night, who were just as likely to sink their fangs into female flesh—or even the flesh of a child—as into the throat of a red-blooded male.

And so the clichés of old were replaced, at a single stroke, by a new approach—which in turn was to become a cliché in itself.

Hammer made sixteen vampire films in all, many of them iconic. Without them, we would likely not have had *Dark Shadows*, *Buffy the Vampire Slayer*, *Interview with the Vampire*, *Twilight* or just about any other vampire film, television series, comic book or video game since 1958, at least not in the forms in which they are now recognisable. Hammer did not invent the vampire film, but it perfected it. It crafted the rules that all of its imitators followed. We are still seeing their influence in the media of today.

For those of you who might believe it to be a form of abuse to expose a young child to Hammer's original *Dracula* (which, of course, I begged to see at the time), I would point out that it never gave me nightmares but it did furnish me with a lifetime of inspiration. That August afternoon, lost to time, inspired me to learn all that I could about films and filmmaking, eventually leading me to make my own; it inspired me to read Stoker's novel when I was eleven and to begin writing when I was twelve, which led eventually to books and screenplays, and to a life devoted to artistic creativity. It inspired the volume that you hold in your hands.

Let us now explore what it was that made the Hammer vampire so special.

Prologue: The Vampire Film before Hammer

The guardians hastened to protect Miss Aubrey; but when they arrived, it was too late. Lord Ruthven had disappeared, and Aubrey's sister had glutted the thirst of a VAMPYRE!

—John Polidori, *The Vampyre: A Tale* (1819)

He drags her head to the bed's edge. He forces it back by the long hair still entwined in his grasp. With a plunge he seizes her neck in his fang-like teeth—a gush of blood, and a hideous sucking noise follows. The girl has swooned, and the vampyre is at his hideous repast!

—James Malcolm Rymer, *Varney the Vampyre; or, The Feast of Blood* (1845-7)

London After Midnight (Edna Tichenor, Lon Chaney)

It took the vampire a while to enter the dark realms of the cinema—surprising, in view of the fact that the undead had been a mainstay of both fiction and drama for nearly a century before film was invented. There were a number of false starts; film pioneer Georges Melies's 1896 short, *Le manoir du diable* (US: *The Haunted Castle*), is sometimes referred to as the first vampire film, but in fact it merely features the first example of what later would become a staple of vampire films: a bat transforming into a man—in this case, Mephistopheles. There was no actual vampirism involved in this two-minute short.

Nor were any supernatural bloodsuckers to be seen in Louis Feuillade's ground-breaking serial *Les vampires* (1915-16). The vampires in question were merely a gang of criminals, one of them a woman called Irma Vep (Musidora), whose name was an anagram of 'vampire'. Indeed, early vampires of the screen were most often 'vamps', such as Theda Bara (real name Theodosia Goodman), whose screen name was also an anagram, of 'Arab Death'. In her most famous film, *A Fool There Was* (1916), Bara was the epitome of the man-eating vamp, hissing 'Kiss me, you fool!' to her leading man. An outrageous personality both on and off the screen, she was often photographed surrounded by snakes and skulls. By the early 1920s, the fashion for vamps had faded and sweet, innocent types like Mary Pickford found public favour instead.

One of the last examples of 'vampish' cinema was Robert Wiene's *Genuine* (1920; aka *Genuine: A Tale of a Vampire*), a dream-like follow-up to the same director's seminal *The Cabinet of Dr Caligari* (1919). Fern Andra plays Genuine, a *femme fatale* who also happens to be the high priestess of an ancient cult. She ends up enslaving the hero to her will, but again, there is no genuine bloodsucking in sight.

Although the record shows a Hungarian production of 1921 called *Drakula halála* (aka *The Death of Drakula*), produced by one Károly Lajthay, this early version of the Stoker novel would appear to be a 'lost' film about which little is known. Recent research in Hungary

Nosferatu (Max Schreck)

has revealed that the film opened in Vienna in February 1921, but contemporary journals make it sound more like an adaptation of Gaston Leroux's *The Phantom of the Opera* than Stoker's *Dracula*. The few photos that survive show a sinister-looking, caped 'Drakula' played by Paul Askonas, but it seems to be the case that the name was 'borrowed' from Stoker, rather than the plot, which, according to the IMDb (Internet Movie Database), had to do with a girl (Margit Lutz) experiencing 'frightening visions after visiting an insane asylum where one of the inmates claims to be Drakula.. she cannot be sure whether they [the visions] were a nightmare or real'. No mention is made of vampires, real or imagined. It was left to master German filmmaker Friedrich Wilhelm Murnau to create the first (albeit unauthorised) screen version of Bram Stoker's tale, *Nosferatu, eine Symphonie des Grauens (Nosferatu: A Symphony of Horror*; 1922).

Many critics deem *Nosferatu* a masterpiece, not just of the horror film, but of cinema as a whole. It is the earliest 'true' vampire film to have survived—a miracle in itself, given that Stoker's widow Florence, on discovering that it was in effect a pirated version of her late husband's book, arranged for all copies to be destroyed. Fortunately, several copies escaped the reach of her legal facilitators.

While the basic plot of *Nosferatu* follows Stoker's novel fairly closely, the devil is in Murnau's detailing. The brooding Count Dracula is transformed into the balding, rat-headed Count Orlock (Max Schreck), who carries the plague to the German city of Bremen by exchanging his mouldering castle for an equally mouldering house across the way from that of pretty young Nina Hutter (Greta Schroeder). In the film's emblematic climax, it is she, not Stoker's Professor Van Helsing, who destroys the vampire by keeping him by her side until sunrise. At dawn, Orlock dissolves in the purifying rays of the morning sun, a metaphorical method of vampiric destruction that was entirely absent from Stoker's novel. It has since become a convention in vampire films.

Nosferatu (Max Schreck)

Now considered to be one of the greatest of all silents, *Nosferatu* did not exactly set the world on fire in 1922. To the contrary, the film itself was almost burned out of existence by legal writ. But mere breach of copyright could not keep a good vampire down for long; Florence Stoker's order to destroy all prints was unenforceable in Germany, although the lawsuit did force Murnau's production company, Prana Film, out of business. But all of the material relating to *Nosferatu*, including outtakes, was sold to Deutsche Film Produktion. A somewhat altered version, called *Die Zwoelfte Stunde* (*The Twelfth Hour*) was eventually released, and this was altered again before the film debuted in the United States in 1929.

This bowdlerised version, titled *Nosferatu the Vampire*, was reviewed in *The New York Times* on June 4, 1929. The critic, Mordaunt Hall, was singularly unimpressed by Murnau's epic, which surprisingly was still being sold as an adaptation of Stoker's *Dracula*. He wrote: 'Because of its age and also the extravagant ideas, *Nosferatu the Vampire*, a film supposed to have been inspired by the blood-curdling *Dracula*, is not especially stirring. It is the sort of thing one could watch at midnight without its having much effect upon one's slumbering hours. In fact yesterday at the Film Guild Cinema, where this production is now on view, there was at least one man who dozed audibly and another who was either terrified or was enjoying a forty or more winks.' Hall, who would later favourably review director Tod Browning's own adaptation of the novel, continued: 'It is a production that is rather more of a soporific than a thriller. Max Schreck's movements as Nosferatu are too deliberate to be lifelike.' Talk about missing the point!

The next vampire film of importance, and one that is often cited as the first American vampire feature, was Tod Browning's 1927 *London after Midnight* (UK title: *The Hypnotist*). In reality, however, this was just another *faux* vampire movie, which was actually a mystery with horror overtones. The great Lon Chaney played two roles, those of a London police detective and an alleged 'vampire', who turns out in the end to be the detective in disguise. But what a disguise it is!—Chaney's make-up being only slightly less grotesque than that of Max Schreck in *Nosferatu*. Chaney's vampire is all bulging eyes and teeth filed to points, adorned in top hat and opera cape as he prowls the foggy streets of London town. Again, not exactly the kind of vampire popularised in literature by John Polidori in his 1819 short story 'The Vampyre', in which the character of Lord Ruthven, a womanising, blood-drinking fiend, was largely modelled on Polidori's one-time employer and mentor, George Gordon, Lord Byron—from whom the kernel of the tale had also been pilfered.

Perhaps the most famous 'lost film' of all time, *London after Midnight* was very successful in 1927, despite the fact that it was one of the very last silent films to come out of Hollywood. Unfortunately, the last-known print of the film was destroyed in a fire in the M-G-M studio vaults in 1967, although rumours persist that another print (under its British title) still survives somewhere in Hollywood. Whatever the case, enough stills from the film existed to enable restoration specialist Rick Schmidlin to 'reconstruct' it from its original script for broadcast on American cable television channel Turner Classic Movies in 2002.

The extant photographs suggest that Chaney crept around like a spider when playing the vampire, with a hideous rictus grin on his face that was enhanced by the light from the antique lantern that he carried. This visage was so frightening to audiences at the time that it was actually used as part of the defence in a murder case: Robert Williams, who stood accused of slitting the throat of Julia Mangan in London's Hyde Park on October 23, 1928, attempted to convince the jury that he had acted out the deed in a state of 'epileptic automatism' brought on by a vision of Lon Chaney, whose bizarre countenance and performance he had just seen in *The*

London After Midnight (Marceline Day, Lon Chaney)

Hypnotist. The jury in the case was not that credulous and Williams was convicted of the crime regardless.

(Another interesting fact about the M-G-M film is that Browning regular Edna Tichenor, who played Lon Chaney's nocturnal accomplice Luna, set the pattern for vampire women for years to come. With her pale face, piercing eyes and long, dark hair, she inaugurated the image of the female of the species that pertained right up to that of American television horror hostess Vampira in the 1950s.)

London after Midnight may not have been a 'true' vampire film, but it was directed by the man who was instrumental in bringing the real thing to cinema audiences around the world. Kentucky-born Charles Albert 'Tod' Browning's sound version of *Dracula* (1931) not only established the benchmark for all that followed but, along with James Whale's *Frankenstein* in the same year, virtually created the genre of the 'horror film' as we know it today.

The fact that Universal and Tod Browning chose to base their film version of *Dracula* on the Hamilton Deane/John L Balderston stage play, rather than Bram Stoker's novel, is at once its greatest strength and also its most obvious weakness. The play had enjoyed much success on Broadway in 1927 and had firmly established the haughty character of Count Dracula—and, by extension, that of most male vampires—in the mould of the Byronic villain that Polidori had originally created. As portrayed on stage and later on-screen by Hungarian-born Bela Lugosi (Browning's first choice for the role, Lon Chaney, had died before the film was made), Dracula was no longer the elderly aristocratic gentleman of the novel, who became younger as events progressed through the ingesting of blood; he was instead an attractive and seductive figure, immaculately-attired in top hat, tails and opera cape.

In many respects, the Browning version set the stage for vampire films—indeed, all horror films—to come. Unlike *London after Midnight*, there was no 'trick' ending in *Dracula* to explain it all away as a plot to catch a killer; the vampires in the film were supernatural beings, through and through. Universal was so unsure of the efficacy of this new approach that they advertised *Dracula* as 'The strangest love story of all!' before its initial opening. Once audiences started to show up in droves, however, the ad lines became bolder: 'The human vampire is out! The dreaded terror of the undead is abroad in the land! Here he is! Count Dracula—dead 500 years—comes to life after sundown and returns to his grave before sunrise, after feasting on the blood of the living!—in the most sensational and amazing motion picture of all time!'

Bela Lugosi

It certainly impressed *The New York Times*'s critic Mordaunt Hall more than *Nosferatu* had. In the February 13, 1931 edition, Hall wrote: 'It is a production that evidently had the desired effect upon many in the audience yesterday afternoon, for there was a general outburst of applause when Dr Van Helsing produced a little cross that caused the dreaded Dracula to fling his cloak over his head and make himself scarce.' In an aside, Hall noted of actor Dwight Frye that he 'does fairly well

Dracula (Bela Lugosi)

Drácula (Carlos Villarias, Eduardo Arozamena)

as Renfield'; Frye was to become as identified with that role as Lugosi would be with Count Dracula.

To accommodate the demands of the burgeoning South American film market, a second version of *Dracula* was produced at Universal concurrent with that of Browning; the English-speaking version shot during the day, and George Melford's Spanish-language version shot at night on the same sets as Browning's and utilising most of the same costumes. Melford's film is superior to Browning's in almost every respect; there is more *décolletage* on display, the camerawork is more fluid and the film on the whole is a more polished affair. The Spanish crew had the advantage of being allowed to view the 'dailies' of the bigger-budgeted Browning film before labouring on their own version throughout the night. As a result, they attempted to top the official studio version by coming up with more imaginative camera angles, more overt hints of sexuality and more textured lighting.

Whereas much of Browning's *Dracula* is a case of staginess and missed opportunities, Melford's film fills in the blanks; it runs some twenty minutes longer and the direction is far more cinematic. Carlos Villarias is no Lugosi, and he tends to leer his way through the role of the count, but everything else about the production is first-rate. In accentuating the sexual element of the myth, it also pointed to the future—unlike Browning's film, which seemed to be afflicted by a certain prudishness in that respect.

The vampire film was finally beginning to make its mark, but the next past the post was a very different concoction. Danish director Carl Theodor Dreyer's *Vampyr* (aka *The Strange Adventure of David Gray*; 1932) is a free-wheeling, almost unrecognisable adaptation of Joseph Sheridan Le Fanu's 1871 novella, 'Carmilla'. Dreyer was one of the finest filmmakers of his time; his silent 1928 film *La passione de Jeanne d'Arc* (US: *The Passion of Joan of Arc*) is widely regarded as a masterpiece. Known curiously in the US as *Not Against the Flesh*, Dreyer's only vampire film is

Vampyr (Henriette Gérard)

suffused with surrealism. Made independently by Dreyer with the help of friends, and with his chief financial backer, Julian West, in the leading role, *Vampyr* is an exercise in atmosphere and impression—a mood piece that attempts, and invariably succeeds, in creating the sensation of a very curious dream.

Dreyer turned the tale of 'Carmilla' on its head. Le Fanu's Carmilla was a beautiful young woman who happened to be a vampire; Dreyer's version transformed the character (renamed Marguerite [Henriette Gérard]) into a white-haired, withered old crone—more or less the clichéd depiction of a witch. This drained the film of the adolescent sexual tension inherent in Le Fanu's story, but then that was not what Dreyer was looking for. Nevertheless, *Vampyr* does contain one sensually-striking scene, in which virginal innkeeper's daughter Gisèle (Rena Mandel), confined to her bed, suddenly becomes aware of her vampiric nature; her features gradually contort into a devilish grin, like that of Lucy in Hammer's later *Dracula*, which seems to promise both the torrid and the terrifying in equal measure.

Apparently, subtlety was not what audiences of the time were looking for. As with *Nosferatu*, some vampire films which are now considered masterpieces were overlooked in their day, and *Vampyr* was another victim of audience expectation. In *The New York Times* of January 15, 1933, under the headline 'Paris views new films and theatres', an anonymous writer noted, 'It is a hallucinating film, "dubbed" from the German, which either held the spectators spellbound as in a long nightmare or else moved them to hysterical laughter, thus entirely counteracting the truly weird effects of the photography and story.'

Other Hollywood studios soon began to cash in on the success of Universal's *Dracula*. 1933 also saw the release of Majestic's *The Vampire Bat*, starring Lionel Atwill and Fay Wray, which, like the Spanish *Dracula* before it, was shot cheaply at night on Universal's *Frankenstein* village set. However, the 'vampire' in the tale was a mad scientist (Atwill) who has created an artificial life-form that needs blood

Mark of the Vampire (Carol Borland, Bela Lugosi)

Dracula's Daughter (Gloria Holden, Otto Kruger, Irving Pichel)

to survive. Invincible's *Condemned to Live* (1935) featured a mad doctor (Ralph Morgan) whose mother had been bitten by a vampire bat during pregancy, which produces the predictable result in her unfortunate offspring.

Tod Browning's third and final vampire film, *Mark of the Vampire* (1935), is one of the most frustrating films of its kind ever made. Bela Lugosi was back in his Dracula cloak as 'Count Mora'—the surname culled from Dreyer's *Vampyr*—complete with a screen daughter named Luna who was portrayed by the hauntingly-beautiful Carol Borland. The original story by Guy Endore had an incestuous undertone which presaged many of the Hammer 'vampers' of later years, but censorship assured that all such references would be struck out of the final film. What is left is one of the most visually atmospheric vampire films of all time, stunningly photographed by James Wong Howe—and with one of the most disappointing endings in the history of horror. *Mark of the Vampire* is actually a thinly-disguised remake of *London after Midnight*, in which everything eerie is explained away at the climax when a detective (Lionel Barrymore) succeeds in exposing a murderer with the help of actors portraying supernatural creatures! Too bad; there is a moment in the film when Borland *hisses* at one of her victims, something that Hammer's vampires would specialise in. But the fact that Borland sprouts bat wings at one point in the proceedings is never explained—how could an actress out to trap a murderer achieve such a feat?

More often than not, female vampires were given short shrift in early films of the genre; they were either old hags, as in Dreyer's *Vampyr*, or angst-ridden, sexually-repressed young women, as in Lambert Hillyer's *Dracula's Daughter* (1936), Universal's belated sequel to *Dracula*. Supposedly based on 'Dracula's Guest', a discarded chapter of Bram Stoker's novel which was omitted for reasons of length and published as a stand-alone short story in 1914, *Dracula's Daughter* has nothing to do with Stoker beyond the fact that its protagonist is female. The original tale had to do with the haunted tomb of a Countess Dolingen of Gratz; the film features the enigmatic Gloria Holden as Countess Marya Zaleska, in reality the daughter of Count Dracula but herself a somewhat reluctant vampire. A clever and rather sophisticated film for the era, *Dracula's Daughter* is mainly remembered today for its implicit lesbianism, specifically in the scene where Zaleska attempts to put the bite on a streetwalker whom she has picked up (Nan Grey). It was the first vampire film to touch on the inherently-androgynous nature of its supernatural fiend, but there would be many more when censorship went the way of the wind in the late 1960s.

It is the brothers Siodmak's often-maligned *Son of Dracula* (1943), however, that may well be Universal's most interesting vampire movie from a thematic standpoint. Although some critics found fault with the casting of Lon Chaney Jr as Count Alucard, who is either Dracula's son or the Count himself (take your pick; it is never satisfactorily explained), *Son of Dracula* foreshadows the Hammer approach in many ways. Directed with considerable style by Robert Siodmak from a story by his brother Curt, *Son of Dracula* is one of the few vampire movies of any era to explore the notion that someone might actually *choose* to become a vampire. Katherine Caldwell (Louise Albritton) is decorously described as 'a woman with a taste for the morbid', and she is drawn to Count Alucard, whom she 'marries' in a midnight ceremony. She willingly submits to Alucard, becomes a vampire herself, and proceeds to attack her former lover (Robert Paige). Laden with surrealist imagery and heavy hints of deviant sexual behaviour (Caldwell *marries* the count, after all—so vampires are inferred to have a sex-life), and with a downbeat ending unprecedented in horror films of the period, *Son of Dracula* was also the first film to graphically depict the physical power of Stoker's 'Un-dead', thanks to Chaney's imposing presence. Robert Siodmak would go from here to the more aberrant psychological territory of *The Spiral Staircase* (1945).

Lew Landers's more conventional *The Return of the Vampire* (1943) is usually referred to as a 1944 release, but in fact it played in America's hinterlands as early as November 1943 before opening in New York in January 1944. Lugosi predictably plays Armand Tesla, who acts the innocent but looks suspiciously like Dracula. Instead of a gibbering Renfield, Tesla is alotted a werewolf named Andreas (Matt Willis) for an assistant, who has a change of heart at the end of the film and drives a stake through his master—whose waxen face then melts to bone in a close-up that was removed from British prints. A serviceable and entertaining Columbia B-movie, *The Return of the Vampire* was stylishly directed by Landers and novel in that it was set contemporaneously in war-time (Nazi bombers actually help in defeating the monster!), but it added little new to the genre.

By the mid-1940s, the Universal horrors had begun to run out of steam and its series of 'monster rallies', which pitted all of the studio's monsters—Dracula, Frankenstein, The Wolf Man and more—against one another in the same films, kicked off with *House of Frankenstein* (1944). John Carradine played Dracula for the first of several times in his career, and a very suave and sophisticated count he was, too. Reduced to a pile of bones at sunrise in *House of Frankenstein*, he somehow managed to turn up unscathed in the following year's *House of Dracula*, in which vampirism was treated for the first time as a physical 'disease'—another theme which would resurface at Hammer. Attempts to cure him of his affliction fail, however, and he succumbs to skeletal mode once more.

A minor gem of the genre came in the form of Republic's *The Vampire's Ghost*, in which John Abbott played bar-owner and centuries-old vampire Webb Fallon in the unlikely setting of darkest Africa. One scene has Fallon survive a potentially fatal

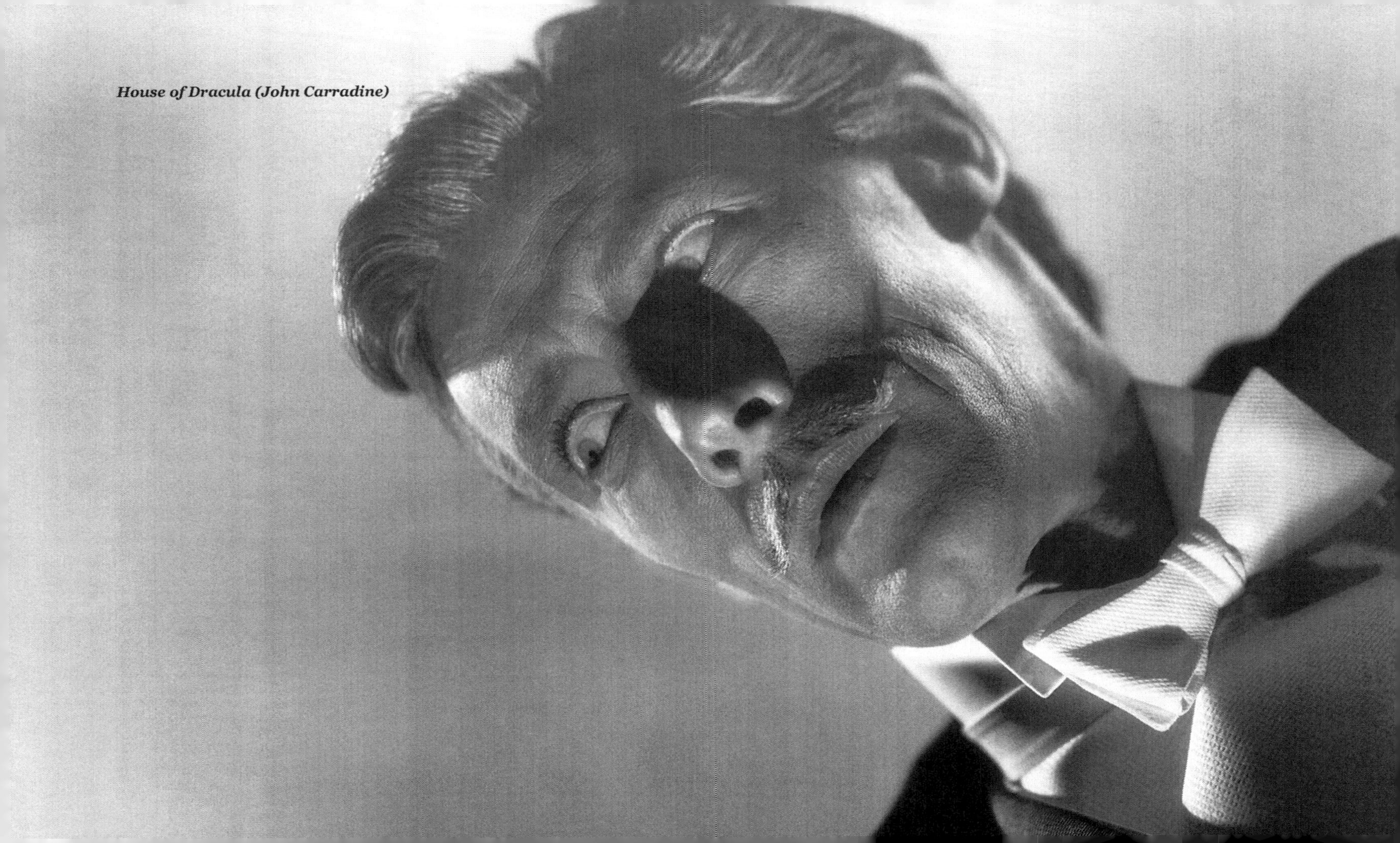

House of Dracula (John Carradine)

Abbott and Costello Meet Frankenstein (Bela Lugosi, Lou Costello)

spear-thrust by regenerating himself in the light of the moon, and screenwriter Leigh Bracket cited Polidori's 'The Vampyre', in which Lord Ruthven employs the same means to survive a gunshot wound, as the main influence on the film.

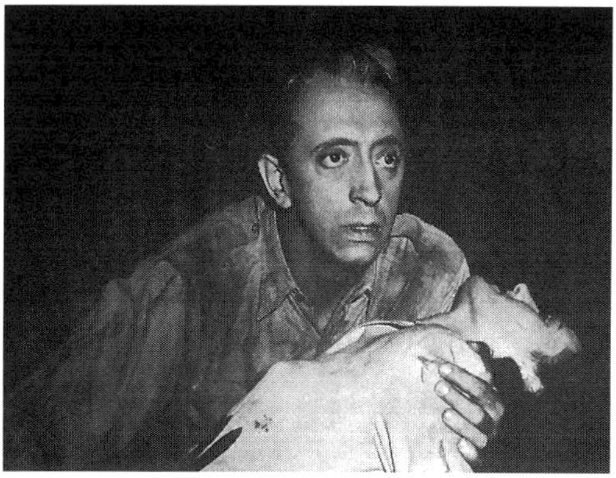

The Vampire's Ghost (John Abbott)

Bela Lugosi reprised the role of Dracula in *Abbott and Costello Meet Frankenstein* (UK: *..Meet the Ghosts*, 1948) and somehow managed to retain his dignity in the process. One of the great comedy-horror films of all time, *Abbott and Costello Meet Frankenstein* was also the final nail in the coffin of Universal horror. In his sixties at the time of its production and already addicted to drugs, the ailing Lugosi was no longer regarded as a sex symbol. The whole Universal horror cycle died with this and succeeding Abbot and Costello pastiches, and Lugosi's career died along with them. One of his last appearances was as the now-stereotypical vampire count in 1952's *Old Mother Riley Meets the Vampire*—a minor programme-filler that was not exactly the highlight of anyone's career, including that of writer-director John Gilling, who would go on from there to helm many a Hammer horror.

One of the more unusual adaptations of Stoker's novel, *Drakula Istanbul'da* (1953) was a Turkish take on the story. Rarely seen by Western audiences, it is a relatively faithful version of the book, with Atif Kaptan making an imposing figure of the count and sporting bat-like teeth, similar to those of *Nosferatu*. The Christian icons of the traditional vampire myth were replaced by those of Islam; this vampire

El Vampiro (Ariadna Welter, Germán Robles)

did not fear the cross but copies of the holy *Quran*. It offered a unique slant on the tale, but it was one which ultimately had no influence on the genre outside of its native country.

Drakula Istanbul'da (Atif Kaptan)

Early in 1953, a rechristened Universal-International (derived from the old Universal Pictures) touted its plan to produce a 3-D film of Le Fanu's 'Carmilla', no doubt spurred by the box-office success of Warners' *House of Wax*. *The New York Times* of February 3 reported on the proposed feature under the headline, 'U-I plots movie about a vampire'. Thomas M Pryor's article read, in part: 'Universal-International is in the market for an actress who would like to play a vampire, perhaps in three dimensions. The studio has a suitable story property in *Carmilla*, a novel by Sheridan Le Fanu, in which the heroine, if such she may be called, comes out of her grave in the dark of night, kills a couple of unsuspecting persons and then sets out to get revenge on a few of her one-time lovers. DeWitt Bodeen is writing the screen play, and Ross Hunter, producer, is on the hunt for an actress to take over where Bela Lugosi left off some time ago in the Dracula-type high jinks..' Think about it: a 3-D version of 'Carmilla', written by the screenwriter of *Cat People* (1942) and produced by a man who was soon to be famous for lightweight romantic comedies featuring Doris Day and Rock Hudson? Needless to say, the project died on the vine, doomed to exist only in what

I vampiri

Famous Monsters of Filmland editor Forrest Ackerman used to call 'The Realm of Unwrought Things'.

Bela Lugosi died in August 1956, at a time when the fortunes of Hollywood vampires were at their lowest ebb (his last role had been in Ed Wood's *Plan 9 from Outer Space*). When he was buried in his Dracula cloak, it was the end of an era: science fiction had replaced horror, and vampires and ghosts had been sidelined by atomic mutations and blobs from outer space. The image of the vampire on screen, which had prevailed for more than a querter of a century, was the image of Lugosi, and it seemed for a while that the book on Gothic bloodsuckers was now closed. But that was about to change: the king-vampire may have been laid to his final rest, but a new king was waiting to ascend the throne.

Quietly, the first stirrings of a Gothic revival were beginning to be felt in some surprising parts of the world. In the year of Lugosi's death, Italian director Riccardo Freda—with a little help from cinematographer, Mario Bava—made *I vampiri* (US: *The Devil's Commandment*), the first horror film to have been made in Italy since the war. The 'vampires' in *I vampiri* were of the scientific kind, experimenting in the rejuvenation of corpses through the use of blood drained from female victims, but the film was redolent with Gothic atmosphere and its plot was plundered from Mary Elizabeth Braddon's 1896 short story 'Good Lady Ducayne', as well as the real-life escapades of historical 'vampire' Elisabeth Bathory, who reputedly bathed in the blood of virgins to preserve her youthful looks. The legend of the 'Bloody Countess' was one to which Hammer would also turn, some years further down the line.

In 1957, a Mexican director by the name of Fernando Méndez devised an old-fashioned, non-science fictional vampire film called, simply, *El vampiro*. Although styled largely after the old Universal classics and elegantly photographed in glowing monochrome, its vampire Count Karol de Lavud (Germán Robles) briefly sported for the first time what has since become the cinematic norm: fangs. Not the jagged rat-

I vampiri (Gianna Maria Canale)

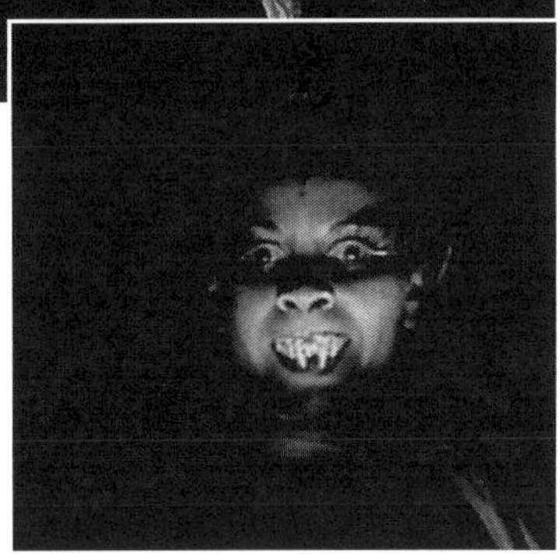

Blood of Dracula (Sandra Harrison)

teeth of Schreck or Kaptan, but the elongated canines of Stoker's count ('..*the sharp, canine teeth lying over the red under-lip..*') that have graced the maws of these creatures of the night in nearly every vampire film since.

In the wake of 3-D and the sc-fi 'boom' that followed it, American studios of the late 1950s remained in thrall to the mutant possibilities of science: Herbert L Strock's generically-titled *Blood of Dracula* (UK: *Blood Is My Heritage*) from American-International produced only a hybrid 'vampire' in pretty Sandra Harrison, after she fell foul of a nutty chemistry teacher intent on saving the world from atomic armageddon by subjecting her to bouts of hypnotic regression. (AIP's B-movies were more than usually populated by such scientific 'pioneers'.)

But one American vampire film from that era presaged of things to come. 1958's *The Return of Dracula* (UK: *The Fantastic Disappearing Man*) from director Paul Landres may still have featured a fangless vampire in former matinee idol Francis Lederer, but alerted by the imminent release of a new and gorier version of Stoker's novel, the mainly black-and-white film was distinguished by a single colour 'insert' of a phallic stake being driven into the chest of a buxom vampire woman (Virginia Vincent), bright red blood welling up around the wooden shaft. (A previous Landres effort, called simply *The Vampire*, had featured the creature in name only, when an experimental scientist [John Beal] accidentally ingested bat-blood and transformed himself into a Jekyll-and-Hyde monster with an uncontrollable urge to kill.)

However, the real revival in popularity of the Un-dead came from England that same year. The cultural *zeitgeist* seemed to be moving in the direction of an injection of new blood into the horror film as a whole and the vampire legend in particular. The cinema audience hungered for it. And it came, finally, from a small production company based at the tiny Bray Studios complex on the banks of the River Thames, near Windsor.

A company called Hammer Film Productions.

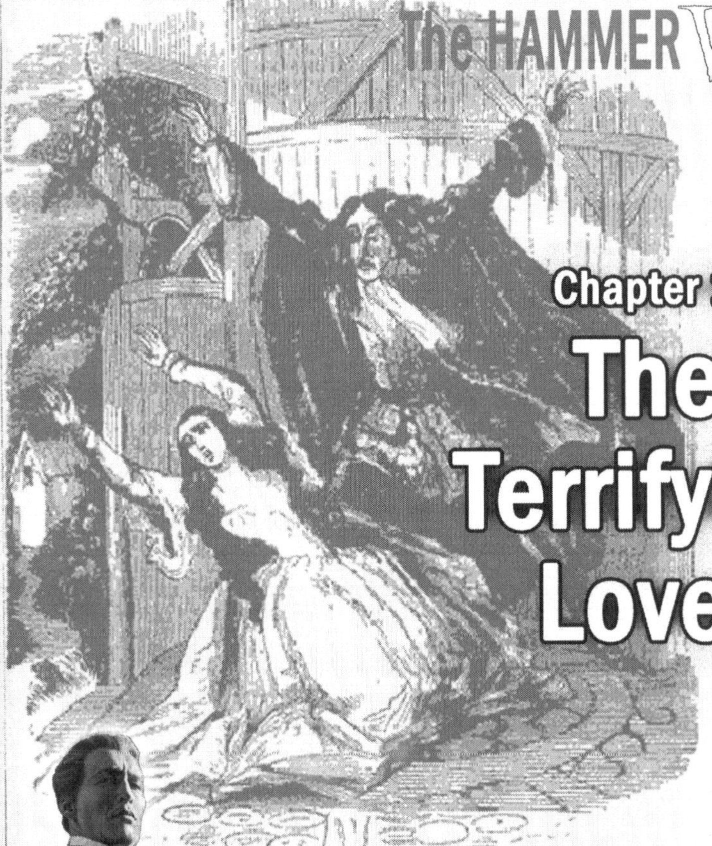

Chapter 1: The Terrifying Lover

'With a mocking smile, he placed one hand upon my shoulder and, holding me tight, bared my throat with the other, saying as he did so: "First, a little refreshment to reward my exertions. You may as well be quiet; it is not the first time, or the second, that your veins have appeased my thirst!" I was bewildered, and, strangely enough, I did not want to hinder him. I suppose it is a part of the horrible curse that this happens when his touch is on his victim. And oh, my God, my God, pity me! He placed his reeking lips upon my throat!'

—Bram Stoker, *Dracula* (1897)

Dracula (Peter Cushing)

Hammer Film Productions had hit it big in May 1957, when Warner Brothers released its first colour Gothic horror film, *The Curse of Frankenstein*, upon an unsuspecting public. After years of making low-budget but highly efficient B-movies for release on the bottom half of double-bills, Hammer had tested the waters of the horror/sci-fi genres with *The Quatermass Xperiment* (1955), based on Nigel Kneale's famous BBC Television serial. But that had been made in Hammer's usual B-movie style, featuring a fading American star (Brian Donlevy), and filmed in black and white. *The Curse of Frankenstein*, on the other hand, was in lavish Eastman colour (courtesy of brilliant lighting cameraman Jack Asher) and featured an entirely British cast, headed by Peter Cushing as Baron Frankenstein, Christopher Lee as the creature and Hazel Court as the damsel in distress, heaving her ample bosom in a variety of low-cut gowns. It was a formula that clicked with audiences from the off.

Just how much it clicked is evident in Hammer managing director James Carreras's breathless letter to his production partner Eliot Hyman on July 7, 1957: 'I enclose a new batch of figures which are quite fantastic. England is sweltering in a heat wave and NOTHING is taking any money except *The Curse of Frankenstein*.. Tony Hinds and Michael are busy on *Blood of Frankenstein* and I feel sure that we have another terrific winner on our hands.. Reply before July 22nd please. PS. DRACULA???'

It made perfect sense; Hammer had revived the Gothic horror movie with its own version of Mary Shelley's *Frankenstein*. The Universal horrors of the thirties and forties had often put Dracula and Frankenstein features together on double bills, and sometimes even paired the characters in the same movies. Bram Stoker's *Dracula* was the other great classic of Gothic literature, after *Frankenstein*; to re-do *Dracula* was the next logical step.

The rights to the book, however, were confusing. Jimmy Sangster, a former production manager for Hammer who had written the screenplay for *The Curse of Frankenstein*, was naturally assigned to pen its version of *Dracula*. As he later pointed out in his book, *Inside Hammer*, there was a lot of legal wrangling to be done first: 'It very nearly didn't get made at all. An author's work doesn't reach public domain until fifty years after his death. Bram Stoker had died in 1912, meaning that it would be 1962 before his novel *Dracula* would become public property. In other

words, Hammer had to search around to see who owned the rights. It was a long and arduous business. There had been at least half-a-dozen dramatisations based on *Dracula*, both on screen and on stage. Hammer went to Universal, who had bought the rights in 1930 from Stoker's widow, to make sure they hadn't sold them on. Apparently they hadn't and, after long negotiations, Hammer bought the rights with one of the conditions that Universal acquired worldwide distribution.'

Hammer was not interested in basing its version on Hamilton Deane's stage play, as Universal had done. Company co-director and house producer Tony Hinds wanted to go back to the novel. Hammer lawyer Edwin Davis drew up an 80-page contract granting Universal-International the distribution rights in exchange for granting Hammer permission to produce the property. U-I would retitle the film *Horror of Dracula* in the States so that it would not be confused with the Lugosi version, which they had re-issued several times. In the UK, however, the film was known simply as *Dracula*.

An article in the July 29, 1957, issue of *Today's Cinema* announced the upcoming feature: 'James Carreras [said] on Friday that Exclusive, who have the rights on *Dracula*, are planning a big-scale remake of the famous thriller. To be made in colour, *Dracula* will go on the floor at an early date. *The Curse of Frankenstein*, by the way, is now the sixth highest grosser in America—this picture can't go wrong!'

Sangster had received a mere £500 to write *The Curse of Frankenstein*. In his book, he told of his reaction to the request from Hinds that he now write the screenplay for *Dracula*: 'Do I get paid?' he asked. The answer was yes, but not very much. Sangster continued: 'Hell, I'd only been writing about eighteen months. What did I know about what writers were supposed to be paid?'

Sangster was given his orders regarding his adaptation of Stoker's novel, in which solicitor's clerk Jonathan Harker famously travels to Castle Dracula in the Carpathian mountains to finalise the count's purchase of an estate near Whitby, only to discover that his host is in fact a centuries-old vampire intent on relocating to England and feeding off the populace of his chosen domicile: 'Once again, aspects of the script were controlled by the budget restrictions that Hammer worked under. I truly believe that one of the reasons Tony Hinds employed me as much as he did at the off was because he knew I was aware of Hammer's way of working and I wasn't going to write anything into my scripts that they couldn't afford to shoot. Therefore—no night-time voyage in a stormy sea. Better to keep the whole piece in Ruritania/Transylvania land.'

Aside from those instructions, however, Sangster was given a free rein. Hammer had encountered some censorship problems over *The Curse of Frankenstein*, but it was exactly those controversial elements that had made the film such a success. There was blood, there were intimations of illicit sex in those heaving bosoms, and it was all set in a heightened and highly-coloured atmosphere of Gothic grotesquery. Why tamper with a winning formula?

No sooner was *Dracula* sanctioned for the Hammer 'treatment' than Hinds thought to extend the company's incursion into the world of vampires by optioning the rights to author Richard Matheson's 1954 novel, *I Am Legend*. The novel told of a world overrun by vampires, and of one man's struggle to survive in a fortified home against nightly assaults by hordes of the blood-sucking beasts. Hinds signed *Quatermass*'s Val Guest to direct and the author himself to provide the screenplay, but the project was not to stay on Hammer's schedule for long; censors on both sides of the pond immediately took fright at Matheson's mix of violence and profane language and the proposed film version of his book, under its new title of *Night*

Dracula (Christopher Lee)

Creatures, was given an unequivocal thumbs down. The screen was not yet ready for a full-on onslaught of fanged fiends, or the graphic means by which they had traditionally to be destroyed. *Night Creatures* was sold off to second-feature producer (and former Hammer partner) Robert Lippert, and Hinds was forced to be a little more cautious over bringing folklore's most fearsome monster bang up to date for a modern audience.

And so *Dracula* alone went into production on November 11, 1957, with the same team behind the scenes who had created *The Curse of Frankenstein*: director Terence Fisher, producer Hinds, lighting cameraman Asher and art director Bernard Robinson. Once again, Peter Cushing was the star (in this case vampire-hunter Van Helsing) and Christopher Lee was the 'creature' (Dracula). Valerie Gaunt, who had played ill-fated maid Justine in *The Curse of Frankenstein*, returned as the count's vampire 'bride' (whom Hammer economies had pared down to a mere one from Stoker and Universal's original three!) Other cast members included Michael Gough as Arthur Holmwood—another expedient combination of Stoker's several stalwart antagonists—and Melissa Stribling as his wife, Mina.

Sangster had completely streamlined the novel. The action of Stoker's sprawling Gothic epic was now confined to Jonathan Harker's ill-fated visit to Castle Dracula, followed by the count's pursuit of Harker's fiancée and others in her immediate family before Van Helsing settles his hash at the climax. Many of its more famous characters were missing altogether in the revision, as he noted in *Inside Hammer*: 'I've been asked on numerous occasions whether or not I omitted the character of the fly-eating Renfield for budgetary reasons. The answer to this is no. The character in the book spends most of his time in a cell and would have cost very little to shoot. If I'd thought he added to the plot, I would have kept him in. But when making decisions like this, as well as the budget, one has to bear in mind the running time of

***Dracula* (John Van Eyssen, Valerie Gaunt)**

Dracula (John Van Eyssen)

the finished movie. Remember, way back then, a programme consisted of two features, along with news and trailers, so the idea was to keep 'em short. The final running time was eighty-two minutes.'

Sangster may have kept it short, but what he did include was more interesting than what he chose to leave out. This time, the Victorian women upon whom Dracula preyed were all too willing to give in to his advances. Instead of being mesmerised into submission by the count's hypnotic gaze, they lay in wait for him in their beds in a state of sexual tension, as though anticipating a midnight visit from a secret love. Sangster, along with Fisher and Hinds, was intent on remaking the image of the predatory vampire into much more of a 'demon lover' than Lugosi had ever been: 'The terrifying lover who died—yet lived!' as the ads were to proclaim. Helped enormously by Lee's characterisation of the count, Dracula was no longer to be feared simply because he was a monster; now he was to be feared twice over because he was also devilishly

***Dracula* (Valerie Gaunt, John Van Eyssen)**

attractive—he still brought terror and death to his victims, but he was to promise them a sexual thrill-ride along the way.

Just as importantly, Hammer's *Dracula* wasted no time in revealing to the audience how deadly the female of the species could be. Gaunt's vampire woman gets to show her fangs before Dracula does when she bites the unwitting Jonathan Harker (John Van Eyssen) on the neck before the count bursts onto the scene, eyes blazing, mouth caked with blood. It is one of the watershed scenes of the British horror film—indeed, of horror cinema as a whole. The 'library scene', as it has come to be called, established the iconography of Hammer Horror perfectly, and Fisher's theories about the 'attraction of evil' were never more graphically illustrated: the vampire woman is full-bodied, her voluptuous lips intimating not only a lust for blood but a lust for the flesh, while Dracula, who previously has been presented as an urbane, well-mannered aristocrat, suddenly shows himself to be a demon from Hell. Masterfully staged by Fisher, complete with well-timed shock-cuts, it is an extraordinary scene that perfectly captures the tone of Stoker's book: '*I was conscious of the presence of the Count, and of his being as if lapped in a storm of fury. As my eyes opened involuntarily I saw his strong hand grasp the slender neck of the fair woman and with giant's power draw it back, the blue eyes transformed with fury, the white teeth champing with rage, and the fair cheeks blazing red with passion. But the Count! Never did I imagine such wrath and fury, even to the demons of the pit. His eyes were positively blazing. The red light in them was lurid, as if the flames of hell-fire blazed behind them. His face was deathly pale, and the lines of it were hard like drawn wires.. With a fierce sweep of his arm, he hurled the woman from him.*'

The scene that follows takes place in Dracula's crypt beneath the castle and deviates slightly from Sangster's screenplay. Sangster wrote the staking of the vampire woman to be filmed quite explicitly; Fisher chose to have the camera cut from Harker raising the hammer to a shot of his shadow when he drives the stake into her body. Then there are a series of shock cuts: Dracula lying in his coffin, his eyes jerking open when the woman screams; then back to a medium close-up of Harker as he drives the stake in again until the woman is still. By that time, however, Dracula has seen the sun setting outside the window of the crypt, and he smiles grimly at Harker's poor timing—not to mention the fact that Harker, who in Sangster's script is an ally of Van Helsing out to destroy vampirism forever, has made the fatal mistake of staking Dracula's bride *before* proceeding to the count.

Fisher then cuts to the woman in the coffin; she has been transformed into a wrinkled crone and is now played by another actress, an old lady on whom no special make-up was required. As Fisher later pointed out: 'She suggested that she remove her false teeth to draw in her face. The only thing she didn't like one little bit was getting into the coffin. She was very upset about that, so I gave her a kiss, which reassured her it was all in fun.'

Fisher departs from Sangster's script again at the end of this sequence. Page 25 of the screenplay has Harker turn from the woman's coffin to discover that Dracula's coffin is now empty. As written, the script reads:

> **EYELINE TO DOOR**
>
> **The door of the mausoleum is just swinging shut. Even as we see it, it slams hard with a solid clunk and practically all light is cut off.**
>
> **After a moment there is a shuffle of feet, a small gasp, then there is silence again.**
>
> **The silence stretches and stretches for as long as it can be held.**
>
> **Then there is a scream, a wild, pain-filled scream, that pierces the silence**

like a knife. On the high point of the scream we
DISSOLVE

In *Inside Hammer*, Sangster finds a problem with this scene as Fisher filmed it: 'The film has Harker turn from the empty coffin of Dracula towards the doorway at the top of the stairs, where Dracula makes an entrance. Fine, but it raises the question, where has he been? At least, it does with me.'

It is safe to say that few audiences at the time had this concern; they were too busy screaming their heads off. When I first saw the film as a child, I recall one particular smart-aleck of a teenager making a comment when the camera first settled on Valerie Gaunt's voluptuous body lying in the sarcophagus. 'She's faking!' he sniggered—'You can see her breathe!' But the youngster shut his mouth quickly when the stake came down and I distinctly remember a boy, probably about my own age, running down the aisle of the theatre at this point. He never came back.

The censors had done what they could to prevent scenes such as this from reaching the screen, however. Hinds had submitted Sangster's second draft of the script to John Nicholls, Secretary of the British Board of Film Censors (BBFC), on October 8. Reader Audrey Field was outraged, as she wrote on October 14: 'The uncouth, uneducated, disgusting and vulgar style of Mr Jimmy Sangster cannot quite obscure the remnants of a good horror story, though they do give one the gravest misgivings about treatment. I never read the original story, and do not remember the first film, though I know it had a great effect on me when I saw it at the age of sixteen or thereabouts. It seems to me that there is nothing censorable in the story as a whole but a good deal to complain of in details. The curse of the thing is Technicolor blood: why need vampires be messier feeders than anyone else? Certainly strong cautions will be necessary on shots of blood. And, of course, some of the stake-work is prohibitive.'

Nicholls went into further detail in his letter to Hinds dated October 21: 'It is important that the women in the film should be decently clad, not seen in transparent nightgowns or with bared breasts, or in unduly suggestive garments. I would add that anything which cross-emphasises the sex aspect of the story is likely, in a horror subject of this kind, to involve cuts in the completed film.'

Although the budget for *Dracula* was relatively modest (£81,412), as was usual for Hammer, the production values were lavish, thanks in large part to Bernard Robinson's magnificent sets and Jack Asher's splendid colour photography. To ensure the film of a certain freshness, Sangster, Hinds and Fisher had decided that this Dracula would avoid the clichés which the Universal canon had established; in Sangster's script, Van Helsing is quick to dismiss the idea that vampires can transform themselves into bats and wolves: 'A common fallacy,' he announces dismissively. As Denis Meikle points out in his book *A History of Horrors: The Rise and Fall of the House of Hammer*: '*This* Dracula was a creature of flesh and blood—warm flesh and blood, at that. His potency lay in his *charm*—no need of "hypnosis" to subdue his victims. From a female perspective, he was an idol of *desire*.' In an interview for the BBC-TV documentary *The Studio that Dripped Blood*, Hinds remarked, 'I didn't want the old florid, puffy-faced Dracula of Lugosi; Christopher Lee was sexually attractive.'

Quoted by Wayne Kinsey in his *Hammer Films: The Bray Studios Years*, Fisher said that he held definite views from the outset as to how he intended to approach the character of the count: 'Even when I came to shoot the Dracula films.. I still did not consult Bram Stoker's novel or the Transylvanian vampire legends. I think my greatest contribution to the Dracula myth was to bring out the underlying sexual element in the story. I also believe that the first Dracula film is just about the best thing I ever did for Hammer and it still looks a very successful film; everything seemed to hang together for once during the shooting.'

But more elements than the count were given a fresh lick of paint in Hammer's adaptation. In the film, Dracula's castle appears relatively new and well-kept, unlike Lugosi's mouldering ruin. This was all thanks to Bernard Robinson's magnificent sets, as his widow Margaret explained to Kinsey: 'When he designed the first Dracula sets, he found out later that there had been a discussion as to whether or not to pay him off and get another art director, because those sets were so different from what they expected. They were scared of them. And then, I suppose, thrift got the better of them and they decided to risk it and go ahead and keep the sets he designed. I must say, I found those sets a bit puzzling myself. I said, "Bernard, there were no cobwebs. Who did the cleaning?" I told Bernard that it didn't seem very logical. "Of course it is," he said. "Magic!"'

(I mentioned in the prologue to this book how much *Dracula* had affected me as a child. Much of that effect, oddly enough, had to do with Robinson's sets. Near the house where I grew up was an old 'root' cellar. This became Dracula's crypt to my childish mind. A barn just down the road was the castle, and its silos were turrets. And there were the ruins of a previous house on the property, including a six-foot-long portion of stone wall. This, of course, became Dracula's stone sarcophagus.. and so on.)

Robinson's sets might well have been wasted had they not been photographed by someone of Jack Asher's talent. Years later, Asher told Kinsey: '*The Curse of Frankenstein* was a try-out, a debut of my ideas for photographing colour.. In

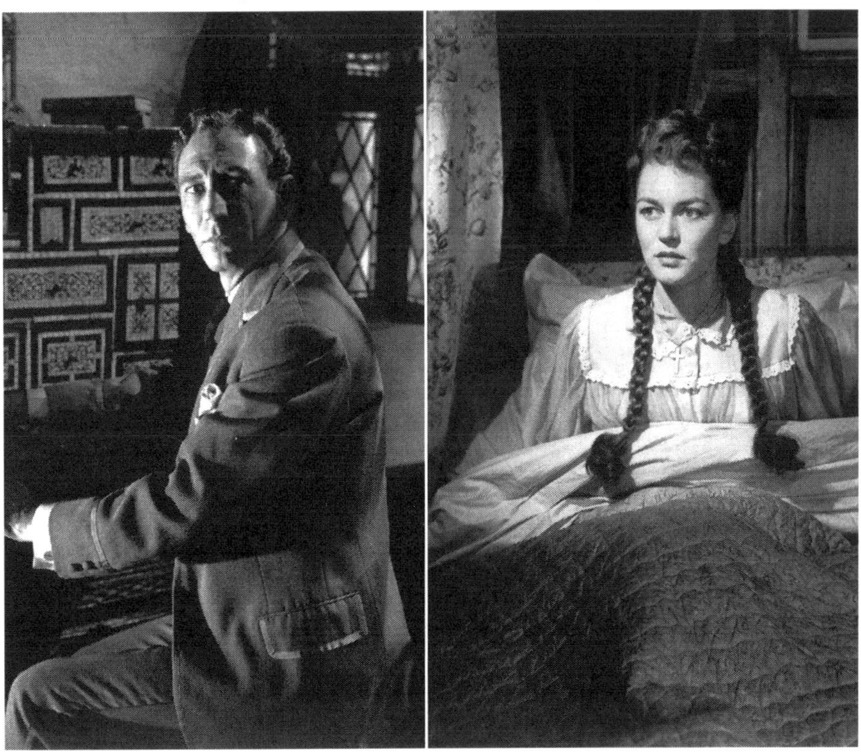

Dracula (John Van Eyssen, Carol Marsh)

retrospect, just to realise that it worked so well is really great. When we started *Dracula*, I felt a settling-down, a maturing of style. I began to feel that we had something special, perhaps transcending all previous versions.' As Meikle writes in *A History of Horrors*, 'It is the lush Technicolor photography that endows the whole with the breath of life. In *Dracula*, the shadows deepen; the velvet shades of mortuary drape mask the festering aura of death and decay that always lies just beyond the pinpoint pools of light in which the principals play.'

***Dracula* (Christopher Lee, Carol Marsh)**

And what principals they are. Like Lugosi before him, Christopher Lee came to look upon *Dracula* as both a curse and a blessing to his career but, in 1958, he had his (fatal) moment in the sun. Cushing, fresh from playing the amoral Baron Frankenstein, is the epitome of good as Van Helsing, despite the fact that he drives in those stakes in with such purposeful ferocity. The little medical bag containing his vampire-killing accoutrements quickly became *de rigeur* for all vampire films that followed—the kit-bag of a doctor of metaphysics, containing at least one hammer, several stakes, some garlic, a phial of holy water and the obligatory crucifix or two.

But while Lee and Cushing are iconic in the film (and they are), it is the ladies who represent the biggest break from previous excursions in the genre. Carol Marsh as Lucy is a revelation. The young actress was already well-known for playing Pinkie Brown's put-upon girlfriend in John Boulting's film of Graham Greene's *Brighton Rock* (1947), as well as for essaying the role of Lewis Carroll's daydreaming heroine opposite a cast composed almost entirely of puppets in a 1949 live-action version of *Alice in Wonderland*. Possessed of a delicate, haunting, child-like beauty, Marsh was perfect for the role of the doomed Lucy. As Fisher explained in later years, 'Dracula preyed upon the sexual frustrations of his woman victims.' The scene in which she is 'seduced' by Dracula as she lies tremulously in her virgin's bed is a masterpiece

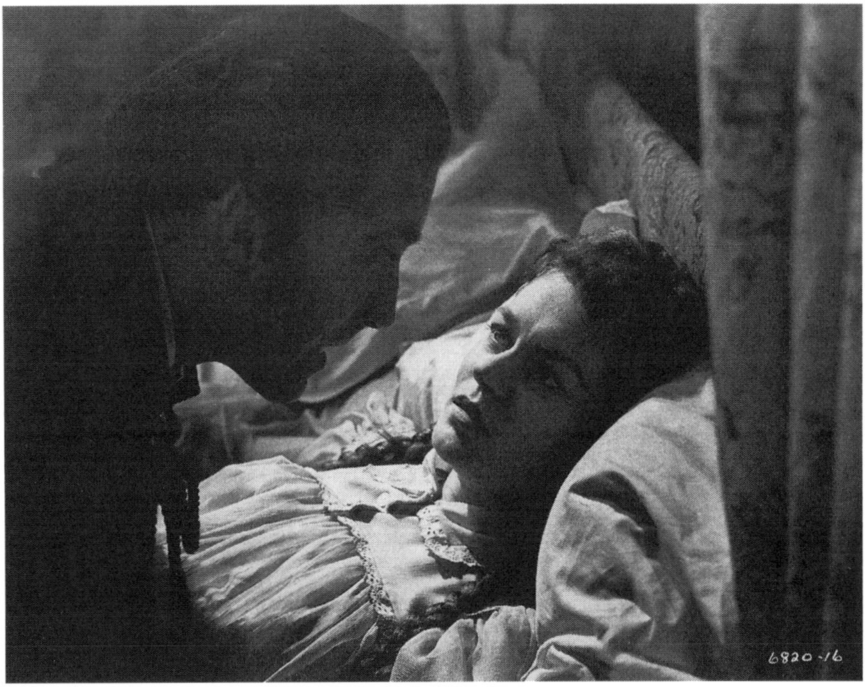

Dracula (Christopher Lee. Carol Marsh)

of sexual suggestion. Fisher once told Ronald V Borst, former publisher of *Photon* magazine: 'Both female characters in *Dracula* were so loosely written that it didn't mean a thing. I had to emphasise that these two women who were involved with Dracula were under a special influence. I think what I dragged out from between the lines was a little more than possibly was ever implied within the script. That may be pompous, but I believe it's true.'

Indeed, when one compares Sangster's screenplay to the finished film, there are numerous differences—not so much in structure, but in directorial interpretation. Sangster's script outlines the basics of the scene, but it is in the detail that Fisher excels. Lucy unlatches the French windows in her bedroom and returns to her bed in anticipation of Dracula's arrival. The autumn leaves blow in the chill wind of the courtyard as James Bernard's ominous music swells on the soundtrack; there is the hint of an enigmatic 'Mona Lisa' smile on her face as she awaits her fate, breathlessly, and in the darkness, like a bride on her wedding night.

As Fisher later commented: 'It's almost ballet the way she opens the doors, goes back and lies down again, her eyes focused, waiting for him to appear. You know, it's a distortion of the so-called true love, and this is the power of evil working from a distance. Dracula could cause himself to appear there right at the moment when he realised that any resistance to him she might have had was gone.'

The only sequence that seems to have been totally cut from the film is the opening of Sangster's screenplay, in which several minor characters are in the coach with Harker en route to the castle. All of the actors concerned were contracted; Stedwell Fulcher as a fellow-traveller, Judith Nelmes as his wife, Humphrey Kent as a portly merchant and William Sherwood a priest. Whether this scene was actually shot or not is unknown, but if one looks closely at the opening scene in the film itself, there do appear to be other people in the coach besides Harker. Ultimately, a voice-over from Harker was used in place of this planned establishing scene, in which sundry

locals were to have warned Harker about the nature of his destination, as it smacked too much of all those Universal clichés that Hammer was trying to avoid. Even Sangster admits this in his book: 'I certainly don't object to VO's and in this case it works quite well. I wasn't around at the time, but I imagine this change was made for budgetary reasons. A coach, possibly with back projection, five actors, half a day to shoot it.. lotsa money. I see from an original cast list that all these parts were cast, so it was possibly the schedule that forced them to cut it. One of the rare occasions when budgetary restrictions actually improve on the original.'

Principal photography on *Dracula* was completed on Christmas Eve, 1957, with inserts and pickup shots scheduled for after the break. The film had been shot on a six-week schedule, something which soon became the Hammer norm and from which it rarely varied—not much time there to shoot the so-called 'Japanese' versions which have so often been rumoured to exist in film vaults somewhere. These stories apparently arose as a result of publicity stills that circulated in magazines and journals but did not feature in the finished film. *Dracula* producer Tony Hinds helped to inspire such rumours by telling *Picturegoer* in 1957: 'The Japanese want more blood so we're making them a special version.'

But are tales of these special versions merely apocryphal? In the case of *Dracula*, the rumours swirled around three key scenes: Jonathan Harker's demise, Lucy's staking and Dracula's destruction. According to Meikle again: 'In the case of Harker, an emaciated corpse was constructed but was abandoned during production on advice from Soho Square (although after its inclusion in promotional material)'—3 Soho Square was the headquarters of the BBFC. As for the other two scenes, they were indeed shot, but not as gorier editions for the Japanese market; they were shot because they were in the script and if they had to be cut, they would be. As it turned out, the American market was more liberal in terms of the amount of blood which could be shown on screen, so we yanks were allowed the full sequence of Lucy's staking, including close-ups of blood spurting from her chest as the stake is driven home. British audiences had to settle for cutaways of her husband leaning against the wall of the crypt for support, even at the 'X'certificate age of sixteen or over.

As for the count's climactic disintegration, Hinds ordered editor James Needs to remove a shot of Dracula clawing at his decaying face as the skin peels off it. A photo of that excised scene soon found its way into periodicals such as *Famous Monsters of Filmland*, fuelling the rumours of a much bloodier 'Japanese version'.

The finishing touch to *Dracula*, and the most grandiose, was 'house' composer James Bernard's pulse-pounding musical score. In 1975, I visited Bernard at his flat in London, and he played the main theme to *Dracula* for me on his piano, making much of the fact that he had composed it to sound like 'Dra-cu-la'. It was a simple but tremendously effective approach to the composition of a film score and Bernard used the technique again and again for Hammer; if one listens to his scores for *Frankenstein Created Woman* (1966), *Frankenstein Must be Destroyed* (1969) and *Taste the Blood of Dracula* (1969), one can hear the titles of the films echoed in their musical themes.

According to John Trevelyan, Secretary of the BBFC, Bernard was asked to write 'sex music' for *Dracula*—whatever had been meant by that. Certainly, his music for Lucy's 'seduction' is sinuous and exotic, and it is employed again when she leaves her crypt as a vampire and goes wandering in the night in search of the young Tania. But the scoring in the scene in which Mina is assaulted by Dracula is much louder and more insistent; it is the main title-theme again, but played with variations. The metaphorical message is clear: if Lucy is 'seduced', then Mina is raped—in spite of

Dracula (Melissa Stribling)

the fact that she has already fallen victim to Dracula's caresses at least once. Fisher said time and time again that he felt his main contribution to Dracula on the screen was the 'sexualisation' of the vampire. Of course, Stoker himself (intentionally or otherwise) filled his novel with such inferences, but it could fairly be said that it

was Terence Fisher who brought them out of the closet. In an interview quoted by Wayne Kinsey and others, Fisher stated: 'The [Holmwood] marriage was one in which she was not sexually satisfied and that was her weakness as far as Dracula's approach to her was concerned. When she arrived back after having been away all night she said it all in one close-up at the door. She'd been done the whole night through, please! I remember Melissa saying, "Terry, how should I play this scene?" So I told her, "Listen, you should imagine you had one whale of a sexual night, *the* one of your whole sexual experience. Give me that in your face!" And she did, of course.'

The scenes involving the vampiric Lucy, passed over so decorously in Tod Browning's 1931 version, are here the centrepiece of the tale. And there is even more suggestion of sexual aberration; the young Lucy, once so child-like herself, now becomes a child-molesting creature of the night, seeking out Tania, the daughter of the Holmwoods' maid. These are some of the most atmospheric and chilling scenes in the film, with an enshrouded Lucy flitting about the benighted countryside and taking little Tania by the hand, to lead her into a graveyard world strewn with flickering lamps and eddying leaves.

The sequence is straight out of the novel, but in all of the filmed versions, the scenes with Lucy—the 'bloofer lady' (a child's attempt at saying the word 'beautiful' in the story)—have never been bettered. Stoker envisaged the

Dracula: Bernard Robinson's graveyard set (Carol Marsh, Janina Faye)

scene in which Van Helsing and Holmwood discover Lucy in the crypt thus: 'When Lucy—I call the thing that was before us Lucy because it bore her shape—saw us she drew back with an angry snarl, such as a cat gives when taken unawares; then her eyes ranged over us. Lucy's eyes in form and colour; but Lucy's eyes unclean and full of hell-fire, instead of the pure, gentle orbs we knew.. As she looked, her eyes blazed with an unholy light, and the face became wreathed with a voluptuous smile. Oh, God, how it made me shudder to see it!' As in the novel, she approaches Holmwood; Van Helsing springs forward out of the darkness and advances towards her holding a crucifix at arm's length, finally pressing it against her forehead; the image of the cross is burned into her flesh, and Lucy screams and flees to the supposed safety of the tomb. It is an extraordinarily powerful scene of supernatural terror, unmatched in its sheer Satanic suggestiveness by any other film until *The Exorcist* (1973).

But there is more to come. The inevitable staking of Lucy—which is performed in Sangster's script partly by Holmwood but in the film entirely by Van Helsing—becomes an agonising excess of blood and screams. Although Hammer and Fisher were criticised for making this sequence too brutal, Bram Stoker's 'penny dreadful' description of events is even more harrowing: 'The Thing in the coffin writhed; and a hideous, blood-curdling screech came from the opened red lips. The body shook and quivered and twisted in wild contortions; the sharp white teeth champed together till the lips were cut, and the mouth was smeared with a crimson foam.'

In his *Photon* magazine analysis of *Dracula,* Borst quoted Fisher as answering his detractors thus: 'The critics who attacked me for being explicit never understood that what I wanted to show in the vampire films was the triumph of good resulting from the act of staking; that it was a release for the victim tainted with vampirism. I filmed the first staking in *Dracula* using shadows because it would have been far less exciting to have filmed them all the same way. But you can't show the destruction of the vampire solely by shadows or implications; you've got to be explicit since it is important that the release from vampirism be shown, just as it's important to show the resulting look of peace upon the victim's face.'

Of course, there are other implications in the staking of Lucy. Dracula's 'bite' has turned her into a wanton creature of the night—an unnatural being who seeks out innocent children to to satisfy her strange new desires; the only way that she can be dealt with is to be destroyed physically, so that the perception of sexual normality can once again be restored to this oddly middle-European Victorian family (Hammer set its version entirely within the locality of Dracula's castle; another of Sangster's budgetary expedients). But the fact that the purgative stake can be seen as a phallic symbol gives the sequence of two men setting out to violate a woman in her coffin an unmistakeable air of necrophiliac rape; Lucy is figuratively freed from her unnatural urges in a very sexist and old-fashioned way by the men in her life, whether dead or alive.

In the book, the sequence ends on an even more horrific note: 'Arthur bent and kissed her, and then we sent him and Quincey out of the tomb; the Professor and I sawed the top off the stake, leaving the point of it in the body. Then we cut off the head and filled the mouth with garlic.' Bram Stoker may not consciously have grasped the full import of the symbolism in which he was dealing, but it is surely no coincidence that Freudian theory was gaining ground around the same time as the publication of his novel. In the film, the same sequence ends with Holmwood gazing adoringly at Lucy's peaceful face, the mark of the cross now vanished from her forehead.

DRACULA takes MINA into his arms. She moans quietly. He gently

brushes her forehead with his full lips.. then her cheek.. then her neck. MINA stops shuddering, holds her breath.

Fisher filmed the scene of Mina being taken by Dracula exactly as Sangster wrote it. From here, the film races to its conclusion, condensing the continental sweep novel so that the pursuit of Dracula (who has kidnapped Mina from her own bedroom) to his castle takes place entirely by coach, rather than by sea and horseback as Stoker has it.

After throwing Mina into an open grave and attempting to bury her alive in order to reawaken her later, the count takes flight into the castle, pursued by the agile Van Helsing, while Holmwood rushes to his wife's side. The climax of the film is now the stuff of legend, and Fisher and Cushing devised bits of business to aid the dynamic of Dracula's destruction that were not in Sangster's script. On the page, Van Helsing was to have pulled a crucifix out of his pocket and back the Count into the sunlight. Cushing felt that he had been pulling a few too many crosses from his pocket throughout the film and did not want to appear to be, in his words, 'a salesman for crucifixi'. Sangster described the alterations that were wrought on the floor during shooting: 'We all know what happens next. Dracula dissolves to dust. Just as we know how the scene contrived by Terry and Peter goes, namely with Van Helsing jumping onto the huge table, running along it, leaping up and pulling down the floor-length curtains. Much better.'

Bela Lugosi's count had been destroyed off-screen, to the accompaniment of a half-hearted groan. Hammer reinstated the blood and thunder that Stoker envisioned, and effects expert Syd Pearson and make-up artist Phil Leakey collaborated on the final disintegration scene, as Pearson described to Wayne Kinsey: 'On discussions with Terry Fisher, the director, we decided we would attempt the sequence in a series of cuts—we would cut back to reaction shots of Peter Cushing as Van Helsing, then Chris Lee in his dying throes, once the shaft of light had hit him.' In fact, Dracula's hand crumbling to dust in startling close-up belonged to Pearson himself. The sequence has since become a classic combination of shock-effects and precision editing—an extraordinary climax to an extraordinarily influential horror film.

When *Dracula* opened in Britain at the Gaumont cinema in London's Haymarket on May 22, 1958, television outside broadcast cameras were there. One member of the audience exiting the theatre announced, 'I love to see the blood spurt.' It was perhaps such a remark, as much as the film itself, that dismayed the British critics. 'I came away revolted and outraged,' shrieked Nina Hibbin in the *Daily Worker*. Peter John Dyer, writing in similarly reactionary vein in the July issue of *Films and Filming*, noted, 'There are boring horror films and there are tasteless horror films. *Dracula* is a boring, tasteless horror film.. Blood dripping on Dracula's coffin, trickling down his chin, streaming over Mina's nightie, you get it all over your hands and our neck and your teeth, and it's pumped into you and out of you, and no wonder the make-up man's name is Phil Leakey.' Paul Dehn (who happened also to be James Bernard's partner), in the *Daily Chronicle*, was a lone voice of approval in the wilderness: 'What is an X Certificate *for*,' he asked pointedly, 'if we may not see a stake being Hammered into a lady's heart?'

The critical reaction in the States, however, was quite different. Even though American audiences were treated to extra gore, *Horror of Dracula*, as the film was retitled so as not to be confused with the Lugosi version, received mostly glowing reviews. *Box Office* called it 'A top notch horror drama' while *The Hollywood Reporter* raved, 'A lavishly mounted, impressive production.' Only *The New York Times* took a more blasé tone: A H Weiler wrote, 'Perhaps the constant hunt for haemoglobin

Dracula (Christopher Lee, Melissa Stribling)

is slowing our villain down, for this time there are strong indications that the once gory plot is showing definite signs of anemia.. Christopher Lee is grim but not nearly so chilling as Bela Lugosi in the title role, and Peter Cushing is proper and precise as the meticulous researcher who finally turns our monster into dust.' But perhaps Jimmy Sangster summed up the variance in critical reaction best when he pointed out how the film was reviewed upon its re-issue some 38 years later: 'Then, in 1996, the movie was re-released as part of a Hammer anniversary bash at the Barbican Centre in London. Again, I quote from a couple of the reviews: "Romantic cinema that transcends genre.. unimpeachable and unsurpassed." "A model of lucid economy.. a fine film." Which goes to show how tastes have changed over the past forty years. Either that or the critics have grown up.'

When shots excised from the original British release print were restored to a new print of the film in 2007, the BFI (British Film Institute) released it again to similar acclaim. There is no doubt that Hammer's *Dracula* was a ground-breaking horror film; it confirmed the company's Gothic credentials after *The Curse of Frankenstein* had established the fundamentals and improved upon them. In one fell swoop, it enshrined the concept of a 'Hammer' vampire that would hold sway on the screen for years to come and would influence countless other producers and scriptwriters: to Lugosi, Chaney and Carradine's elegant bloodsuckers, it had added the 'tigerish ferocity' of the vampire in violent action, graphic bite-marks, the bloodshot eyes of the fiend in full flow, and the tell-tale trickles of blood from the corners of the mouth when he takes to his rest. These and more became the trademarks of the Hammer vampire. When all is said and done, and taking into account the many other versions of Stoker's novel which have been made since, it remains the most exciting of them. Francis Ford Copolla's *Bram Stoker's Dracula* (1992) may have had a multi-million dollar budget, but it did not have the skills and slick craftsmanship of Terence Fisher, Tony Hinds, Peter Cushing, Christopher Lee,

***Blood of the Vampire* (Donald Wolfit, Barbara Shelley)**

Curse of the Undead (Michael Pate)

James Bernard, Jack Asher or Bernard Robinson. As a horror film, *Dracula* is one of the best. As a vampire film, it is a masterpiece.

Christopher Lee has been quoted as saying that Universal-International was saved from bankruptcy by *Dracula*. It is an assertion that remains unsubstantiated, but there is no question that Hammer's first vampire film was a resounding success all over the world. Lee has also claimed that *Dracula* made back eight times its production cost—which would make it, in terms of profit recouped from investment, more successful pound for pound than James Cameron's *Titanic* (1997).

In the wake of Hammer's *Dracula*, vampire films were once again the flavour of the month among enterprising exploitation companies around the world—but others were surprisingly slow to react to the new and vibrant Romanticism of the full-blooded Hammer variant. In Britain, only Monty Berman and Robert Baker's Artistes Alliance dared to confront Hammer directly by employing *Dracula* screenwriter Jimmy Sangster to come up with an alternative take on the myth that nevertheless would enable it to cash in on *Dracula*'s success. The result was *Blood of the Vampire*, a genuine penny-dreadful admixture of themes and ideas, in which Dr Callistratus (Donald Wolfit), impaled as a vampire before the credits, is revived via heart-transplantation and endeavours to experiment on the prisoners in his asylum in order to try to perfect the blood transfusions that he needs to stave off said organ rejection. The film was gory and gaudy, but Technicolor and amputations aside, it looked to have been produced in the 1940s when viewed alongside the ultra-professional polish of the Hammer Gothics.

In America, Hammer's US distributor Universal-International came up with a vampire film which had more to do with the current popularity of western series on television than it did with the Gothic sensibility of Byron or Polidori, or even Bram Stoker. Despite its Stoker-esque title, *Curse of the Undead* featured a 'wild west' vampire in the form of Don Drago Robles (Michael Pate), a cuckolded suicide who returns to life as bloodsucking gunslinger 'Drake Robey', only to be laid permanently to rest by the silver bullet of concerned Preacher Dan Young (TV's *Rawhide* trail boss, Eric Fleming). But by the time *Curse of the Undead* hit US drive-ins in May 1959, U-I was content to leave vampires and their kith and kin in the more practised hands of Britain's Hammer Films.

By 1959, Universal was itching for a sequel to Hammer's hugely successful *Dracula* of the previous year. In response, Hinds had asked Sangster to pen a screenplay for such a sequel, which Sangster titled *The Disciple of Dracula*. It was a Dracula film with very little Dracula—the character of Baron Meinster was introduced into the mix instead, to obviate the necessity of revivifying the count and dispense with the need to woo Christopher Lee, who was now proving reluctant to reprise the role for fear of typecasting. (Sangster may have been borrowing from his own scripts at this juncture, as he was sometimes wont to do; there had been a 'Professor Meister' in his *Blood of the Vampire* for Baker and Berman.) At the climax of *Disciple of Dracula*, however, the count was still required to make a belated appearance when the hero, Latour, is forced to summon the *spirit* of Dracula to dispatch the 'renegade' disciple.

Hammer had now been granted the rights to remake Universal's library of classic horror films. *The Mummy* was next to go before the cameras, but as early as March 1959, the sequel to *Dracula* was in the planning stages. At the time, Christopher Lee was in Italy filming a vampire spoof called *Hard Times for Vampires* (aka *Uncle Was a Vampire*); the role had him playing a vampire who looked suspiciously like Hammer's count, but instead of battling an Italian Van Helsing, he found himself up against comedian Renato Rascel. Minor romps like this were part of Lee's current bid for international stardom.

To add to the confusion, Hammer had announced the sequel to the trades in June as *Dracula the Damned*, though this title was soon erased from the schedule. As Sangster noted in *Inside Hammer*, the gestation of the film was long and complicated: 'Tony Hinds asked me to do a *Dracula* sequel, but "let's not go overboard with Chris Lee". Tony felt he was playing hard to get. In fact this was exactly what he was doing, moving to mainland Europe where he hoped to build an international reputation based on his huge success as Dracula. And who could blame him.. so on Tony's instructions, I wrote the "Christopher Lee" part down and made the character of Baron Meinster the principal vampire. It turned out that Lee was playing even harder to get than Tony thought and he flatly refused to do the picture. So I was paid for it and it was shelved. But like all good vampire legends, it was destined to be reborn.'

According to Denis Meikle in *A History of Horrors*, Hammer screenwriter Peter Bryan (*The Hound of the Baskervilles*; 1959) was then asked by Hinds in September to rework Sangster's screenplay for *The Disciple of Dracula* with one important caveat: get rid of Dracula entirely! The result of Bryan's efforts saw the

The Brides of Dracula (Yvonne Monlaur)

aforementioned vampire baron inadvertently released from magical captivity by an innocent schoolteacher, after which—and in line with sexual undercurrent which had been introduced into the first film—he sets about preying on the nubile young virgins at the nearby girls' academy where the teacher is employed. As Jonathan Harker unwittingly led the count to a fresh source of sustenance in *Dracula*, so Marianne was to do the same to Meinster in the sequel; the difference this time was that all of the vampire's victims were to be *female*.

Bryan came up with a new and novel way to dispatch Baron Meinster at the end of the film, which consigned the proposed reappearance of Dracula/Lee to history: instead of summoning up the spirit of the count, a plague of bats was summoned from Hell to destroy the bad baron. In the end, even this new climax was jettisoned in favour of something more 'traditional', but the rite was eventually pressed into service in Hammer's next vampire film, *The Kiss of the Vampire* (1963), as was the opening of Sangster's *Disiciple* script, in which Latour impaled a female vampire by thrusting a shovel through the lid of her coffin—which goes to prove that Hammer never wasted a good idea!

In Sangster's script, the foremost of its *two* heroines had been named Margaret. Bryan changed her name to Marianne—a moniker that surfaced again for the female lead in *Kiss*. Bryan also restored Van Helsing to the story, demoting the original's Latour to the role of manservant to the Meinsters. In the process, he broke the rule which had been established by Hinds and Sangster for Hammer's *Dracula* by allowing the baron to transform into a bat, and he introduced a sub-plot in which he became 'engaged' to Marianne so he would have a more 'legitimate' reason to visit the girls' academy.

Perhaps most importantly, Peter Bryan came up with a new title: *The Brides of Dracula*. It was a perfect choice to indicate the direction in which Hammer planned to take its vampires, the female of whom were soon to become far more deadly than their male counterparts.

In November 1959, the Sangster/Bryan script was sent to Cushing in the hope

that he would reprise the role of Van Helsing. As there was now no Dracula in the story, the casting of Cushing was considered to be all-important: Hammer needed a star. Cushing, however, did not like the script and did not want to do it. Hinds contacted a third writer, the venerable Edward Percy, whose work in the theatre was much admired by Cushing. Percy was now a 69-year-old who merely added a few period touches, but they were enough for Cushing who agreed to star on the strength of them.

The rewrites on *Brides* had pushed the start of production beyond Christmas 1959, and Hammer was due to deliver the film to U-I the following May. Hinds was becoming increasingly concerned about the anomalies in the script which had come about from combining the two quite separate drafts, noting later, 'I had a hell of a time setting it up.' Sangster had written the role of Baroness Meinster, the baron's mother, as 'a tainted, monstrous matriarch' who, as the story unfolded, seemed to be a vampire herself; in Peter Bryan's revision, she had become a lonely and embittered old woman, who ultimately became a victim of her own son. As Hinds tinkered the shooting script into shape himself, uppermost in his mind was the fact that it had not yet been submitted to the BBFC for approval, as was the usual practice, even as production was about to begin.

The Brides of Dracula went onto the floor at Bray Studios on January 26, 1960. The cast and crew assembled for Hammer Film Production #65, as it was called, were among the best ever garnered for the company. First and foremost, director Terence Fisher was back in charge of proceedings. He was quoted as saying of the titular character's absence in the film's pressbook, 'In the last picture we destroyed him when we had him disintegrate into a pile of dust at its conclusion.. but the wily old Count had many disciples—men and women—all steeped in the blood-lusting craft. And it is with one of these that the new film deals.'

Almost the entire production team behind *Dracula* was retained for the new film, among them production designer Bernard Robinson, lighting cameraman Jack Asher and camera operator Len Harris. One of the Hammer regulars who was not scheduled for a return was composer James Bernard, who was replaced by 'Master of the Queen's Musick' Malcolm Williamson on this occasion. 'Well, I couldn't do all of them, could I?' he once quipped to me.

In terms of the cast, Peter Cushing was now very much a star in his own right, but Miles Malleson, a familiar British character actor and writer who had been in everything from *The Thief of Bagdad* (1940, which he also co-scripted) to *Scrooge* (1951) was a favourite player of the director's; Malleson had a small part in *Dracula* and a more memorable one in Fisher's *The Hound of the Baskervilles*—in *Brides*, he was promoted to the larger role of Dr Tobler, who assists Van Helsing in dealing with 'the seal of Dracula'.

Another of the more pleasurable aspects of working on *Brides* for Cushing was the opportunity to act alongside Henry Oscar, who was to play Herr Lang, owner of the Lang girls' academy. Oscar had helped Cushing early in his career when, in 1942, the young actor had begged him for a job at London's Drury Lane Theatre, where Oscar was director. In the magazine 'Dark Terrors', Oscar recalled, 'I well remember him bursting into my room. He looked thin, dishevelled and in need of a good hot meal. From his excited manner and wild appearance I decided he must either be a madman or a genius.' He decided that Cushing was the latter and cast him in Noel Coward's *Private Lives*.

But the film was to be dominated by its duo of '*grande dames*'—Martita Hunt and Freda Jackson. The two had appeared together in director David Lean's classic

The Brides of Dracula (Yvonne Monlaur, David Peel)

The Brides of Dracula (Martita Hunt)

The Brides of Dracula (Freda Jackson)

Great Expectations (1946), but according to Hinds, they hated each other! Hunt, in particular, was a highly-respected but much feared stage actress, amusingly described in Alec Guinness's autobiography, *Blessing in Disguise*. Guinness had taken acting lessons from her and found her to be quite demanding: 'Have I made her appear a dragon?' he inquired, rhetorically. 'Well, although only thirteen years older than me, she could appear dragonish and had a sharp tongue.' Bernard Robinson's widow Margaret said, 'She was more terrifying off-stage than when I saw her in the film..' Hunt's predilection for alcohol (especially wine) was as legendary as her imposing presence; continuity lady Tilly Day remarked in the magazine *Little Shoppe of Horrors* that at 8 o'clock in the morning, 'she would sit at the head of the table and while I'd be doing something or other she'd ask, "Would you like a glass of warm wine, dear?"' Years later, Jackson was quoted on her experience of making the movie in *Dark Terrors*: 'It was filmed during the icy months of January and February. I had to be up at 5:30 every morning and drive for an hour and a half in a freezing fog to the studio forty miles from where I live. I had to be on a cold, dimly lit dungeon set at 8:30. Then, the director ordered me to get down to my knees and simulate an acute form of hysteria. Believe me, it's no joke in the conditions I've mentioned to work yourself up into a state of high hysteria!'

As for the 'brides' themselves, leading lady Yvonne Monlaur (Marianne) had been spotted by Hinds in the Italian film *Avventura a Capri* (1956) and in French magazines. Hammer, of course, was always on the lookout for beautiful 'glamour girls' to feature in what *Time* magazine termed its 'girl and ghoul' movies and Monlaur was one of the more memorable choices, as studio publicist Dennison Thornton's pressbook for *Brides* noted breathlessly: 'She's France's latest sex-kitten.. tawny-haired, exciting, twenty and magnetically feminine.. Last year Yvonne was picked by a Paris magazine as 1959's "sexiest screen newcomer". Yvonne, who gives her statistics as 89-56-89 (centimetres!) says, "I am most proud of this honour. But I am more proud of the award I received recently from an Italian newspaper as this year's most promising actress. You see, sex is important. It gives a girl confidence.

Marie Devereux

But for me, talent and ability are even more important."' Monlaur was accompanied to the set each day by her mother, who 'chaperoned' her throughout the shooting; the actress had just been through a long convalescence, recovering from facial burns she received while making a film in Italy.

The remaining brides were Andree Melly, sister of writer and jazz singer George, who was noted in the pressbook as being 'twenty-five and with a personality described as "highly distinctive"', and the statistically-stunning Marie Devereux, who had just appeared in Hammer's *The Stranglers of Bombay* and was described as 'a dark beauty with aggressive statistics charting her figure'—which was a diplomatic way of saying that Devereux, whose real name was Patricia Sutcliffe, was particularly well-endowed in the bust department, as her brief but memorable appearance as a sadistic she-devil in *Stranglers* had demonstrated.

The Hammer Vampire

(Melly had an interesting observation to make about Devereux to Oscar Martinez in *Little Shoppe of Horrors* that revealed much about how Hammer sold its films. Melly recalled, '[Devereux] was not at that time actually an actress in that I don't think she'd ever had any speaking acting parts, but she had a good figure and particularly large boobs.. I asked, "How did you come to be in the film?" She said, "Oh, they always want me in these films because I've got such big boobs and they like to put them on the posters.. I get some small part in the film and then I get put on the posters." And I thought that was really a sad fate, in a way.')

Finally, there was Baron Meinster himself: the enigmatic David Peel. In an article in *Little Shoppe of Horrors* entitled 'I Met David Peel', Carl Del Vecchio wrote, 'Peel had very pleasant memories of filming *The Brides of Dracula*. Cast and crew were almost like family and he particularly enjoyed working again with Peter Cushing, recalling that Peter was a complete professional and a true gentleman.. he informed me that the two of them had appeared in a BBC television adaptation of *Beau Brummel* in the early 1950s. The one unhappy memory for Mr Peel about *Brides* is a bit amusing. A small hairpiece was weaved into his own locks just above his forehead. Hammer insisted on "the curl" and Mr Peel grudgingly went along with it. He also commented on having to wear "lifts" in his shoes for this picture in order to make him appear taller!' While composer Williamson had more tart comments to make about Peel ('David would bring his two poodles onto the set.. he was an extremely *sweet* actor, if you know what I mean'), he had no such reservations about the film's star: 'I met Peter Cushing several times and to meet him is to love him. I think no one in the world would say other than that.'

Principal photography was completed on March 18, with some final location work in Windsor's Black Park involving the coach sequence that opens the film. Another Hammer Gothic was in the can, and U-I (soon to change its name back to plain old Universal) could not wait to take delivery of it. The print arrived in the US in April, just two days before a penalty clause would have come into effect. But to Universal's beleaguered executives, it was to have been worth the wait.

The BBFC had eventually forwarded its criticisms in March 1960, after the film itself was in the can! Sangster and Bryan must have been amused by some of the remarks: 'Obviously written by an insane but very precocious schoolboy' was one. 'Quite the stupidest vampire film so far, but no nastier than the others on the whole,' they continued. The censors were especially nervous of the sexual aspects of the script, particularly the hints of lesbianism in the scene in which a student named Gina arises from her coffin and advances on Marianne: 'All this loving talk between the lady vampires is dangerous,' they commented, 'and the line, "We can both love him, my darling," very steep indeed and not likely to pass.' Their indictment of the screenplay concluded with, 'What next? Dracula, the homosexual vampire?' As David Peel, the actor chosen to play Meinster, was in fact homosexual, the Board completely missed the fact that Hammer had already countered the potential for a much worse inference in the film by having him prey only on women!

Despite the misgivings of the readers at the BBFC, the film got off relatively lightly; Hinds was a master at sleight-of-hand when it came to dealing with the censor and when the Board balked at the sight of a stake being pounded into the aged chest of Baroness Meinster, Hinds protested that a similar scene had been allowed to pass in the first *Dracula*. It had not, but no one checked and the scene in question remained in the film.

In Britain, *The Brides of Dracula* was released by Rank, and the premiere of the film was held on July 6 at London's Marble Arch Odeon. Hammer boss James Carreras lived up to his 'showman' image by turning the evening into a media event. Yvonne Monlaur arrived in a horse-drawn carriage—the same as that used to transport Martita Hunt's baroness in the film; as the invited audience filed in, four 'brides of Dracula' in diaphanous gowns presented them with cardboard fangs and crosses as souvenirs. Special guests for the evening included cast members Henry Oscar and Mona Washbourne, as well as executive producer Michael Carreras and associate producer Anthony Nelson Keys; also present were *Quatermass* director Val Guest and *The Curse of Frankenstein*'s Hazel Court, who was accompanied by her husband, actor-director Don Taylor.

It was a triumphal opening, and the film launched just as successfully—if not quite as splashily or star-studded—in the US. On July 11, James Carreras sent a memo to Hinds with an American status report: '*Brides of Dracula* is taking a packet in the USA.. which makes me think that we can start another one for Universal sometime in 1962. Would you please put the wheels in motion so that well before that time we can have a script which has been approved by Universal?'

Hinds did as he was charged but, in the meantime, Hammer could take pride in the fact that its second vampire opus had re-energised the myth once more and completely remodelled the screen image of the vampire into one that was not only sexier and more audacious but also more attractive to a young audience weaned on Cliff Richard and Adam Faith, rather than Frank Sinatra and Benny Goodman.

The Brides of Dracula opens with one of Hammer's most atmospherically-charged scenes, complete with ominous narration ('Count Dracula, monarch of all vampires, is dead—but his disciples live on..'), a coach careering through a suitably mist-shrouded forest, and the tense accompaniment of Williamson's evocative score. The gist of this prologue is simplicity itself: Marianne is en route to the town of Badstein and her new position as teacher at the Lang academy. But Fisher does wonders within this establishing premise; the coach driver (Michael Ripper) sees what he thinks might be a 'dead 'un' in the road, which has startled his horses. It soon turns out to be nothing more than a fallen log, obscured by the mist. But a mysterious wayfarer (Michael Mulcaster) creeps into frame, hitches a lift on the

The Brides of Dracula (Michael Mulcaster)

rear of the coach out of sight of the driver, and shadows Marianne to the intermediate destination of a village inn.

The sense of foreboding is palpable. At the inn, Marianne is shunned by the locals but engaged in conversation by a second night visitor: the Baroness Meinster. The entrance of the baroness is also impressively handled; she is presented as an elderly woman of mystery, an object of fear to the villagers. Sad, melancholy, and apparently starved for company, she invites Marianne to dine with her at a nearby chateau. The viewer is aware that some dastardly reason must underlie her seeming generosity, but is not yet privy to what that reason might be.

The interior of the Chateau Meinster is a riot of baroque design. Robinson's production design was allowed the kind of freedom that only success can bring, and his sets are awash with mouldering velvet, sinuous staircases, secret rooms, mysterious locked portals, carved gryphons, richly-coloured candles and other assorted bric-a-brac. The chateau's Gothic expanses are lovingly crafted, like a fairytale castle that is dreamed of by children, but with something decadent and darker lurking beneath all the velvet and chintz. And that darker something forms the crux of the story.

Having glimpsed a handsome stranger on the battlements from the window of her bedroom who is seemingly in need of help, Marianne's curiosity gets the better of her and, Pandora-like, she steals out in the night to investigate a locked chamber. She gains entrance to the hidden room and, for whatever reason—infatuation; sheer recklessness; the young baron's hypnotic stare (is he a Prince Charming, Rapunzel in drag, or a frock-coated pop star?), she releases him from the silver chain that is manacled to his leg..

Paul Jensen, John McCarty and other genre critics have pointed out an apparent 'inconsistency' with regard to this chain: if Baron Meinster can transform into a bat,

The Brides of Dracula (Yvonne Monlaur)

they ask, how could a chain prevent him from escaping? The answer is obvious: the chain is made of silver—and since the forties, silver had become as accepted a cliché of pure goodness in Hollywood films when it came to dealing with demonic creatures as, say, crucifixi or holy water. The fact that its power originated in the imagination of Curt Siodmak and his film *The Wolf Man* (1940), rather than with Sheridan Le Fanu or Bram Stoker, and it was thought up to deal specifically with werewolves, is neither here nor there; nor is the fact that *The Brides of Dracula* was not Hollywood product. Screenwriter Peter Bryan was no doubt familiar with the concept from his own film-going youth, and he employed it here with flair and originality.

Baron Meinster is one of the best examplars of Terence Fisher's theories on 'the attractiveness of evil'; what makes it so seductive, according to the director, is that it often presents itself in a more beguiling guise. The lurid American trailer for the film trumpeted that Meinster was 'blindingly handsome', combining the looks and appeal (including the hated 'curl') of a flaxen-haired pop star with the sudden vampiric venom that fans had been primed to expect from Hammer's new breed of screen monster.

The scene in which Meinster shows his true colours after he is released from his prison and chooses his own mother to be his first (incestuous) victim is another example of Hammer daring to break sexual taboos in its Gothic horrors—although it came about as an expedient, as the baroness was originally written as vampire herself and the various redrafts had somehow to return her to that state so that Van Helsing could despatch her with hammer and stake. The film also breaks new mythic ground with its elaborate explanation (written by Hinds himself) of how the baron became a vampire in the first place: Meinster has, in modern parlance, been hanging with the wrong crowd and for the first time on screen (it would resurface in Hinds's own script for *The Kiss of the Vampire*), vampirism is equated with sexual and moral degeneracy. As Greta (Freda Jackson) intones over the now-prone body

The Brides of Dracula (Andree Melly, Yvonne Monlaur)

of the baroness, 'You spoiled him—oh, yes. He was always self-willed and cruel, and you encouraged him—aye, and the bad company he kept, too. You used to sit and drink with them, didn't you? Yes.. and you laughed at their wicked games. Till in the end one of them took him; made him what he is..'

This monologue, which is preceded by Marianne's discovery of Baroness Meinster's blood-drained corpse and by the howling of wolves outside the chateau ('He's got 'em all stirred up,' Greta gloats) is a prime example of the attention to character that is one of the hallmarks of *Brides*: the wan old baroness, beautifully portrayed by Hunt with her gaunt, birdlike face and body, radiates that aura of aristocratic decadence that is pure Hammer; racked with bitterness and guilt—and shame at eventually becoming a vampire herself, she is one of the classic icons of the Hammer vampire film.

As Van Helsing creeps around the chateau in search of his prey, a woman flits into shot behind him like a ghost. It is the baroness—and when he turns to confront her, she tries to conceal her newly-minted fangs from him by covering her mouth with her veil, as though she were a schoolgirl embarrassed by an angry spot. Hunt had apparently resisted wearing the fangs, so Fisher came up with the idea of trying to conceal them; what began as a compromise between actress and director ended as a memorable nuance which added more depth to the myth as Hammer was now delineating it: 'You know who I am?' the baroness inquires. 'I know who you were,' Van Helsing replies.

The baroness is then despatched in prescriptive manner, to the accompaniment of Malcolm Williamson's own liturgical 'ode to joy', but it is the scene that follows which marks the (literal) rise of what was now to become the 'Hammer vampire'.

In one of the most unforgettable scenes in the film, and one of the creepiest in any horror film, Marie Devereux's vampire 'bride' is urged to leave her grave by the half-mad Greta. As this is her first outing as one of the Un-dead, she needs some encouragement to claw her way through the earth to the welcoming air above, and the most remarkable aspect of the scene is its queasy subtext: Greta acts as though she were a midwife to a woman in the process of giving birth. She lies straddled across the grave, whispering to its occupant, 'No, I can't help you; you've got to be strong. Yes, I know it's dark, but you've got to push..' The ground atop the grave is disturbed from within, a coffin-lid is finally thrown back, and the 'infant' vampire rises out of a coffin that appears, incongruously, to have been only inches beneath the surface. Clad in a diaphanous shroud, her face pale and blue, her fangs slightly bared, she smiles.. 'There's my little beauty! Ah, she's a clever one!' Greta cackles.

As Paul Jensen summarised: 'Most of the relationships in *Brides of Dracula* are distortions of normal affections, of acceptable loves. The mother–son tie develops implications of incest, with the Baron taking his mother's blood. The faithful attentions of a nurse are perverted into a struggle to keep her vampire charge safe.' It is Greta who then takes on the matriarchal role during the second half of the film. She will stop at nothing to protect her 'children', and she meets her own end as a result of her obsessive devotion to Meinster: when Van Helsing encounters the vampires in an old mill, Greta rips the crucifix from his grasp, losing her footing in the process and falling to her death from a balcony.

The other 'bride of Dracula' is Gina, who is deployed as a counterpart to the character of Lucy in Stoker's novel, in the same way that the baroness in Hammer's sequel stands in for the character of Jonathan Harker. Gina's slow and suspenseful release from *her* coffin is another of the film's memorable scenes, which screenwriter Peter Bryan borrowed unashamedly from the climax of M R James's short vampire

The Brides of Dracula (Yvonne Monlaur, David Peel)

story 'Count Magnus'. Marianne is asked to guard Gina's coffin, which has been sited in the stable of the Lang school. Suddenly, one of the locks on the casket falls to the floor. Then the other follows, its clasp still intact. As if by magic, the lid opens and Gina steps out, baring her fangs. 'Say that you forgive me for letting him love me,' she croons, in a scene that was to inaugurate the whole 'lesbian vampire' tradition at Hammer. 'Put your arms around me, please—I want to kiss you, Marianne,' Gina implores, and in a further 'perversion' of conventional sexual mores, suggests, 'We can both love him.' Andree Melly, who played the role, said repeatedly in interviews that Fisher was at pains to point up the lesbian angle to her and she carries it off with conviction. Her offbeat, somewhat exotic looks and unusually mannered accent give the sequence a dream-like, otherworldly quality.

Against these, Yvonne Monlaur as the film's heroine fares somewhat less well. The script rewrites had made her character inconsistent: she seems surprised when Meinster tells her that his mother is dead, yet she has seen the corpse herself at close range; after Gina rises from her coffin, she appears to be in denial when she says to Van Helsing, 'It looked like Gina, but it couldn't have been. She's dead.' As Denis Meikle explains in some detail in *A History of Horrors*, the Marianne character was actually in league with the baron and helped to procure him girls from the academy to feed his 'habit' in Sangster's original draft; Peter Bryan's restructuring of Sangster's screenplay was not altogether successful at eliminating this aspect of the story, and her contradictory behaviour is testament to its failure to iron out the anomalies that resulted. Coupled with the fact that Monlaur was not speaking in her native tongue and that films are largely shot out of sequence (so actors are not always aware of the consistency or otherwise of their characters' motivation till they see the finished product), it is remarkable that Marianne's often strange behaviour

in context still goes largely unnoticed in the fast-moving swirl of events after Meinster has made his getaway from the chateau.

David Peel's Baron Meinster is the physical opposite of Lee; light instead of dark in dress and demeanour, boyish and charming instead of mature and intimidating. The 39-year-old (at the time of shooting) Peel had been a regular in British television drama throughout the fifties and he had come to the attention of Hinds in a BBC serial called 'The Infamous John Friend'; aside from a brief appearance in *The Hands of Orlac* (1960), his subsequent film career was short-lived, but he invests Baron Meinster with such a stylish air of decadence and sexual ambiguity that he more than substitutes for the absence of Lee's Dracula. Baron Meinster in this film is the first 'modern' screen vampire—the first to throw off the Victorian opera-cloak of tradition and to recast the archetype in the mould of a movie star, complete with 'kiss-curl', heroic good looks and perfect diction. In both male and female form, the archetype of a 'Hammer vampire'—a sexy, seductive, slavering monster, attractive yet repellent at the same time—was finally formulated in *The Brides of Dracula*.

The licentious antics of Baron Meinster and his vampire harem were made more topical at the time of the film's production through the contrast with Cushing's ultra-conservative vampire hunter. While the world teetered on the brink of a sexual revolution, the two sides who were to stand in opposition to each other could not have been depicted more clearly—Van Helsing's Christian Right versus 'free-love' libertarians and 'amoral' social reformers. Cushing played Van Helsing a total of five times for Hammer, but such was the change that *Brides* wrought on the basic myth-structure that his Christian scientist was replaced in the next few outings for the count or his disciples by an expedient combination of priests and agnostic young things, with whom the new 'youth' audience could more readily identify.

Flaws apart, *The Brides of Dracula* is Terence Fisher's greatest film. Everything that was delivered in the original *Dracula* is expanded and improved upon. It is also Jack Asher's masterpiece; he outdoes his work on *Dracula* with delirious dream-imagery—a magnificent palette of Gothic hues that must be seen on a cinema screen to be fully appreciated. Like some sumptuous Victorian sofa, *Brides* is stuffed to bursting with lush period atmosphere, well-rounded characters and the mythic battle between good and 'evil' in the form of a reinvented remnant of the 'pagan' religion with which producer Hinds professed himself to be enamoured.

The notion of the Hammer vampire is firmly established in a magical movie that perfectly adheres to its own nightmarish logic. With 'dashes of Freud and Tennessee Williams', as the American *TV Guide* was later to put it, *The Brides of Dracula* is both Fisher's magnum opus and Hammer's greatest Gothic fairy tale; indeed, in many ways, it even surpasses *Dracula* itself.

> 'Just at that instant,' he says, 'I felt a blow on my foot. Hastily enough I drew it back, and something fell on the pavement with a clash. It was the third, the last of the three padlocks which had fastened the sarcophagus. I stooped to pick it up, and—Heaven is my witness that I am writing only the bare truth—before I had raised myself there was a sound of metal hinges creaking, and I distinctly saw the lid shifting upwards..'
>
> **—M R James, 'Count Magnus'/*Ghost Stories of an Antiquary* (1904)**

Chapter 2:

The Nature of the Beast

Walpurgis Night, when, according to the belief of millions of people, the devil was abroad—when the graves were opened and the dead came forth and walked. When evil things of earth and air and water held revel. This very place the driver had specially shunned. This was the depopulated village of centuries ago. This was where the suicide lay; and this was the place where I was alone..

—Bram Stoker, 'Dracula's Guest' (1897)

The Kiss of the Vampire (Jennifer Daniel, Barry Warren)

The Brides of Dracula may have established the template for what was to become the Hammer vampire, but other producers remained intent on harnessing their own vampire variants to movies designed to cash in on the upsurge in popularity of the horror film by the turn of 1960.

As it happened, the sudden leaning towards lesbian vampires was not confined to Hammer Films. French director (and former husband of fifties' screen sex-kitten Brigitte Bardot) Roger Vadim sought to capitalise on the international success of his 1959 film *Les liaisons dangereuses* by mounting a contemporary adaptation of Le Fanu's 'Carmilla' in widescreen and Technicolor, which he entitled *Et mourir de plaisir*. The end result featured a high-value cast in Elsa Martinelli, Annette Vadim (formerly Stroyberg, the director's current wife) and Mel Ferrer, and it was distributed outside France by Paramount as *Blood and Roses*. As photographed by Claude Renoir, it was luscious to look at and contained some memorably poetic images, but with the Gothic sensibility of the original sidelined in favour of romantic intrigue, it was short on horror and shorter still on genuine vampires—figurative ones becoming the mainstay of a psychological plot in which the spirit of Millarca von Karnstein possesses the two female stars in turn.. or is it all in their fevered imaginations? Vadim's overly-artistic interpretation, with its chamber-music score and Cocteau-esque dream sequence, did little to help matters; the film provided few answers and consequently made few friends, but it was the first serious attempt since Dreyer's *Vampyr* to tap into Le Fanu's unique take on the myth, with its own dark undercurrent of same-sex adolescent infatuation.

A more potent entry into the field came from Italy. After salvaging *I Vampiri*, *Caltiki—il mostro immortale* (UK: *Caltiki, the Immortal Monster*) and Steve Reeves starrer *La battaglia di Maratona* (*The Giant of Marathon*) when their original

Blood and Roses (Annette Vadim)

directors—Riccardo Freda and Jacques Tourneur respectively—gave up on them, cinematographer and special effects wizard Mario Bava was at last offered an official directorial debut. The project he chose was *La maschera del demonio*, which was loosely based on a folk-tale and short story by Russian author Nikolai Gogol called 'Vij'. The seductively-sinister features of former British Rank starlet Barbara Steele catapulted her into the lead as centuries-old vampire/witch Asa Vajda, who returns from the grave alongside lover Javutich (Arturo Dominici) to wreak vengeance on the descendents of those who condemned them both to death.

Bava's black-and-white film was a grim and sombre shock-fest of graphic gore and mouldering corpses, topped off with hints of incest and necrophilia, and in its English-language incarnation, as *The Mask of Satan*, it proved too much for British censors who promptly banned it (as they had also banned *Caltiki* the previous year). Drive-in specialists American International Pictures picked it up for US release

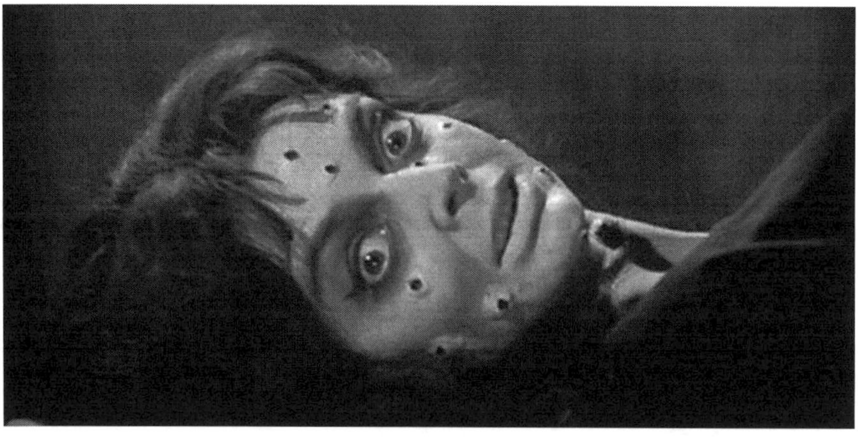

The Mask of Satan (Barbara Steele)

and distributed it in cut-down form, and with a new musical score (by its own Les Baxter), as *Black Sunday*. Notoriety and good word-of-mouth ensured that it took a fortune, but it did little to advance the cause of vampire cinema as Bava had decided against the fangs that he had ordered to be made for Steele (and Dominici) during the shooting, so Steele's character was perceived to be more witch than vampire in the finished version. Another decade was to pass before the film was eventually awarded an X certificate in Britain, albeit with cuts, and under the more accurate guise of *Revenge of the Vampire*.

Bava's way with the Gothic consequently held no sway over British producers, and the new fleshly variety of screen vampire remained the exclusive property of Hammer Horror for now.

Hammer and US distribution partner Universal had both been so pleased with the box office results of *The Brides of Dracula* that James Carreras had sent a memo to Universal dated August 4, 1960, which read in part: 'Tony Hinds has already started an outline on *Dracula 3* and would appreciate your OK on this subject as soon as possible. I have no doubt that there is room for another one.'

There was room alright—but it would not be for another two years, by which time much else would have changed. The 'sequel' that came to be known as *The Kiss of the Vampire* was, in essence, another Dracula film without Dracula. It is certainly set in the same 'country of the mind' as *Brides*, and there are several scenes that echo Hammer's earlier entry in the series. Both feature a scene of a woman clawing at a grave, entreating its occupant to feel her way out; the lead character of Professor Zimmer is a partial clone of Van Helsing; both feature beautiful, seductive vampire women; the climax, in which a plague of bats lay waste the vampires' lair, was originally intended as the ending for *Brides*. And both films feature a heroine called Marianne.

But Hammer had suffered several setbacks in the meanwhile, so *The Kiss of the Vampire* featured new talent both behind and in front of the camera. The leading role was taken by Welshman Clifford Evans, whose Professor Zimmer was a remodelling of the character of Latour in Sangster's *Disciple of Dracula*; Evans had played Oliver Reed's adoptive father in Fisher's *The Curse of the Werewolf* (1961) and, as was common practice with Hinds, had automatically been signed for another of the same. Many of the other actors were also recruited from Hinds's unofficial 'stock' company. Isobel Black, who would play the most prominent female vampire in the film, had been discovered at age 15 by future Hammer producer (and ex-Hammer actor) Harry Fine, for his ITV series *The Invisible Man*. And Australian-born Don Sharp stepped into a director's chair now vacated by Terence Fisher, who was in Germany directing *Sherlock Holmes and the Deadly Necklace* with Christopher Lee (which guaranteed that there would be no Dracula in 'Dracula 3') but who was also being sidelined by Hammer after the commercial failure of his previous Gothic, *The Phantom of the Opera*, despite a long and hugely successful run with the company. Hinds had admired Sharp's second unit work in British action films, and hired him after 'hitting it off fine'. For his part, Sharp (who at one time had also been an actor) said of *Kiss*, 'I felt that the picture had to have a style about it; it had to have a feeling of elegance and decadence.' That was what he delivered, and in spades.

The Kiss of the Vampire went into production at Bray Studios and at Black Park near Pinewood on September 7, 1962. Hinds also replaced regular Hammer cinematographer Jack Asher with newcomer Alan Hume, 'both for quality reasons and because he was fast'. The latter was the more important reason to Hinds, as there were certainly no quality issues with Asher. Years later, he admitted that Asher had probably been the best cameraman at Hammer, but that 'Jack was rather slow'.

The Hammer Vampire

Don Sharp had wanted 'classical actors' to portray the key roles in the film, as the concept of a regulation Hammer Horror picture was something entirely new to him. 'I met with Tony Hinds and told him that I'd never seen a horror picture,' he recalled. 'He said to me, "Well, from what I've seen of your work I think you'll be able to handle it, but why don't I run a few for you?" So over the next few days I saw *The Curse of Frankenstein, Dracula* and *The Stranglers of Bombay* at Hammer House in Wardour Street. What intrigued me about them was that after about twenty minutes I was totally hooked despite a totally absurd situation. I thought it was wonderful—here was a genre with its own ground rules and self-contained world, and you could be theatrical but treat it realistically to grab the audience and make them believe something absurd.' In consequence, all of the film's leads—Evans, Edward de Souza (who also starred in Fisher's *The Phantom of the Opera* and was cast as Marianne's husband, Gerald Harcourt) and Noel Willman (as Dracula *in absentia*, Dr Ravna)—had vast stage experience. Sharp was a particular admirer of Willman as both an actor and stage director; the latter had played a small role in Hitchcock's 1956 version of *The Man Who Knew Too Much* but a more prominent one in John Guillermin's seminal British gangster thriller *Never Let Go* (1960).

In the process of injecting some new blood into the traditional Bray product, Hinds and Sharp saw an opportunity to enlarge upon the established motifs of the Hammer vampire. Their joint approach, in the view of female lead Jennifer Daniel (Marianne), was 'to break the partnership of Peter Cushing and Christopher Lee. They wanted to see if they could find new combinations.' Hinds's intriguing script for the film (written under his pen name of John Elder) already benefited from various sequences discarded from Peter Bryan's draft of *Brides*. But there is a case to be made for the idea that it also borrowed from Universal's 1934 Boris Karloff/ Bela Lugosi starrer *The Black Cat*, directed by Edgar G Ulmer. Certainly, the basic situation is identical: a honeymooning couple (David Manners and Jacqueline Wells in *The Black Cat*) find themselves stranded in a mittel-European village, where they become involved in a battle of wills between two old enemies and fall foul of a 'Satanic' cult; in the *Kiss of the Vampire*, the similarly-stranded Harcourts are befriended by the mysterious Dr Ravna, who holds Marianne captive while her husband tries to persuade some uncooperative locals, specifically the mean and moody Professor Zimmer (Evans), of the need to tackle the 'cult' of vampirism in their midst. On top of that, *The Kiss of the Vampire*'s main theme of a 'kidnapped' heroine whose existence is denied by everyone with whom she previously has come into contact was lifted wholesale from the 1950 British thriller *So Long at the Fair*, which was directed by Terence Fisher!

While Sharp approved of the Hammer approach in general, he felt that the company was 'piling on the agony a bit too much'. His idea was to make a Hammer horror film that 'suggested' more than it actually showed, much in the style of RKO 'house' producer Val Lewton, whose 1942 *Cat People* and others made under his aegis had personified the 'less is more' school of horror in the sensitive period of wartime, which ultimately had the effect of bypassing the more restrictive censorship.

Pre-production on the film was about eight weeks and the shooting schedule took up another six. Typically, the atmosphere at Bray was still one of camaraderie: when I interviewed Jennifer Daniel for 'Little Shoppe of Horrors', she recalled, 'The whole six weeks, one was called at five in the morning, a bit like modern television really, and one would get home at about seven or eight o'clock at night. So it was hard work, but it was great fun.' In fact, everyone I spoke to who had worked on *Kiss*

The Kiss of the Vampire (Jennifer Daniel)

recalled it as 'fun'. Black remembered showing off for the newspapers, who took photos of her having her fangs fitted; 'If you have to be locked into position under camera lights for hours, there's nobody nicer to be locked in with than Edward de Souza,' Daniel said of her co-star. 'We had lots of fun,' de Souza confirmed.

But lest the saccharine become too pervasive, there was Noel Willman to keep things in perspective. The hard-featured actor-director who was now to play Hammer's third 'Dracula' had a long and varied career in London and New York and was highly regarded. Nevertheless, Willman was something of a man of mystery—a 'closet' homosexual who, by all accounts, kept to himself and was not what de Souza might call 'jolly'. 'I'd heard before that he was rather stern,' Daniel said, 'so I was rather worried about meeting him, but in actual fact he was absolutely charming.' Black was less generous. Although she had nothing but praise for the rest of her co-stars, she noted of Willman: 'He was a little less easy to get on with. I don't think I had a lot to do with him. He kept himself to himself a bit.'

De Souza explained the apparent contradiction in Willman. 'He seemed unapproachable because he looked really stern and aloof, but in fact he was a very nice man.' Noel Willman was to turn his austere demeanour to the film's advantage, however: 'I intend to play this part [of Dr Ravna] without changing my expression once,' he reportedly informed de Souza prior to the shooting.

Clifford Evans was the other notable recruited for the film. De Souza said of him, 'Clifford Evans was much larger than life and very mobile—a stage actor, really. He was extremely volatile and Celtic. The thing Don [Sharp] had to do was make him stand or sit still.. I think that's one of the reasons he didn't have very many

closeups. If he didn't have a closeup, he'd be all over the place. Don would make him stand very still, and then of course all that power and intensity would be like a sort of *liqueur*. And very potent indeed.'

The screenplay called for a number of musical interludes, either at the piano or during the masked ball which acts as the prelude to Marianne's 'disappearance', and James Bernard had to step in early to compose the themes, unlike his usual routine of scoring 'to picture' in post-production. A piano concerto designed to literally 'entrance' Marianne was to be played by Ravna's son (Barry Warren) as a climax to the Harcourts' first visit to the chateau; the piece had therefore to be sinuous, exotic and mysterious—'sex music', as it was referred to in Bernard's score for *Dracula*. From this scene was born the notion of using what Bernard called the 'Tooth Concerto' thoughout the film, including over the opening credits.

Bernard was also required to compose 'a sequence of waltzes with one melting into the other' for the ballroom scene, which was conveyed in time-lapse montage. His compositions for piano on a Viennese theme morphed into a sort of mini-concerto, and Leslie Edwards, the Senior Member of London's Royal Ballet, was recruited by Hammer musical director John Hollingsworth to choreograph the dancers. The masked ball sequence is certainly one of the most stylish elements of the film, and it was influenced by a similar scene in *Blood and Roses*; an extravagant *bal masque* was also to become a feature of Roman Polanski's Hammer pastiche of 1967, *Dance of the Vampires* (US: *The Fearless Vampire Killers*).

Shooting wrapped on October 25, 1962. Hinds remembered *The Kiss of the Vampire* as being 'a very happy film. It went through very smoothly. I had a lot of friends on it.' Its director likewise thought it 'a damned good movie'. As did critic Larry Lipskin, who wrote in *The Hollywood Reporter*: 'Departments commonly slighted in production of bloodcurdlers give an outstanding account of themselves in this production. Director and scripter have actually developed a number of characters in this gory yarn and colour photography is generally distinguished. Handling of special FX produces a chilling climactic invasion of bloodthirsty bats that will satisfy the most demanding horror-hungry audience. The jolts that excite come in steady succession.'

But its production marked the temporary closure of Bray Studios, as censorial reaction in the UK to the glut of horror product from 1959 on had clipped the wings of the purveyors of such films, including Hammer, in the wake of the furore that had surrounded the 1960 releases of both Hitchcock's *Psycho* and Michael Powell's notorious *Peeping Tom*. 'Our censors have got very strict since Lord Morrison took over,' Hinds noted in October 1962. American audiences did not get to see *The Kiss of the Vampire* until almost a year after its completion—partly because when the film was delivered to Universal, the powers that be felt that the ending was too similar to scenes in Hitchcock's *The Birds*, which was due for release in the summer of 1963, and so ordered its screening to be delayed. It finally surfaced in September. But the wait in Britain was even longer; the film was released in January 1964, co-billed with Hammer's own 'mini-Hitchcock' psycho-thriller, Freddie Francis's *Paranoiac*.

The 'fun' days at Bray may have been over for the time being, but Hammer's vampires were only just beginning to spread their bat-wings.

The Kiss of the Vampire is an iconic example of the Hammer vampire, and it graphically illustrates how the myth was changing and evolving. In *Dracula*, the count's victims were seen to fear yet exult in his arrival; the sexual aspect of the vampire's 'kiss' was brought to the fore. In *The Brides of Dracula*, the viewer is

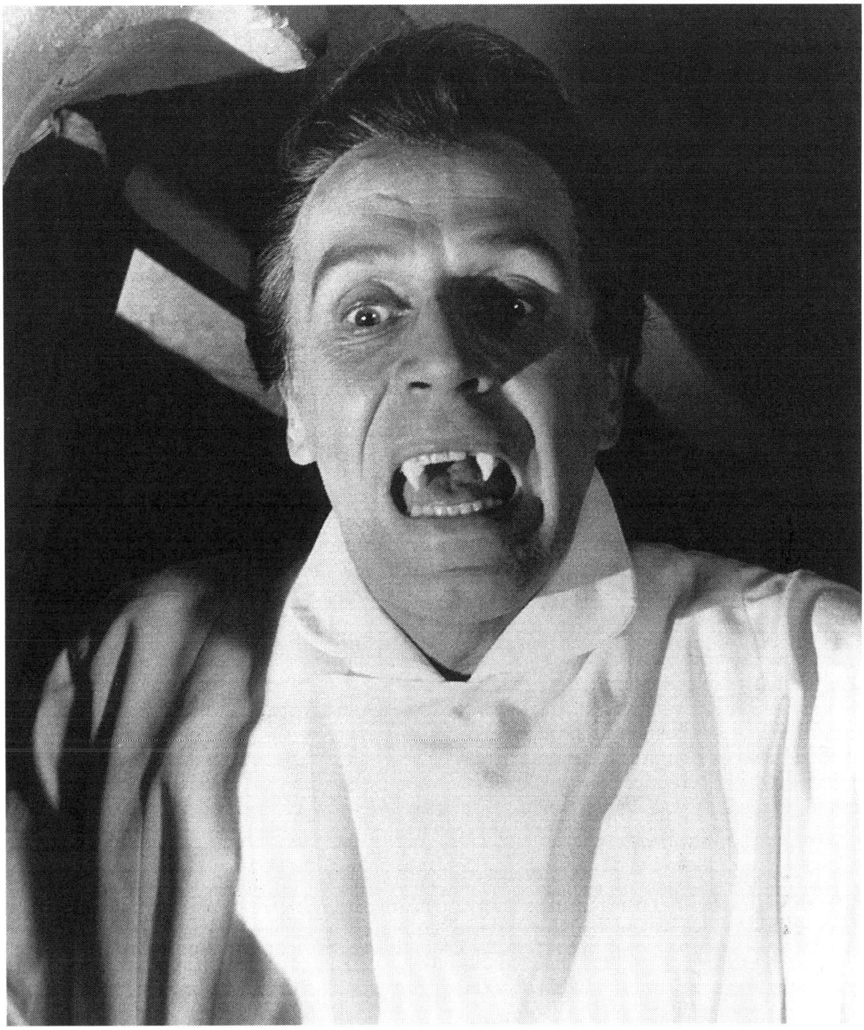

The Kiss of the Vampire (Noel Willman)

never made privy to exactly how Baron Meinster was 'corrupted' by his friends, but the central notion was that vampirism was depicted as being some kind of sexual perversion.

By the time *The Kiss of the Vampire* rolled around, vampirism had gone beyond being a perversion to become a 'social disease': an entire cult of wealthy, bored aristocrats have apparently been infected with the delights and damnations of this particular scourge and now prey on the peasants in their feudal charge. And one of those who has been spirited away by the cultists—'groomed', in modern parlance—is Professor Zimmer's daughter.

The opening scene of the film breaks a number of social and religious taboos. When Zimmer hurls a pointed shovel through the closed lid of his daughter's coffin and into her heart, he not only destroys her but sweeps aside the cinema's traditional reverence for the Church and its rituals in the process. Hinds the writer was forever tweaking the myth of the vampire in ways which were guaranteed to shake up the audience; from this film on, he seemed to take special delight in subjecting the

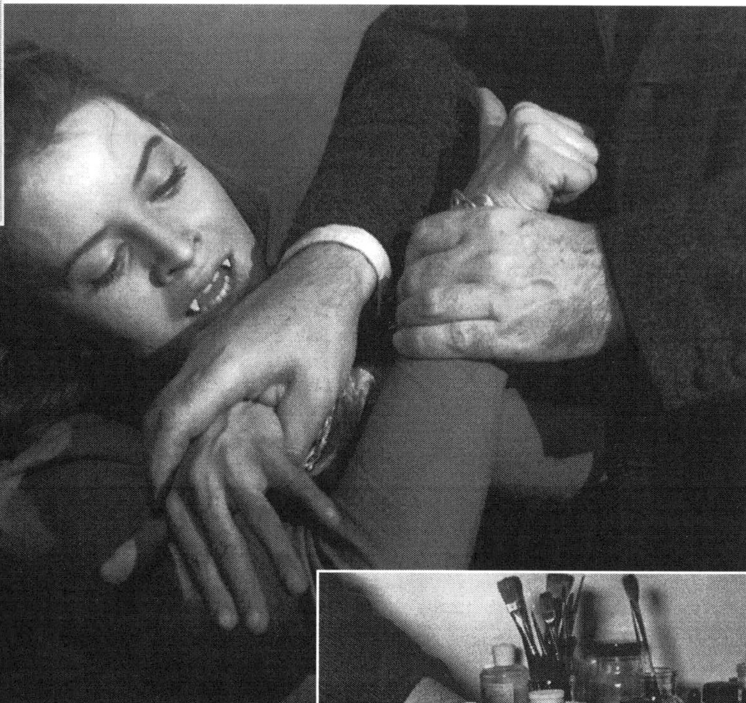

The Kiss of the Vampire (Isobel Black)

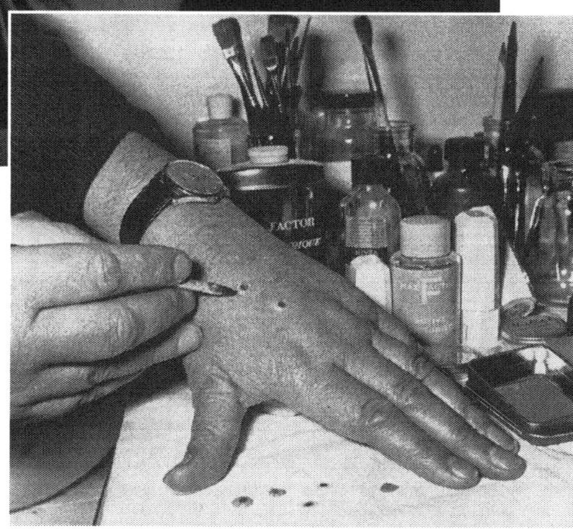

priesthood to all manner of ignominy in the course of his plots. The prologue of *Kiss* is a real eye-opener and it sets the tone perfectly for the elegant and iconoclastic film that follows.

In contrast to the usual cinematic convention, where the monster is held in wait for at least a reel or two, the viewer is introduced to Dr Ravna as soon as the credits fade; he is at a window in his chateau, peering through his telescope at the honeymooning couple in the forest below as they drive unawares in their 1910 De Dion Bouton towards the web of intrigue that he is about to spin around them. 'I like only to be surrounded by beautiful.. things,' he tells Marianne, when she finally gets to meet him in person, but his practised charm is like the ornate edifice in which he and his 'family' reside: old-worldly and attractive on the surface, but cold and dark beneath the cultivated veneer. He tells her that he was once involved in 'a series of experiments, one of which went wrong,' and concludes with a not-so-veiled hint as to the outcome: 'As a result, I have never been able to return to the city of my birth and I'm forced to live here, in this ornate coffin.'

Meanwhile, Zimmer is hovering around the edges of the story in the manner of a 'red herring', until he turns up in the village graveyard to witness the script's clever counter to the 'midwife' scene in *The Brides of Dracula*: Tania (Black) claws at a grave in an effort to entice the professor's daughter to crawl to the surface in the manner of Marie in the previous film. 'Why have you not been to see us, my sweet? —Why have you waited so long?' she coos. But instead of a hand thrust suddenly

The Kiss of the Vampire (Edward De Souza, Clifford Evans)

through the dusty earth into the air above, Tania comes upon the handle of Zimmer's shovel, still embedded in the corpse below..

It is a weird, dream-like scene, beautifully handled by Sharp—all the more so because it was added in afterthought to pile on more than was originally intended of the Hammer 'agony' that the director complained about earlier in the proceedings. This explains the anomaly that is immediately apparent if one were to think about it: would the girl really have been buried with a shovel still stuck in her chest? Of course not. But the scene was appended by Hinds for *effect*, and to quicker establish for Universal's benefit that *The Kiss of the Vampire* was indeed a red-blooded Hammer 'Dracula', and not the genteel Gothic mystery that his original script had made it out to be.

Back at the chateau, Carl Ravna (Barry Warren) embarks upon the planned seduction of Marianne by playing her an hypnotic melody on the piano while his father notes with grim humour how the most pleasant things can often spring from the most unpromising of materials. 'That wine we drank,' he says, 'trampled by the feet of a peasant. Dirty feet, as like as not. That pheasant we ate; it had been hanging for five..' —his daughter Sabena (Jacquie Wallis) cuts him off abruptly. Intercut with this veiled mockery of a conventional dinner-party is a scene in which Zimmer burns the 'kiss' of the vampire, inflicted upon him by Tania, from his wrist, aping that in which Van Helsing burned a bite from his throat in *Brides*. But on this occasion, holy water is replaced by whisky to cauterise the wound!

Hinds already felt that each new Hammer 'Dracula' should bring something different to the table, and not simply trade on past success; to this end, the vampires in *Kiss* were allowed to come and go in the daytime, albeit with reservations: when Carl and Sabena pay a visit to the inn where the Harcourts are staying, Zimmer suddenly appears to announce, 'The weather is improving. It's getting a bit brighter, I think.' The two make a swift exit in the direction of their waiting coach, pull the shades down over the windows, and exhort the coachman to '*Drive*!—Drive like

the devil!' But the most striking realignment of the myth in the Hinds Draculas from *Kiss* onwards was to be seen in the role now played by the Church. The priest in Sangster's *Brides* had been positively proactive in helping Van Helsing beat the scourge of vampirism but, from here on in, the priesthood in Hammer's vampire films would be ineffectual at best and at worst, actively complicit in aiding the fiends to their nefarious ends.

It is in the ballroom scene that the plot begins to thicken. Hinds and Sharp employ the old trick of a *bal masque* wherein characters can switch identity undetected to deft effect: not until halfway through the sequence, via a highly-effective pan along the sea of masked faces, does the viewer realise that every one of the revellers apart from the Harcourts is actually a vampire! It is at this point that the plot takes a turn straight out of Hitchcock: when Harcourt returns to the chateau in search of his wife after having been drugged and thrown out unceremoniously the night before, the Ravnas deny all knowledge of her: 'You come in here, get drunk, have to sleep it off and then ask for someone called Marianne?'

Distraught, Harcourt confides his plight to Zimmer, and screenwriter 'John Elder' enlarges upon the idea that was floated originally in *Brides* and puts into the mouth of the professor Hammer's new philosophy on the nature of vampirism: 'I had a daughter,' Zimmer poignantly relates. 'She was all I had in the world. I idolised her.. When she was very young, she ran away from home. She went to the city. She drifted in with the so-called "smart set". Finally, she ended up living with a certain man. She came home eventually.. What was left of her came home. She was riddled with disease; and she was a vampire. The name of the man who corrupted my daughter was *Ravna*.'

Alan Hume's cinematography, while not as expressionistic as Jack Asher's, is nevertheless beautiful to behold. His sense of colour composition perfectly matches the understated elegance of Sharp's direction and, years later, he would work his way up the cinematic ladder to lens major productions like *Eye of the Needle* (1981) and three James Bond films. Sharp himself had proved to be an exciting find and

Don Sharp directs the vampire 'cult' (right)

The Kiss of the Vampire

Effects artists prepare for the climax of The Kiss of the Vampire

valuable addition to the Hammer 'family'; sadly, the company made little further use of him. He returned to helm *The Devil-Ship Pirates* in 1963 and the equally conventional historical horror *Rasputin—The Mad Monk* two years later, but only *Witchcraft*, a minor foray into 'horror by suggestion' that he made for Lippert Films in 1964, showed any sign of the darkly poetic quality that he managed to achieve in *The Kiss of the Vampire.*

In the 'Dracula' films of Hammer's Tony Hinds, vampirism was akin to a social disease brought about by dissolute living. Buried beneath the surface gloss of the typical Gothic tale is a cautionary and socially-conservative one, which now equated the spawn of the greatest villain in literature with the societal 'evils' of sex, drugs and rock and roll. Zimmer expressed the fears of parents everywhere for daughters who were prone to run away, seduced by the 'smart set', and who ended up living 'in sin'. The moral message is unambiguous: uphold the precepts of family values, be chaste, and avoid at all cost the pointed teeth and impregnating attentions of a 'vampire'! The very thing that Sangster and Fisher had helped to make so attractive in *Dracula*, Tony Hinds seemed determined to return to its rightful place in monster myth as a scourge on society. If *Dracula* appeared to encourage affairs with secret lovers of *mittel*-European origin, *The Kiss of the Vampire* thoroughly condemned them; certainly, the faint hint of disgust on Ravna's face as he bends, befanged, to sup from Marianne's pretty white throat is a far cry from the anticipatory expression on that of Christopher Lee in Hammer's first vampire outing. In with the sixties had come the birth-control pill and its promise of 'free love', and moral majorities the world over were reacting with alarm at what the lifting of Victorian social taboos boded for society in general. *The Kiss of the Vampire* is probably Hammer's most 'contemporary' Gothic; it was a genuine reflection of the change that was rapidly coming about in the real world outside the cosy confines of Bray, but it was also alert to the new and more stringent demands of screen censorship in the wake of the *Peeping Tom* affair. No longer was the Hammer vampire simply evolving; it was changing with the times. And the times were now demanding that it be less sexy and more dangerous.

In Hinds's new world (of vampires) order, even the Church is made to appear powerless in the face of the threat from within; Ravna's cult is defeated not by crucifixi and Van Helsing's unwavering belief in the power of good but by 'black' magic—as blatant a metaphor for the subtle use of pro-Establishment propaganda against the burgeoning counter-culture of the early sixties as it is possible to find. Zimmer chalks a pentacle onto the floor of his room and summons a horde of vampire bats to suck the life-blood out of the vampires massed in the chateau. Thus the evil is turned in on itself, to destroy itself through its own excess. There is no musical accompaniment to the scene; the only sounds are the fluttering of the bats' wings and the screams of the vampires. It is a strangely subdued, almost redemptive climax, and it marked the end of an era at Bray. 'It worked!' Zimmer remarks with relief, but Hammer's concept of the vampire as seducer or siren had been stopped dead in its tracks.

By 1965, Bray was back in full-time action and attitudes at the British Board of Film Censors were beginning to soften with the appointment of a new and more liberal President in Lord Harlech. But the restrictions of the early sixties had seen to it that few horror film producers were willing to follow where Hammer had led since 1957. Of the vampire films which had appeared since *Kiss*, most originated from Italy. In 1964, Antonio Margheriti had pinched the Gothic trappings of Mario Bava's *La maschera del demonio*, as well as his two stars—Barbara Steele and Arturo Dominici, for a ghostly 'vampire' variant entitled *Danza macabra* (US: *Castle of Blood*), supposedly (but not really) based on a story by Edgar Allan Poe; the Poe connection was limited to a reading of part of the author's 'Berenice', which literary critics consider to be vampiric in theme. In the same year, Christopher Lee featured in another version of 'Carmilla', called *La cripta e l'incubo* (UK: *Terror in the Crypt*), but it was as lacking in real vampire action as Vadim's *Blood and Roses* before it.

Before them, Piero Regnoli had aped Hammer's *Brides* in 1960's *L'ultima preda del vampiro* (US: *The Playgirls and the Vampire*), in which Walter Brandi played a David Peel-like Count Gabor Kernassy and his vampire ancestor, and Renato Polselli did likewise in *L'amante del vampiro* (US: *The Vampire and the Ballerina*), also in 1960 and also with Brandi, who returned to the role of vampire again two years later in Roberto Mauri's *La strage dei vampiri* (UK: *Slaughter of the Vampires*). Taking their lead from the title of Hammer's film rather than any of its stylistic elements, all three concentrated effort more on the plight of their vampires' victims, nubile and often near-nude, than they did on atmosphere or plot; as such, distribution outside of their native Italy in the early sixties was limited or not at all.

Several low-budget Italian productions that previously had been thought of as

Slaughter of the Vampires (Walter Brandi)

uncommercial, like Sergio Corbucci's 1961 *Maciste contro il vampiro* and Ubaldo Ragona's 1964 *L'ultima uoma della terra*, were also taken down from the shelf and given a UK release (as *Goliath and the Vampires* and *The Last Man on Earth* respectively; the latter being producer Robert Lippert's version of Hammer's abandoned *Night Creatures* script from 1957), while more recent excursions into the genre had been given higher profile, such as Bava's *I tre volti della paura*, which had gone out with Roger Corman's *The Tomb of Ligeia* as *Black Sabbath*. As in his earlier *Mask of Satan*, Bava had borrowed from a literary source—Alexei Tolstoy's 1839 novella *Sem'ya Vurdalaka* (*The Family of the Vourdalak*)—for the vampire segment of this three-part compendium, in which Boris Karloff's aged 'wurdalak' preyed on his own family for sustenance. But other genre entries had been 'vampire' in name only: 1961's *Seddok, l'erede di Satana* was accurately released in the UK as *Seddok, Son of Satan* but it went into theatres in the US as *Atom Age Vampire*, while Bava's latest offering—*Terrore nello spazio*—went out in both markets under the more exotic moniker of *Planet of the Vampires*. Nevertheless, the impact of the Hammer vampire was being felt far and wide: even 'golden boy' William Holden had turned up as a 'Hammer' vampire, complete with fangs, in the 1964 rom-com *Paris When It Sizzles*!

In Britain, Planet Films had edged into Hammer's own territory with *Devils of Darkness*, from a script by Lyn Fairhurst, the resident film critic of the BBC Light Programme's 'Movie-go-round'. The film was actually set in *Brittany*, but it featured a sub-Dracula vampire named Count Sinistre (Hubert Noel), whom *Films & Filming* classified as 'a new streamlined fangless vampire' when he surfaced onscreen in November 1965. Unusually for a (non-Hammer) British horror of the time, *Devils of Darkness* was shot in colour, but its distinct lack of the requisite X-certificate ingredients sank it without trace.

Of more concern to Hammer in general terms was a previous 1965 release, which had been shot in both Technicolor *and* Techniscope and had put the Amicus

Dr Terror's House of Horrors (Max Adrian, Donald Sutherland)

Productions of producers Max J Rosenberg and Milton Subotsky fairly and squarely on the horror film map: *Dr Terror's House of Horrors* had originally been offered to Columbia in 1962 in black-and-white, but it was turned down on grounds of cost; the idea was then sold on to Paramount, and the result had been released in February. In setting up shop in competition with Hammer, Amicus had taken full advantage of the range of skills on tap at its opposite number over at Bray: *Dr Terror* had starred Cushing and Lee, been photographed by *The Kiss of the Vampire*'s Alan Hume, and was directed by Oscar-winning cinematographer Freddie Francis, who had helmed *The Evil of Frankenstein* and several psycho-thrillers for Hammer. The film itself was comprised of five short stories, the fifth of which concerned vampires; Donald Sutherland had been called upon to plunge a stake into the heart of wife Jennifer Jayne, but kindly doctor Max Adrian turned out to be the real vampire at large in an agreeable spoof of the company's conventions. Trade magazine *Variety* called the Amicus venture 'a usefully chilly package which will offer audiences several mild shudders and quite a lot of amusement.' But Hammer was to be less amused by the antics of Amicus as time went by.

Having lagged behind the market for a couple of years, Hammer determined to reclaim the territory that it had once thought of as its own; with a dearth of alternative horror product around for audiences to get their teeth into, plans were laid to resurrect the one vampire who counted most at the box-office.

In late 1964, *The Curse of Frankenstein* and (*Horror of*) *Dracula* had been reissued as a double bill for American audiences. Under the tagline, 'Frankenstein spills it!—Dracula drinks it!' the pairing made a tidy sum in the States, where they

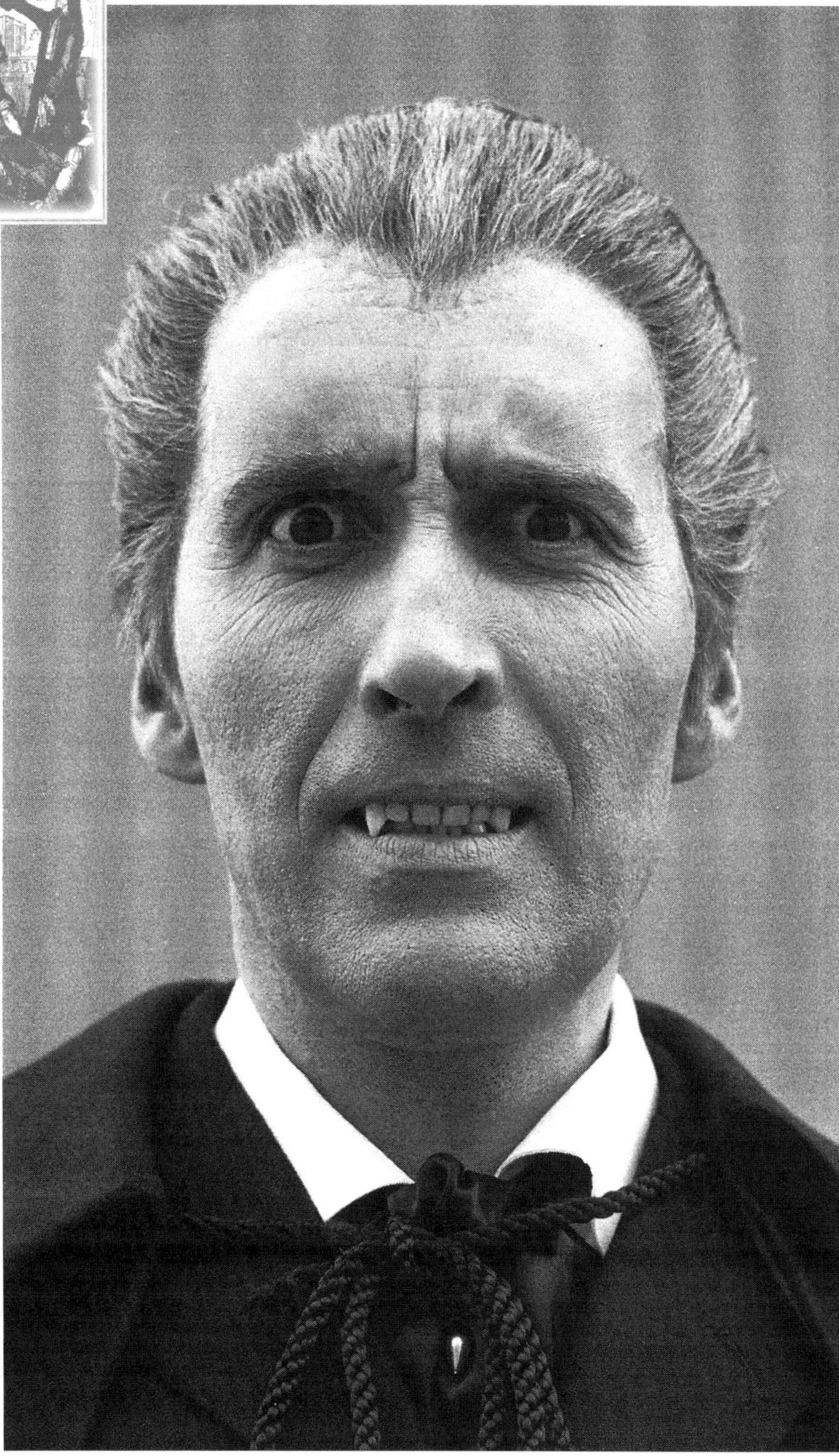

Publicity shot for Dracula—Prince of Darkness

were released by a company called 7-Arts, in which Hammer's US business associate Eliot Hyman was a partner. In 1965, 7-Arts teamed up with Hammer and 20th Century Fox to produce a programme of films, the first of which was to return its most famous monster to the screen.

Dracula—Prince of Darkness was Hammer's fourth 'Dracula' but the first official sequel to its 1958 success; finally, with his disciples out of the way, Count Dracula himself returned in the imposing form of Christopher Lee, who had recently returned to England from a self-imposed tax exile in Switzerland. Jimmy Sangster was brought in to rewrite an old treatment of his called *The Revenge of Dracula*, which was originally intended as the sequel to *Dracula*, but he would do it under another name. As Sangster explained in *Inside Hammer*, 'So why did I decide to call myself John Sansom on the titles? I asked for the pseudonym to be used because I was fed up with Gothic horror movies and felt that my career had moved well past this phase.'

'Some people claim that I used my pen name because I wasn't satisfied with the final movie. They're wrong on a couple of counts. Firstly I didn't even get to see the movie until it was ready for exhibition with the screen credits already in place and second I thought the final movie was pretty good.. Another point of controversy was why Dracula didn't have any lines. In the previous movie, the first *Dracula*, he had half-a-dozen lines at the beginning of the movie when he introduces himself to Jonathan Harker. He needed those lines because nobody knew he was a vampire at that time. Once his true colours were revealed he never opened his mouth again, except to suck blood. This time, we know exactly who he is when he first appears. He is Count Dracula, king of the vampires. And vampires don't chat. So I didn't write him any dialogue.'

Although Lee was now willing to reprise the role that had made him famous (partly because he was also offered the role of Rasputin in *The Mad Monk*), there were things about the screenplay with which he was not happy. According to Sangster, 'Chris Lee has claimed that he refused to speak the lines he was given. On the other hand, there's a story that Chris called Peter Cushing and told him he was about to do this movie, written by Jimmy Sangster, and he hadn't been given any lines to say. Peter told him to be thankful for small mercies!'

In a letter to his fan club dated May 9, 1965, Lee wrote: 'I hope people will not be disappointed by a graying Dracula. And, incidentally, as Dracula I never say a word. As I am already a vampire from the word go there is nothing I can say—not even a courteous, "Well, here we are again.."' And in relation to the controversy about his lack of dialogue, Lee wrote in his autobiography *Tall, Dark and Gruesome*: 'Much gore had flowed under the bridge in the eight years since we'd made the original *Dracula*. In this new one I never said a word. I hissed, I spat, I snarled, but no word escaped my ruby lips. I had read the script. I realised that it was impossible for anyone to write convincing lines for me. Rather than say the lines written down, I said nothing.'

Sangster, however, lays claim to the last word on the subject of the count's sudden silence: 'So you can take your pick as to why Christopher Lee didn't have any dialogue in the picture. Or you can take my word for it. I didn't write any.'

In any event, the deal with 7-Arts and Fox was for the new Dracula to be back-to-back with Hinds's own screenplay for what was now entitled *Rasputin—The Mad Monk*, utilising the same sets and many of the same cast. This was a cost-saving measure which also applied to each film's co-feature, *The Plague of the Zombies* (with *Prince of Darkness*) and *The Reptile* (with *Rasputin*). Producer Anthony Nelson Keys was assigned to bring in each film at around £100,000 apiece; in fact,

The Hammer Vampire

The Reptile was the only one of the four completed on budget and the total cost for all four came to £429,648—still a very economical sum for four period Gothic horror films.

Straight away, *Dracula Prince of Darkness* fell foul of the censors. The BBFC registered objections to several sequences, especially one in which Dracula is resurrected via a gruesome ritual. A visitor to his castle is stabbed to death and hung, upside-down, over Dracula's sarcophagus; his head is then cut off and a torrent of blood rains down on the count's ashes.. This scene and its conclusion were considerably altered in the film from how they were envisaged in the script: 'The decapitated body is jammed into the trunk, drained of all blood, and the head has been put on the top, from where it grins towards camera, its lips pulled back over the teeth.' So wrote Jimmy 'The Nasty' Sangster. As it was later shot, Alan Kent's demise is still one of the strongest moments of 'hammer horror' in the company's canon, but in this case, the censor's intervention may actually have improved it.

Most of the crew of the original *Dracula* returned, including Bernard Robinson, who 'refurbished' the count's castle for the sequel, and James Bernard, who composed a variation on his original *Dracula* theme. The new director of photography was Michael Reed, who would go on to lens one of the best of the James Bond films, 1969's *On Her Majesty's Secret Service*. But more importantly, Terence Fisher was back at the helm.

Principal photography on *Dracula—Prince of Darkness* began on April 26, 1965 with a typically fine cast. Lee's nemesis on this occasion was not Peter Cushing but Andrew Keir, as the warrior-monk Father Sandor. An outstanding actor, Keir was a robust Scotsman who had played the role of Thomas Cromwell on stage in Robert Bolt's award-winning *A Man for All Seasons* in 1960; he had also featured in Joseph L Mankiewicz's *Cleopatra* (1963), among many other film appearances. Cushing had been unavailable to don his Van Helsing persona, so the script had been rewritten with Sandor as stand-in for the doctor. As the climax of the 1958 *Dracula* was to open the new film, Cushing—who had waived formal payment for his appearance in the clip—was rewarded by having Hammer pick up the bill for repairs to his cottage in Whitstable. But the creation of a new character who was a religious figure also opened the way for some interesting subtext to the franchise which would be explored more fully in subsequent features.

Another important cast-member was model-turned-actress Barbara Shelley as Alan's wife Helen. Shelley had been the star of one of the first British horror films of the fifties, Alfred Shaugnessy's *Cat Girl* (1957), a thinly-disguised reworking of Jacques Tourneur's 1942 classic *Cat People*; the red-headed beauty was also the female lead in Henry's Cass's *Blood of the Vampire* and had co-starred with George Sanders in Wolf Rilla's trend-setting *Village of the Damned* (1960), an adaptation of the John Wyndham sci-fi novel *The Midwich Cuckoos*. For Hammer, she had recently starred in *The Gorgon* (1964; with Lee and Cushing) and had played a secondary role in *The Secret of Blood Island* (1965).

Francis Matthews, as Alan's brother Charles Kent, had played the assistant to Peter Cushing's baron in *The Revenge of Frankenstein* (1958) and had also appeared in Robert Day's *Corridors of Blood* for Producers Associates, along with Lee, Boris Karloff and Hammer regular Francis De Wolff; his previous outing for Hammer had been in its 1959 comedy *I Only Arsked!* Screen newcomer Suzan Farmer had also starred opposite Karloff, but in American International's 1965 adaptation of the H P Lovecraft short story 'The Colour Out of Space', called *Monster of Terror (US: Die, Monster, Die!)*; she was cast as Charles's wife Diana.

Dracula—Prince of Darkness (Philip Latham)

The key role of the unfortunate Alan Kent, who was to come to such a bloody end in the dungeon of Dracula's castle, went to Australian Charles Tingwell, a regular on British television, whose credits included *Danger Man* and *Emergency Ward 10*. Others in the cast were Philip Latham as Klove, the count's 'manservant', and Fisher favourite Thorley Walters as the Renfield-like Ludwig. The only actor other than Lee to return from the 1958 *Dracula* was West Countryman George Woodbridge, who once again played the role of an innkeeper. The ruddy-cheeked Woodbridge was a Hammer regular, often appearing as a tradesman or a police constable in films like *The Revenge of Frankenstein* (1958), The Mummy (1959) and *The Curse of the Werewolf* (1961), though he had briefly been elevated to the ranks of the aristocracy for his role in the Sangster-scripted *Jack the Ripper* in 1959.

Sangster's draft of the screenplay included a few nods to Stoker's novel that he had seen fit to leave out of *Dracula*. The character of the insect-eating Ludwig was one, as well as the idea that vampires can only cross a threshold if they are 'invited' in by someone already inside and that they cannot cross running water. (Dracula's castle in the first film was fronted by a fast-flowing stream!) This latter would be employed to provide the climax to *Dracula—Prince of Darkness*.

Robinson and his assistant Don Mingaye recreated the facade of Castle Dracula, complete with its anomalous ice-covered moat, over the village square set that had been constructed for *The Gorgon*. For long shots of the castle, the filmmakers used the model that FX artist Les Bowie had built for Chateau Ravna in *The Kiss of the Vampire*. *Dracula—Prince of Darkness* and *Rasputin—The Mad Monk* were both shot in Techniscope, a cheaper (and cruder) widescreen process used in many European films of the time. But this proved to be a problem when Hammer decided to 'drop in' the climax from the 1958 film, which had been shot in standard 'Academy' ratio; Hinds's solution was to frame the sequence in a halo of billowing fog, which masked the sides of the Techniscope screen.

Dracula—Prince of Drakness (Christopher Lee)

The plot of the film was a simple one, and it was intended originally to have provided the sequel to *Dracula*: on a visit to Transylvania, Alan and Charles Kent and their wives find themselves stranded at Castle Dracula, where they are welcomed by Klove in lieu of his dead master. During the night, Alan is murdered by Klove and his blood used to resurrect the monstrous count. Helen is turned into a vampire, but Charles and Diana flee and are forced to take refuge in a nearby monastery, under the protection of Father Sandor. Dracula comes after them but, in a partial repeat of the finale from the first film, he is pursued back to his castle and trapped on the ice-covered moat; shots are fired, the ice breaks, and he falls through it to his doom (for now) in the swirling waters below.

Production of the film went smoothly, aside from the expected problems with props. Lee may have had no dialogue, but such was not the case for all of the film's vampires: Shelley found it tricky to speak while wearing her fangs. She later noted, 'I hadn't realised there would be any difficulty. I had to walk toward Suzan Farmer, who was out of shot, and I had to walk into a big close-up and look at her and say the line, "You don't need Charles." The fangs were a tremendous impediment and so it came out like, "Hew gon't gleed Kharlz," at which, of course, everybody just roared with laughter, and I had to go into my dressing rooom for about twenty minutes and practise very carefully speaking around the fangs.'

There were several mishaps in the shooting of the climax. Years later, Bowie recalled, 'I've lost count of the times I've killed Christopher Lee. Syd Pearson finished him off in the first Hammer *Dracula*, but I handled the falling through the ice sequence in the second one.. We utilised a number of methods to get these scenes.. sometimes we used real blocks of ice in a swimming pool for a few of the close shots.. for other shots we used wax.. if you pour wax on water it forms a coating on the surface. For the final shots of Dracula sliding under the ice we used a circular section of plaster mounted on pivots.' (Christopher Lee also suffered one of his numerous on-set accidents when make-up artist Roy Ashton accidentally dropped one of Dracula's contact lenses onto the salt-covered wax and put it back into Lee's eye without cleaning it; this caused the hapless actor a deal of pain, and makes it easier to understand why he has so often complained about having to wear contact lenses for the role.)

To cap it off, Lee's stuntman Eddie Powell was almost drowned! Powell recalled, 'The ice.. was on a swivel thing and.. the water underneath came right up to the underside. Chris did his bit, then I came in. I had arranged it so that I had an air bottle on the bottom—it was only about ten feet deep—because when it closed, you need some air, because they were shooting from a distance. So I worked everything out, I knew where everything was. I thought, "Terrific!" and on "Action", it tipped up, went down and this bloody thing closed behind me, which it was supposed to do, but of course it was pitch black. I hadn't thought of that. Now I'm looking for this bloody thing down below to get an air line and thinking, "Christ, I've had it," because the water's up to the underside of this sort of ice and there's no air up there. Eventually I found it, lungs bursting, and they came along and picked me up. But it's silly little things like that that cause these sort of accidents.'

Shooting wrapped for *Dracula Prince of Darkness* in Black Park on June 4, on time but a little over budget after six weeks of principal photography. Location shooting had been scheduled for the final day so that Robinson's and Mingaye's sets could be revamped for *Rasputin—The Mad Monk*, in which Castle Dracula was to become a Russian palace. In post-production, sound editor Roy Baker felt that Shelley's voice was too deep when she screamed, so Suzan Farmer ended up screaming for both of them.

Dracula—Prince of Darkness (Francis Matthews, Barbara Shelley)

Dracula—Prince of Darkness (Barbara Shelley, Christopher Lee)

The double-bill of *Dracula—Prince of Darkness* and *Plague of the Zombies* was released in the UK on December 17, 1965, and became one of the top ten money-makers of the year. When it went out in the US the following spring (to catch the drive-in season), it made a killing there also despite (or because of) a silly advertising campaign, which included the handing out of free 'Dracula fangs' to audiences.

In many respects, *Dracula—Prince of Darkness* is Hammer's most iconic production. The massive advertising campaign which was mounted on its behalf was instrumental in entrenching the company as the House of Horror in the public's mind. Hammer's three previous vampire outings had each explored different aspects of the legend: *Dracula* had introduced the vampire as seducer—basically expanding on the old Lugosi image of a sophisticated and sexually-attractive devil. But in bringing the sexual element to the forefront, Fisher had appended a buxom bride as well. It was only fitting then, that the next in the series would actually be called *The Brides of Dracula* and would deliver a 'Prince Charming' pop star as its monster in the person of Peel's Baron Meinster, whom his 'wild friends' have corrupted to the extent that he feels free to indulge in incestuous relations with his mother, and the first hints of lesbianism and other types of 'abnormal' sexuality also creep into the myth. In *The Kiss of the Vampire*, vampirism has moved on to become a kind of sexually-transmitted disease.

In *Dracula—Prince of Darkness*, the cult of vampirism is taken another step further to become a full-fledged 'religion'. Klove resurrects the 'messiah', whose one purpose is to spread 'the obscene cult of vampirism'. Fisher told of how he decided to film Dracula's resurrection: 'When Klove, Dracula's servant in *Dracula—Prince of Darkness*, cuts Alan's throat to obtain blood to pour upon Dracula's ashes, to resurrect him, the scene could have been played in quite different ways. Klove could have played it with speed and triumph—he cannot wait to see Dracula again—or he

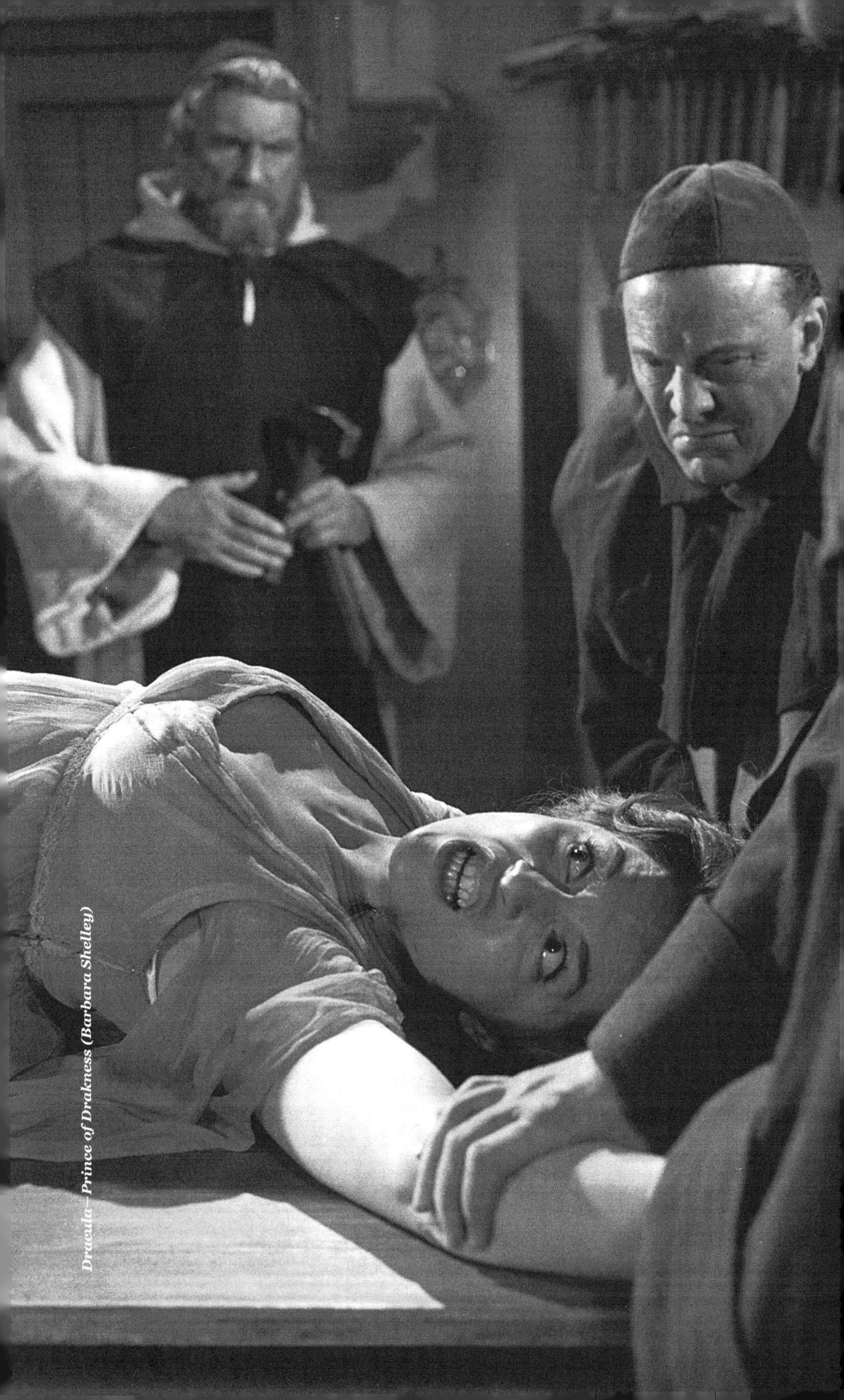

Dracula—Prince of Drakness (Barbara Shelley)

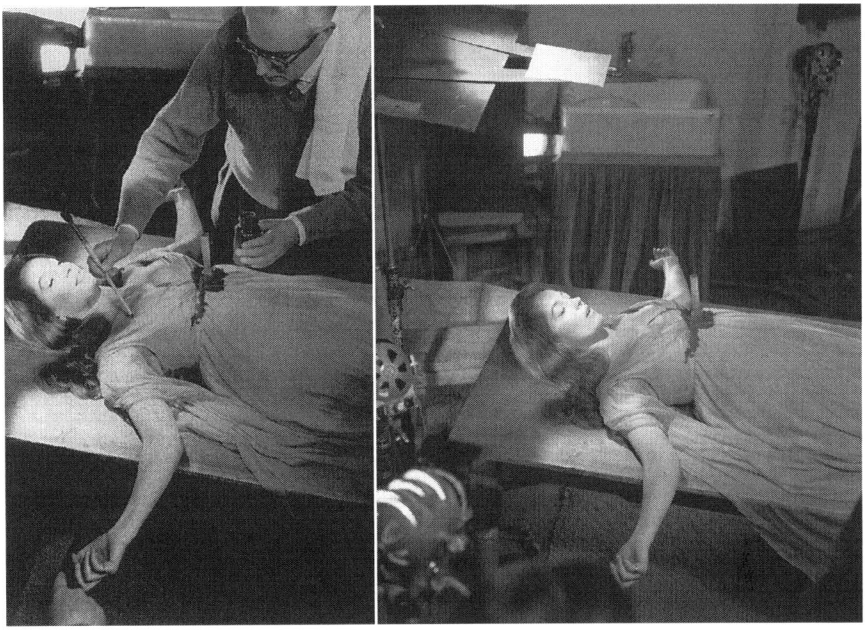

Roy Ashton readies Barbara Shelley for her close-up

could have played it almost weeping and overcome with emotion, causing perhaps bungling and uncertain movements. I chose to play it slowly and ritualistically, in the same way a priest would administer the Sacrament; an anti-Christ ceremony. There was no indication in the script of how this sequence was to be treated.'

Fisher handles the scene brilliantly. With Bernard's ominous music pulsing on the soundtrack, the *mise-en-scène* has a certain grim majesty. Dracula's cloak has been lovingly arranged in the background, waiting to be draped over the bare back of the 'messiah'. Klove reverently pours the ashes into the stone sarcophagus and, emotionless, he slits Alan's throat as though he were simply slitting open an envelope. The blood literally *cascades* onto the count's ashes, and in one of Les Bowie's best-ever effects scenes (though strangely reminiscent of that in *Castle of Blood*, in which a ghost-vampire returns to life in a mist-enshrouded sarcophagus [Margheriti's film was not released in the UK until 1967]), the count's flesh regenerates onto his bones and his hand, complete with crested ring, reaches out of the tomb; it is the climax of a Black Mass, with the Antichrist being born into the world. And it is one of Fisher's, and Hammer's, most masterful sequences.

Prior to this reawakening, the sequel has taken a long while to start moving. As Sangster noted, 'Worth pointing out is the fact that nothing actually happens until we're nearly forty minutes in, when Alan is stabbed by Klove. Up to that point we've had mystery and tension combined with expectation, but that's it. It's a confirmation of my theory of suspense. You can keep the audience dangling for a long, long time providing they know something pretty terrible is eventually going to take place. Then once the action starts it really gets going.'

Aside from the shocking murder and mutilation of Alan, another scene that gave the censor pause was that in which Dracula attempts to victimise Diana. Frank Crofts and Newton Branch of the BBFC wrote, 'Remove the whole incident in which Dracula bares his chest, scratches it and tries to get Diana to suck the wound.' Editor James Needs balked at removing the whole scene and, instead, reduced it. The scene was resubmitted, whereupon Crofts noted, 'The "scratch-and-kiss" scene has been

cut at the point where Dracula, having scratched his chest, advances on Diana and puts his hand on her shoulders. This will do.' This was lifted directly from Stoker's novel, when Dr Seward bursts into the Harkers' bedroom to find the count at work: 'With his left hand he held both Mrs Harker's hands, keeping them away with her arms at full tension; his right hand gripped her by the back of the neck, forcing her face down on his bosom. Her white nightdress was smeared with blood, and a thin stream trickled down the man's bare breast which was shown by his torn-open dress. The attitude of the two had a terrible resemblance to a child forcing a kitten's nose into a saucer of milk to compel it to drink.

Whether or not Stoker intended it, the scene reads like some grim parody of oral sex. As performed by Lee and Farmer, it also plays in the film like a man who is trying to persuade a woman to taste of his 'essence'. It is an inversion of the scene in *The Kiss of the Vampire* in which Isobel Black bares Edward De Souza's chest and scratches it with her fingernails, drawing blood, but the symbolism in that instance was equally clear.

It may be said that the idea of the 'Terrifying Lover' is, to an extent, a dream of rape. Fisher saw in the story of Dracula a tale of repressed lust but, to Stoker, it was something quite different. A great deal of Freudian 'interpretation' has been read into the text over the years, but the truth is on the page. The novel *Dracula* exemplifies the widespread 'fear' of foreigners at the time of its writing, and their ability to 'ravage' the flower of English womanhood and thereby dilute the race. Stoker was alleged by writer and great-nephew Daniel Farson to have died of syphilis; his views on women, as expressed in his final novel *The Lair of the White Worm* (which is filled with symbolism for the Freudians), were the very antithesis of the desire for 'sexual freedom' that was brought out metaphorically by Fisher in his three vampire films for Hammer. Literary critics have misread the novel for years; they fixate on Stoker's obsession with 'blood transfusions' and see in that the implication that all of his male protagonists want to have sex with Mina, when in fact he was merely obsessed with the racial 'purity'. Dracula represented a contagion from abroad, at a period in history when the whole of the British Empire was under threat from unchecked immigration. The concept of the demon lover does not enter into it.

Fisher once told Sue and Colin Cowie, 'He [Dracula] is basically sexual. He has the powers of evil to prey on the victims' sexual feelings so that they believe at the moment he bites it is the culmination of a sexual experience. This is because he is the personification of evil and will always prey on the weakness of every victim, no matter whether it's greed or sexuality. His is the personification of temptation.' This was his own reading of the myth, but 'borrowed' from the films that he had seen in his youth—in other words, the Lugosi personification of the count, rather than the less-than-dashing, mostly unattractive Stoker characterisation. F W Murnau had got it right all along in *Nosferatu*, when he depicted Dracula as a plague-carrier, intent on spreading his pestilence in the west through the body of a young woman. He 'infects' her not with desire but with *disease*—the notion that Hinds brought to Hammer's vampire films. Her blood is 'tainted' by that of a foreigner; no wonder Stoker's widow sued Murnau!

In the Hammer films, Dracula is a dream of desire: the 'continental lover' who gives prim Victorian womanhood what it secretly longs for but lacks the courage to admit. In *Dracula—Prince of Darkness*, Barbara Shelley's character is transformed from shrewish *hausfrau* into a wanton creature of the night thanks to Dracula's bite. In fact, there is something going on between Dracula and Helen even before

Dracula—Prince of Darkness (Suzan Farmer, Christopher Lee)

he is resurrected; she thinks she hears someone calling her name in a dream—the spirit of Dracula? When they do finally come face-to-face, it takes but one nuzzle from the count to turn her into a fully-fledged vampire. No courting of the victim here; perhaps Helen is easier to 'convert' because she so desperately wants to be freed from her repressive Victorian shackles to begin with.

In an interview with Al Taylor in 'Little Shoppe of Horrors', Shelley described the approach that she took to shaking off the constraints of respectability: 'Terry [Fisher] pointed out that when one becomes a vampire, one's sexual proclivities are no longer heterosexual. I did, in fact, do a lot of preparation for this particular role because I wondered how one could play a vampire as the epitome of evil and decadence. So, I went back to my old days when I used to study the old Greek dramas and studied the use of that sort of feeling of the Furies.'

Whether a Fury or a Harpie (noteworthy that both Helen and Diana are classical Greek names), the vampiric Helen is positively demonic. The fires of Hell dance in her eyes when she is captured by monks in a scene that perfectly encapsulates the story's mythic subtext of Christianity versus paganism. As she is held down by several of their number, Father Sandor hammers home the purgative stake; the setup of the scene prompted more than one critic to equate it with gang-rape. British audiences did not get to see the stake penetrate Helen's flesh, but Americans were allowed the phallic goods.

This one sequence can be seen as summarising the 'double-standard' inherent in Hammer's approach to vampire films by 1965: a diaphanously-gowned vampire woman is destroyed by the Church, which casts out the 'lust' in her by driving a stake into her breast. It was a far cry from the old black-and-white Universal vampires—indeed, 'black and white' did not enter into it. There now were numerous shades of grey, and the religious aspects of the myth were coming increasingly to the fore.

Dracula—Prince of Darkness turned out to be the final Hammer vampire film for both Fisher and Sangster. Along with Tony Hinds, these three had virtually created the Hammer vampire. The franchise would be placed in the hands of a number of other directors (though Hinds would continue to write the scripts) and the myth would be further refined and explored. But these first four Hammer vampire films had established the blueprint that all the others would follow and, between them, they had changed the face of the genre forever.

> ..'Speak it. God of Heaven! let me hear it.'
>
> 'A vampyre!'
>
> Henry sprung to his feet. His whole frame quivered with emotion; the drops of perspiration stood upon his brow, as, in a strange hoarse voice, he repeated the words,—
>
> 'A vampyre!'
>
> 'Even so; one who has to renew a dreadful existence by human blood—one who lives on for ever, and must keep up such a fearful existence upon human gore—one who eats not and drinks not as other men—a vampyre.'
>
> **—James Malcolm Rymer, *Varney the Vampyre; or, The Feast of Blood* (1845-7)**

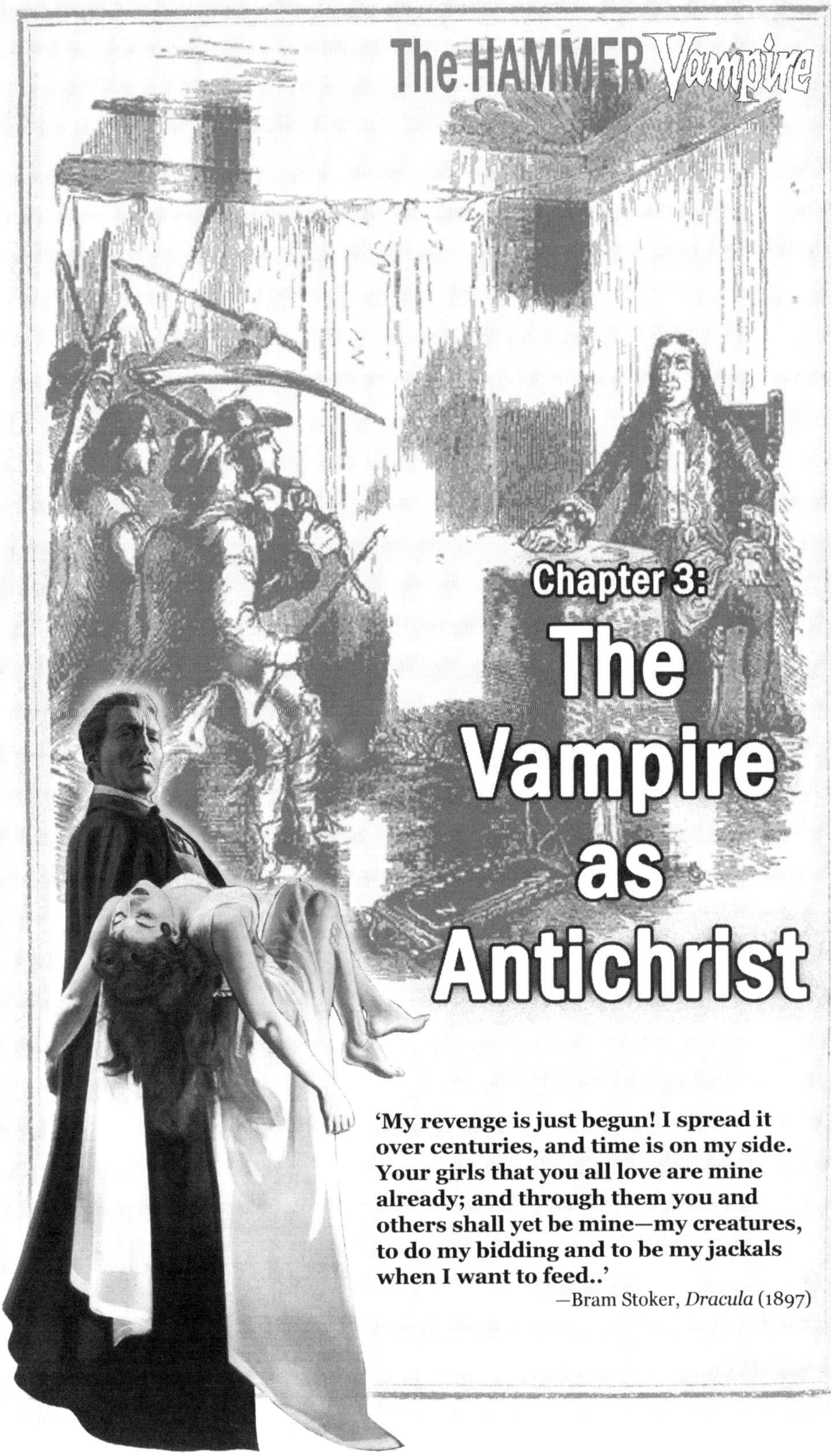

Chapter 3: The Vampire as Antichrist

'My revenge is just begun! I spread it over centuries, and time is on my side. Your girls that you all love are mine already; and through them you and others shall yet be mine—my creatures, to do my bidding and to be my jackals when I want to feed..'

—Bram Stoker, *Dracula* (1897)

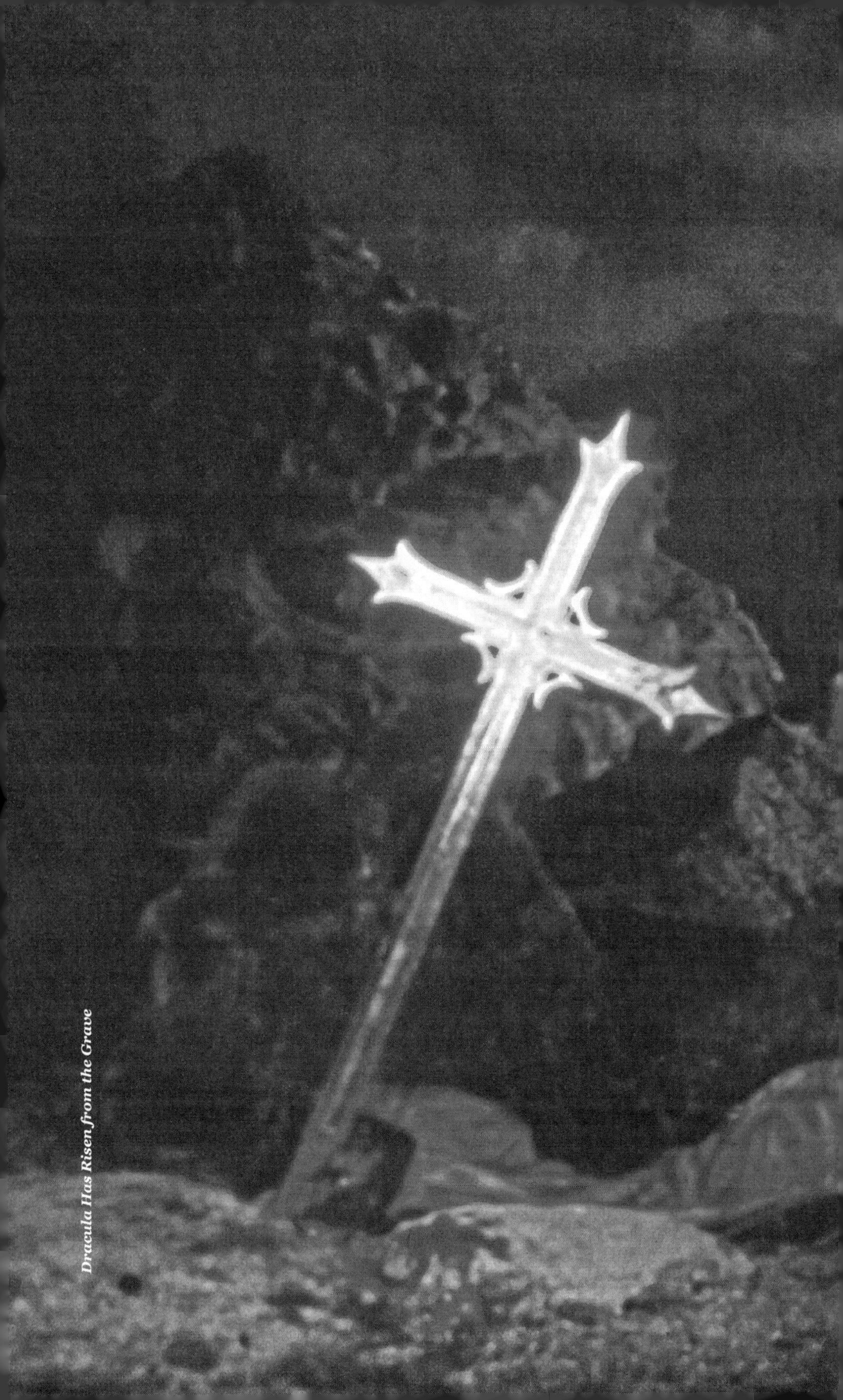

Dracula Has Risen from the Grave

The news in The Christopher Lee (Fan) Club Bulletin for April–May 1968 could not have been any more exciting for Hammer fans. The bulletin always opened with a letter 'from Christopher', and this latest missive from the actor began with a couple of paragraphs on his role in Tigon's *Curse of the Crimson Altar* and his upbeat feelings about Terence Fisher's *The Devil Rides Out* (while also lamenting its US title-change to *The Devil's Bride*). Lee saved the bombshell for last: 'And now, to close, my final tidbit of information. Over the past few weeks, there has been a great deal of slightly hysterical and acrimonious discussion between me, my agent, James Carreras, Tony Hinds and producer Aida Young and director Freddie Francis, about the next *Dracula*, due to start on 22nd April next. If only I had a tape recording of some of the conversations concerned, it would make for hilarious listening. To sum up, they have committed themselves to the making of this film, but they do not appear to think that they are required to pay me my current market price, which I receive from all the other film companies. The arguments and appeals to my better nature, etc., have been remarkable, but I have remained firm and so has my agent, Dick Blodgett... The decision is a very simple one. If they will pay me the salary I receive from all the other companies for whom I work—and I like the script—I will play the part again, bad back and all. If I do not play this role again, you will at least know why. You may be sure that as soon as the decision has been taken, I will let you know at once. The title—*Dracula Has Risen from the Grave*—has already filled me with considerable misgivings.'

The fact is that the film had already been announced to the trade press in February. Disappointing box-office returns for Hammer's two Dennis Wheatley adaptations (*The Devil Rides Out* and *The Lost Continent*) would lead to 20th Century Fox withdrawing from its current co-production arrangement with Hammer, but 7-Arts had partnered with Warner Brothers (Eliot Hyman having bought out Jack Warner) and Hyman remained a great friend to the company; a new co-production deal had been struck between Hammer and Warner Bros/7-Arts, and *Dracula Has Risen from the Grave* was going to be the film that would launch it.

In fact, as far back as May 4, 1967, *Dracula Has Risen from the Grave* had already been mooted as a 'Dracula subject'. A Hammer production meeting had been held on that date and, with James Carreras's usual showmanship, a pre-sale brochure had been issued by August. Obviously, there was no script at that point—in

fact, screenwriter Tony Hinds (under his *nom du cinema* of John Elder) had not even formulated a synopsis at the time.

From this embryonic 'Dracula subject' had grown a provisional title: *Dracula's Revenge*. The final title of ..*Risen from the Grave* may have taken its cue from the mid-sixties craze for using a phrase as a title, much to the chagrin of Lee, who preferred the more austere-sounding 'Dracula Arisen'. Originally, the film was budgeted at £165,000 and was intended to be shot back-to-back with the similarly-titled *Frankenstein Must Be Destroyed*; the fifth film in Hammer's ongoing Frankenstein saga was also made under the deal, but it was not shot back-to-back with *Risen from the Grave*. It was further intended that Terence Fisher would return to the director's chair after the success of *Dracula—Prince of Darkness*.

Set construction began at Pinewood Studios (Hammer having vacated Bray late in 1966) on April 4, 1968, and the schedule was the usual eight weeks. During pre-production, however, Fisher was knocked down by a motorcyclist while crossing the road and ended up with a broken leg, which immediately put him out of commission. He was replaced by Oscar-winning cinematographer-turned-director Freddie Francis, who had now helmed several features for Hammer, including the only Frankenstein that had not been directed by Fisher—*The Evil of Frankenstein* (1964), as well as numerous assorted horrors for rivals Amicus Productions, most recently *Torture Garden* (1967).

Having been drafted into the job, Francis approached it with enthusiasm, saying that he wanted to make the film 'visually interesting and exciting, as opposed to just expecting the audience to go along and see the same old Dracula'. *Risen from the Grave* had originally been set to go into production on March 18 but had been postponed due to Fisher's accident; it was also to have been shot at the ABPC Studios at Elstree, but they were fully booked. Having had to replace the director, Hammer had also to replace the producer: Anthony Nelson Keys had been nominated for the role, having earlier produced *Dracula—Prince of Darkness*, but Keys was in Ireland on another project and he, in turn, was replaced by Aida Young, an old hand of Hammer's and protégé of Michael Carreras from as far back as *Mantrap* (1953) but more recently, associate producer on *One Million Years BC* and *Slave Girls* (1966 and 1967 respectively); as a woman operating in a man's world, Young was a tough, no-nonsense facilitator.

The final hurdle was persuading Christopher Lee to accept the role. Francis said later, 'When I first went onto the movie, we were looking for somebody to play the part, and then suddenly out of the blue James Carreras had met up with Chris, and suddenly Chris was going to do it.' The wily Carreras had convinced his reluctant vampire 'king' to return to the fold; according to Lee, Carreras telephoned him at home and begged him to play the role, saying that if he refused, he would put a great many people out of work. Lee referred to the bind into which Carreras invariably put him as 'emotional blackmail'. Young, on the other hand, suggested that Lee 'was a unique character and he probably wouldn't get a leading role elsewhere..' Though she went on to say, 'Whatever part he got in [another] film would have to be a secondary or tertiary part. With Dracula, he was the king.'

In the more than two-year absence from the screen of the 'king' of vampires since *Dracula—Prince of Darkness*, other producers had finally begun to catch up with the commercial value of the Un-dead, as well as the commercial virtues of Technicolor and/or widescreen.

Hammer may have had things its own way up to *Dracula—Prince of Darkness*,

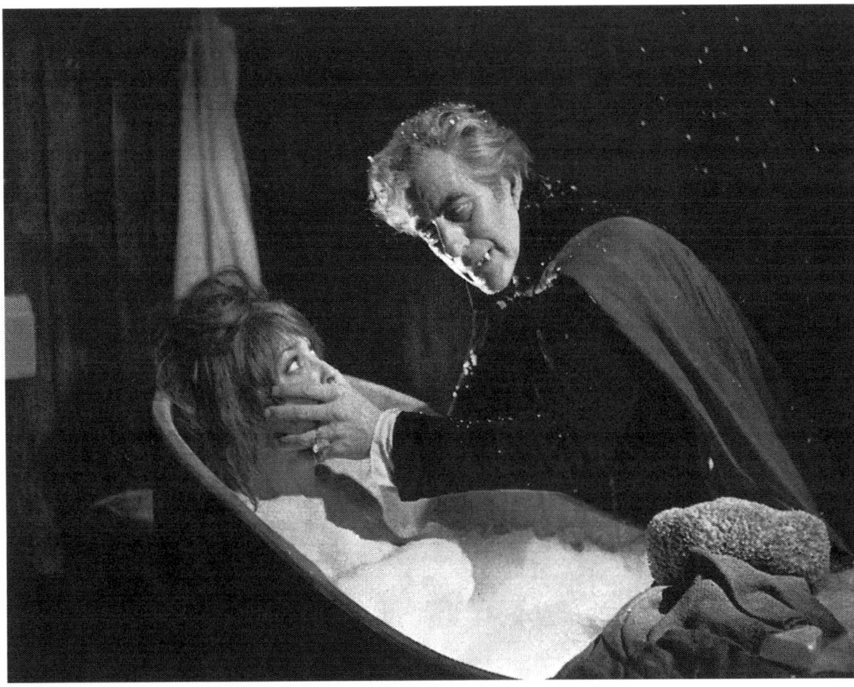

Dance of the Vampires (Sharon Tate, Ferdy Mayne)

but the success of that 1966 release had seen to it that more 'vampire' films followed thick and fast. With the exception of a dubbed German import (*Cave of the Living Dead*) and a couple of minor British entries—*Theatre of Blood* with Christopher Lee and *The Hand of Night*, starring William Sylvester from *Devils of Darkness*—they all seemed to be of the humorous variety, however. Producer Peter Rogers had set the parody ball rolling with *Carry On Screaming*, the twelfth in the successful comedy franchise, in which Fenella Fielding played the 'vamp' while the rest of the cast poked light-hearted fun at all things Hammer. But the real bite had been delivered by rising directorial talent Roman Polanski, a Polish émigré, whose first English-language script had been turned down by Hammer on his arrival in London.

After the critical and commercial success of his Tigon-backed *Repulsion*, the young director had persuaded M-G-M to fund a Gothic horror-comedy called *The Vampire Killers* to the tune of $2 million, and its Dracula-inspired Count Krolock (Ferdy Mayne), elaborate Transylvanian castle-set, voluptuous damsel in distress, sumptuous cinematography and massed disciples of the Un-dead had convinced critics on both sides of the pond that Hammer was indeed the target of its barbs, despite the fact that its director's mid-European sensibility had vested the film with more of Universal or UFA than Bray. Released in the UK as *Dance of the Vampires* and in the US as *The Fearless Vampire Killers*, Polanski's horror *hommage* was a critical and commercial disaster. But the damage was done, and the Hammer vampire as it had come to be recognised over the preceding decade was not to be viewed in quite the same light again. A change of tack was required, and its time was not far off. (Christopher Lee would satirise the character himself in 1969 by appearing in cameo as Dracula [along with Peter Cushing] in the comedy *One More Time*, in which Sammy Davis Jr and Peter Lawford played bungling secret agents Salt and Pepper.)

Until then, and in light of these send-ups, Hammer's next Dracula required to

be a bit more 'knowing', if not downright camp. Freddie Francis's gaudy sense of colour and affectation for lens filters and fish-eye lenses was to ensure it of both.

For *Dracula Has Risen from the Grave*, Hammer assembled its now-regulatory mix of newcomers and seasoned professionals. With Hinds's screenplay completed, it was apparent that *Risen from the Grave* would expand upon the religious overtones of *Dracula—Prince of Darkness* and be more of a morality play than ever. Consequently, his latest plot was to see the count inadvertently brought to life again by the actions of a rogue priest (Ewan Hooper), whom he then enslaves to his will. The target of Dracula's rage becomes the family of the Monsignor (Rupert Davies) who has barred him from his castle in his 'absence' by sealing the door with an ornamental crucifix. (How a Catholic Monsignor came to acquire a 'family' was subject to some tortuous explanation in the script.) Finding refuge instead in the cellar of an inn, Dracula sets about his obligatory revenge..

As the Monsignor, Davies was a distinguished character actor well known to British TV audiences as Georges Simenon's *Maigret*. He had never worked for Hammer before, but he had recently appeared in Don Sharp's *The Brides of Fu Manchu* alongside Lee, and he would move on from this film to feature in Tigon's *The Curse of the Crimson Altar*, again alongside Lee, as well as Boris Karloff and Barbara Steele.

Hammer stalwart Michael Ripper was allotted the role of—need it be said?—the innkeeper, and his barmaid, Zena, was to be played by New Zealander Barbara Ewing, fresh from Francis's *Torture Garden*. The film's leading lady and focus of Dracula's attention was 23-year-old Veronica Carlson, whom James Carreras had spotted in a bikini in the *Daily Mirror*. Carlson had only minor film credits, such as a small role in *Casino Royale* (1967), but ever on the lookout for Hammer Glamour-girls, Carreras put her under contract and shots of her in a negligée in a graveyard set formed a major part of the publicity campaign for *Risen from the Grave*. As Carlson's boyfriend in the film, Barry Andrews was an untried actor who would go on to play the lead in Tigon's *The Blood on Satan's Claw* the following year, but Scots-born Ewan Hooper, who was to play the priest, was a graduate of RADA (The Royal Academy of Dramatic Art) and had written, produced and acted for both television and the stage.

Christopher Lee and James Carreras at Pinewood Studios

The production received another boost when it was announced on April 18—only four days before *Risen from the Grave* went onto the floor at Pinewood—that Hammer was to be the recipient of a 1968 Queen's Award to Industry. The news made international headlines. Throughout the 1960s, Hammer had gone from strength to strength, bringing in almost £3 million in profits between

Dracula Has Risen from the Grave (Carrie Baker)

1964 and 1967. Its biggest American contract had just been signed: the company was to produce a television series called *Journey to the Unknown* for the American ABC network. The Queen's Award was hugely prestigious, and it could not have come at a better time for Hammer.

The first day of shooting for Francis and company—April 22—saw the unit on Pinewood's K stage and consisted of two interiors. There was also a scene in the inn on J stage that highlighted a tavern song whose bawdy lyrics ('Here's to the best man who can drink the most of us/there'll be a maiden waiting in his bed') were a good indication of the direction that the series was now to take. Carlson was the typical virginal heroine, but there also was a lusty female supporting role in Ewing's barmaid, who needed little convincing to become a creature of the night. Ewing fitted the role, but the role fitted her only after she was given a push-up bra; until then, she had not been deemed 'sexy' (that is, busty) enough.

As a sign that Hammer had taken note of the sumptuous look of Polanski's *Dance of the Vampires*, matte artist Peter Melrose was hired to simulate his work on that film and provide some elaborate glass paintings of Castle Dracula and the fairy-tale rooftops of Kleinenberg. Melrose found himself rushed on Hammer's shorter schedule, but the sense of scale that he contributed to *Risen from the Grave* added immeasurably to the big budget look of the film.

Freddie Francis's experience as a lighting cameraman ensured that his approach

to direction was highly visual. While confessing himself to be no great fan of the horror genre, Francis nevertheless had done solid work in the field (notably in the Amicus film *The Skull*; 1965) and was being considered by many as a rival to Fisher on the British horror scene. But in *Risen from the Grave*, he somehow opted to afford more screen-time to young lovers Paul (Andrews) and Maria (Carlson) than to Dracula himself.

Lee had his own problems with the script—which at least allowed him some dialogue this time out; his main concern was a scene in which Dracula had to pull out the stake that has been driven into his heart. In an interview with Tim Stout in the fanzine *Supernatural*, Lee expressed his distaste at the idea of overturning one of basic tenets of vampire lore. Hinds was rewriting the rules again and, as he had it, Paul, who is an atheist, cannot bring himself to pray during the staking of the count, which enables him to survive a situation that should by rights be fatal to any bloodsucker. 'It was all wrong that Dracula should have been able to remove the stake,' Lee opined. 'Everyone knows a stake through the heart is the very end of a vampire. I objected at the time, but it was overruled. It is an extremely gruesome sequence; the blood comes pouring out.'

Lee also had back problems throughout the production, as he outlined to his American fan club president, Gloria Lillibridge: 'The present *Dracula* is going well and I suppose will have its usual worldwide success.. Of course I can't leap about like I used to and several scenes have to be played by my double, Eddie Powell, who has been with me now for several years.. He will be doing any scenes which require me to jump or carry anybody. I am quite relieved about the latter, as the girl I have to carry in the story, Veronica Carlson, is hardly a lightweight and turns the scale at around 120 pounds! As poor Eddie has also had a lot of trouble with his spine, he is also rather apprehensive at the moment.. So far as I can see, I finish the film by being impaled on a crucifix, with the resultant disintegration. I don't like this idea at all, but Hammer are insistent—so I suppose they are already thinking into the future and are reluctant to kill off the proverbial golden goose.'

Freddie Francis, Christopher Lee and Aida Young

It was during the shooting of this 'crucifixion' that Brigadier Sir Henry Floyd, the Lord Lieutenant of Buckinghamshire (where Pinewood Studios is located) came on set to present Hammer with its Queen's Award. Seeing Lee writhing around on the cross, tears of blood streaming from his eyes, led to more than a few raised eyebrows when Sir Henry then observed to cast and crew, 'I know that you have had great success with what are termed "horror films", but I was glad to learn that the word "horror" does not include scenes of actual personal violence, and that in this respect your company feels you have a responsibility towards the viewing public.' James Carreras had seen fit to play down Hammer's 'history of horrors' in light of his

Dracula Has Risen from the Grave: Pinewood's rooftop set/inset: Peter Melrose glass-shot

impending knighthood! As Lee recollected for *Little Shoppe of Horrors*: 'The Lord Lieutenant of Buckinghamshire came down and presented this award.. and then after that they came on the set and they came at a rather violent moment when I was crashing about in the rocks with this cross through me, pouring blood and those awful contact lenses in my eyes. Well, after the Lord Lieutenant and his wife, who I'm sure had never been in a studio in their lives, had been watching all this without any expression at all on their faces.. there was a long, long silence and then, very clearly, and very penetratingly,

he turned to his wife and he said, "You know, my dear, that man is a member of my club".'

Principal shooting on *Dracula Has Risen from the Grave* wrapped on May 31, 1968, on both time and budget. In a letter to Ben Kalmenson of Warner Bros/7-Arts, dated June 24, Carreras wrote: 'I am sending out into New York five minutes of *Dracula Has Risen from the Grave* which has just been shown by Norman Katz to all his salesmen in Europe and others gathered for the sales convention in London. Without a doubt this is the best *Dracula* that has ever been made by Hammer and its box office potential is enormous. I hope you will show this film to all those who will be selling the film in the USA and Canada and start getting them as excited about it as we are.'

On August 6, Lee again wrote to Lillibridge: 'I am told that the latest *Dracula* has been received with glad cries by the distributors, who will doubtless make a vast amount of money, as usual. I have no comment to make except to say that it is virtually the mixture as before. However, it is possible that the direction of Freddie Francis has been more intelligent and less pedestrian than that of Terence Fisher,' he added acidly.

Dracula Has Risen from the Grave was indeed the hit that Carreras had predicted. When it went on general release in the UK, it broke the opening day record on the ABC circuit, despite what were now the usual dismissive reviews. 'Fangs ain't what they used ter be,' was the crude and unfunny assessment of Dick Richards in *The Sun*. But if the count could now pull a stake out of his own heart, the barbs of his critics were to cause him little discomfort: Dracula had indeed risen from the grave, and his resurrection marked a new high in profits for Hammer and its gleeful distributors.

This was all in spite of the fact that Lee, who fortunately was not in charge of Hammer's publicity department, wrote again to Lillibridge, 'The third *Dracula*, which I have not dared look at as I am convinced it is a very indifferent film, is making fantastic sums of money on the London circuit. I have got past understanding any of this by now. The film was made with complete absence of style, taste and production quality. The critics tore it to bits, as they always do with a Hammer film, and yet, according to 7-Arts and Hammer, it is probably the most successful picture they have ever made.'

Despite what Lee may ultimately have thought of it, *Risen from the Grave* evinces considerable style and offers up several worthy performances, including his own. The count is graced with a smattering of dialogue, though not much is made of it ('Who has done this thing?'; 'There is a girl.. bring her to me!'), and Lee succeeds in vesting the character with both his usual ferocity (when he finds the cross affixed to the door of his castle) and an unusual tenderness (as when he nuzzles Maria before sinking his fangs into her virginal throat). And when he is put to the stake, in the scene that he hated the most, he is terrifying; the vampire hunter's worst nightmare—an Un-dead who simply will not die.

Given Francis's concentration on the other characters in the drama, the film is nearly stolen from its protagonist by Barbara Ewing, who plays the role of the sexy barmaid to the hilt. 'Your dumplings are pouring over, Zena,' a patron tells her, while staring at her copious cleavage. Good-natured, earthy and ultimately, the latest evolution of the Hammer vampire, Zena is perhaps the most believable character in the film; when she meets her end mid-way through, *Risen from the Grave* loses some of its own *joie de vivre*. But Hooper is equally fine as the priest who becomes Dracula's unwilling 'disciple', despite the fact that his voice was

Dracula Has Risen from the Grave (Veronica Carlson, Barry Andrews/below: Ewan Hooper, Barry Andrews)

Dracula Has Risen from the Grave (Veronica Carlson, Christopher Lee)

dubbed by a Hammer averse to regional accents (an eventuality which Francis had to warn him about prior to the film's premiere in London). His tortured expressions and growing air of disgust over what he is required to enact on the count's behalf bring a convincing sense of anguish to the character; he seems constantly to be in battle for his soul, a fight that he ultimately wins.

Amid all the fuss and flurry of Francis's psychedelic colour-effects (this *was* the late sixties), Hinds allows himself a line or two that stands out from the usual expedient of dialogue that is simply there to move the plot forward. When Paul tells Max (Ripper) in a sideswipe at the 'hippie' philosophy prevalent among the youth of the time that he is searching for 'the truth', the jaded innkeeper replies 'The truth?—What do you want with that? If you want to be a success in life, *forget* the truth..'

Carlson and Andrews acquit themselves adequately—which is just as well, given the amount of time that Francis devotes to their tryst on and under the roof-tops of Kleinenburg. Hammer always tried to keep one eye on the youth market, and the phenomenal success of Franco Zeffirelli's 1967 film version of Shakespeare's *Romeo and Juliet* (starring Leonard Whiting and Olivia Hussey) may have provided some inspiration in that regard.

Dracula Has Risen from the Grave has been referred to as a triumph of style over substance, but its style *is* its substance. Christian symbolism runs rampant throughout the film. Hammer's vampire films had always been highly successful in Catholic countries like Spain and Italy and in *Risen from the Grave*, Hinds and

Dracula Has Risen from the Grave (Barry Andrews, Christopher Lee)

Francis constructed a horror film that was an overt religious allegory. Paul—the young hero and point of empathy for the audience—is an atheist; Dracula's servant is not the satanic Klove but a priest whom he has bent to his will; the lamb on the sacrificial altar turns out to be the kindly Monsignor. Paul is converted to the 'path of righteousness' at the climax when Dracula is impaled on a golden cross. The atheist's resolve finally breaks down in the face of the threat to his beloved, and he finds himself praying for salvation for both of them.

What Dracula represents in *Risen from the Grave* is sin, with a capital 'S'. He is a corruptor of the flesh—easily, in Zena's case, when she is seduced in the forest; more laboriously in the case of Maria, the neophyte brought up under the protection of the Church by the good Monsignor. Maria's struggle with her moral conscience as to whether or not she should let boyfriend Paul 'go all the way' is metaphorically reflected in her battle of wills with the seductive vampire of sexual Temptation. In the decade of the Pill, Maria's dilemma mirrored that of many of the newly-liberated teens in the film's target audience.

By 1968, Hinds and Francis had seen the writing on the wall: the old rules did not apply any more, in life or in motion pictures. The sexual revolution was in full swing and traditional concepts of morality were being overturned in favour of a different consensus. Similar barriers were being broken down in horror films; good no longer triumphed over evil as a matter of course, as evidenced in George Romero's groundbreaking *Night of the Living Dead* or Michael Reeves's *Witchfinder General*—both of which were released in that same tumultuous year. Gestures to this change had been required, and vampires now no longer died simply by the inflicting of religious iconography upon them—but in the conservative view of Hammer and Hinds, 'atheists' should still convert to the faith when faced with a clear threat to the social order, as represented here by the advance of Sin in the form of Count Dracula and his contaminating 'pestilence'. Ironically, the cinematic rebels of only a decade

before were being forced onto the defensive by the *realpolitik* of the very 'permissive society' which they had helped to encourage.

For all that, Freddie Francis and set designer Bernard Robinson invested *Dracula Has Risen from the Grave* with much visual richness (sadly, it was the last time that Robinson designed a vampire film for Hammer before his untimely passing from a heart attack at the age of 58). The rooftop set on which the lovers rendezvous is one of his finest and adds immeasurably to fairy-tale ambience of the film, while its Grimm's castle, Gothic cellar and benighted woods echo of the same mythical mittel-European world of *The Brides of Dracula*—a country of nightmare, complete with star-crossed lovers, a dark wizard, and a mist-enshrouded edifice that harbours a monster.

Despite a somewhat inconsistent script, *Risen from the Grave* is one of Hammer's most enjoyable genre outings due to its captivating imagery and symbolic subtext. As with all of Hammer's best genre films, it now seems timeless. The company would continue to adapt the formula to the changing times, but Dracula was coming to the end of the road as sole representative of the Hammer vampire. He would continue on his journey to perdition for a few films yet, but more as a reminder of times gone by than as an indicator of the direction to come. That task would fall to the female of the species, and under a new regime of producers and directors at Hammer, she would rise to the challenge of the permissive age in a way that the count had seemed reticent to do in *Dracula Has Risen from the Grave.*

In a personal letter to Gloria Lillibridge—not his fan club—dated August 27, 1969, Lee wrote: 'I have left my most dramatic piece of news to the last. You know how I feel about Hammer films in general and their presentation of the Dracula stories in particular. Imagine therefore my surprise when I discovered on my return from Portugal that my agent, with the very best of intentions, has virtually committed me to playing Dracula for the fourth time in yet another Hammer production, tentatively entitled *Taste the Blood of Dracula*. Words fail me. It is by no means certain, even now, that I am going to do this, because I have not read one word of script. In fact it appears that there isn't one at the moment. I have been assured by many people that the fact that I play Dracula does not in any way mean that I am taking a step backwards into further cheap horror pictures. I only hope they are right and that some of the films that I have appeared in in the last few months will prove positively that I have escaped irrevocably from the rather misleading label which has been attached to me. My agent's excuse for committing me to this picture in all good faith is that I am receiving three times the money I have ever received for any Hammer film. However, there are loop-holes by which I could escape if I decided quite definitely I would not do this picture for them. So, you had better hold your fire on any announcement until you get confirmation from me.'

The 'prestige' pictures on which Lee had worked included Billy Wilder's *The Private Life of Sherlock Holmes* (1970), in which he played the Baker Street detective's brother Mycroft. A beautifully-crafted film, it nevertheless was a box office disaster. He had also completed *The Bloody Judge* for director Jess (Jesus) Franco, whom he called 'one of the most brilliant directors I have ever worked with'. The remark was made before Lee had the opportunity of actually *seeing* any of Franco's films. (*The Bloody Judge* was retitled *Night of the Blood Monster* in the US; at best, it was a rip-off of Tigon's *Witchfinder General*, with Lee's performance as its one saving grace. But it certainly qualifed as a 'cheap horror picture'.)

Things were changing rapidly at Hammer in the late sixties. In the documentary

Taste the Blood of Dracula (Linda Hayden, Christopher Lee, Isla Blair)

Taste the Blood of Dracula/El Conde Dracula (Christopher Lee)

feature *Flesh and Blood*, Don Sharp stated, 'Tony Hinds *was* Hammer.' But Hinds was to leave the company after helping to produce the TV series *Journey to the Unknown*. He would continue to offer Hammer his services as a screenwriter, but his days as the guiding light of Hammer's Gothic horrors were over. The camaraderie and 'family' feeling that had been a major feature of Hammer's operations at Bray Studios had also given way to the assembly-line anonymity of the more industrialised regime at ABPC-Elstree.

Taste the Blood of Dracula was scheduled to begin shooting at Elstree around Halloween of 1969—with or without Lee. His salary demands had become such a headache for Hammer that Hinds had been asked by company business manager Brian Lawrence to pen a script in the style of *Brides*, in which a 'disciple' of the count becomes the main focus of the story. Hinds came up with the intriguing notion of a decadent Victorian aristocrat who conducts a black mass at which he drinks Dracula's blood; he is then beaten to death by three thrill-seekers whom he had persuaded to join him in his blasphemy, but he is reborn as a vampire, and he sets out to revenge himself on the families of the 'gentlemen' who turned on him during the ceremony.

Warner Bros, however, was less than enthusiastic about the idea of a Dracula film without Lee, who had now become as identified with the role to the modern audience as was Bela Lugosi in the thirties. Hinds revised his script to have 'Lord Courtley' turn into Dracula, and Lee was duly reinstated into the production, inflated salary and all. So it was that he wrote to Lillibridge on September 23: 'On November 3rd I start what I hope will be positively my last film for Hammer. The tasteful title is *Taste the Blood of Dracula*.. The only ray of hope is that we have an entirely new director, a young Hungarian named Peter Sasdy. So we can all pray for a fresh approach in the knowledge that at least he is the right nationality!' Lee went on to state that he was also committed to playing the role of 'Bram Stoker's Dracula, as he wrote it,' in a separate European production. 'This will mean that I will have played the part of Dracula five times in all and only once has Stoker wrote it. And it will be with the latter that I will be content.'

The other film that Lee referred to was Jess Franco's *El conde Drácula*, which was released in the UK in late 1970 as *Count Dracula*. Produced by the infamous Harry Alan Towers and shot entirely in Spain, Franco's plodding epic pitted Lee's count against a Van Helsing played by Herbert Lom and portrayed the character as moustachioed, capeless, and ostensibly as Stoker had written him (he was even given some of Stoker's lines), but in an obvious cash-in that was cheap, listless, and completely lacking in any cinematic dynamic. Hammer had sought to prevent Franco's version from going into production, but there was nothing it could do as the novel was in the public domain. As things turned out, the company had little to fear from *El conde Drácula*.

Taste the Blood of Dracula commenced production on October 27, 1969. 'We have a new boy here called Ralph Bates,' Carreras had informed the press in relation to the young actor who had been cast as Lord Courtley—the implication being that he was being groomed to replace Lee; Carreras had spotted him in the BBC-TV series *The Caesars*, in which he had played the Roman emperor Caligula. Bates was intended originally to have carried the whole show, but a telegram from Carreras to Warners on August 15 confirmed that Lee was back on side and Warners was to foot the bill for the difference: 'Budget in your possession carries a memorandum that if Christopher Lee employed, cost will be two hundred and twenty seven thousand pounds sterling.' Warners agreed, and Lee donned the cape once more.

By way of recompense, the supporting cast was one of the finest for a Hammer Dracula film: Geoffrey Keen, John Carson and Peter Sallis were cast as the three Victorians leading a double life of propriety by day and sin and debauchery at night;

Taste the Blood of Dracula
(John Carson, Geoffrey Keen, Ralph Bates, Roy Kinnear)

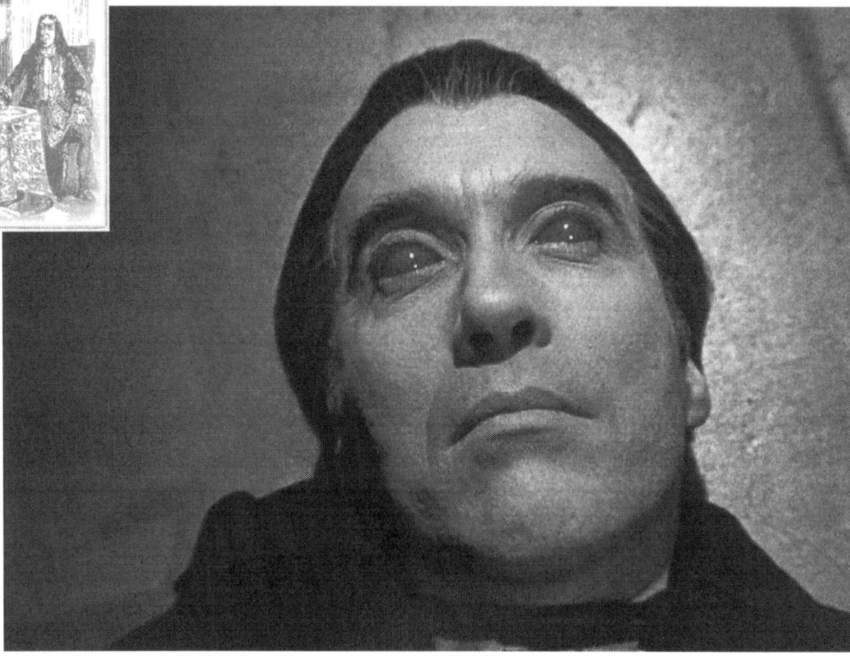

Taste the Blood of Dracula (Christopher Lee)

the star-crossed lovers were Anthony Corlan and Linda Hayden, who would go on to star in Tigon's *The Blood on Satan's Claw*, the salesman whose bill of fare includes Dracula's ashes was ubiquitous British funnyman Roy Kinnear, and the 'Hammer vampire' on this occasion was Isla Blair, in Stokeresque vein as 'Lucy'. With Dracula reinstated into the action, Ralph Bates ended up with only five days work on the film, before his character of Lord Courtley was magically reconfigured as Hammer's famous count.

Aida Young was back as the producer, but Scott MacGregor replaced an ailing Bernard Robinson as art director. MacGregor had the onerous task of following a master, but he took to it energetically and the gloomy Gothic church that provides Dracula with a hideaway in Victorian England is well up to the high standard set by his predecessor. Locations for the shoot included Scratchwood and Aldenham Park. St Andrew's Church in Totteridge Lane was one of two North London locations; the other was the famous Highgate Cemetery, supposedly the site of a 'real' vampire happening in the early 1970s.

In an interview with Al Taylor some years later, John Carson recalled the filming at Highgate: 'The most eerie thing that happened was when we filmed in Highgate Cemetery. Located in North London, it is divided by a road into two halves or two sections. One section is very well kept.. the other cemetery is now totally neglected and overgrown. It's on a steep hill, and many of the graves are cut into the side of the hill. These tombs have been plundered and broken into.. we filmed there on a wet and misty day, and we needed no artificial help to create the atmosphere. We didn't need smoke machines or anything like that. It was very spooky indeed. We all felt it, and we were glad to get out of the place.'

Taste the Blood of Dracula wrapped on December 5. The British press gave the film some good coverage, as it often did with Hammer. Trade magazine *Kine Weekly* for December 13 featured a brief interview with director Sasdy, who 'puffed' the production in the expected fashion, 'One of the most pleasing things about this particular Dracula subject from my point of view is that for the first time the setting is London.. This means that the characters are not strange people in a foreign land, but people who live in and around London in the Victorian period. They are the sort of people whom audiences in Britain and America are going to recognise more readily—ordinary families suddenly faced with terrible evil; real people caught in a vortex of horror. Who, you ask all the time, is going to survive? So we really have a thriller with this horror picture.'

No one appeared to see irony in the fact that Sasdy, who as Lee had pointed out was Hungarian ('the right nationality'), was actually the first director to bring the Count to London, instead of dealing with him on his 'home' turf. He did furnish a fresh approach to the subject, however; whereas Fisher would concentrate on atmosphere and dynamics and Francis preferred a sense of heightened reality, à la Mario Bava, Sasdy spent much of his time developing the characterisation necessary to draw the viewer into the plot. Given that his background was in the more personal medium of television, this change of tack for Hammer's Dracula franchise was not entirely surprising.

Taste the Blood of Dracula was released in the UK in May 1970, on a double bill with Hammer's own *Crescendo*, a 'mini-Hitchcock' psycho-thriller written by Jimmy Sangster and Alfred Shaugnessy and directed by Alan Gibson; the same bill was pressed into service for play-dates in the US in June. Most of the reviews were less than kind. 'Early in the creepy proceedings [a character] whispers, "My God, I don't like this." He proves to be absolutely right,' opined A H Weiler in *The New York Times*.

The American version was shorn of more than five minutes of footage, most of it featuring naked or half-naked tarts in a lively bordello sequence; much of the film's graphic gore was also eliminated. There had been criticism in the US over the new rating system's more liberal attitude towards violence in films and particularly over the G (for General audiences) rating that had been awarded to *Dracula Has Risen from the Grave*, with no cuts at all; what had been certified X in Britain had been considered as 'kiddie fare' in America, a frightening prospect in itself. Films like *Night of the Living Dead*, which had pushed the envelope, were also coming under closer scrutiny now; because of this, Courtley's demise in *Taste the Blood*—battered to death with walking-sticks—was much reduced, and every other murder scene in the film was relieved of a few seconds of gore, including the staking of Sallis by Blair and Hayden.

It was to be the beginning of a new era for Hammer in the US. In the fifties and much of the sixties, American audiences had been allowed more 'Kensington Gore' than their British counterparts. Now the situation was reversed; the extra infusions of sex and gore which Hammer had been enabled to insert into its horror films by virtue of the newly-revised X-certificate, which had raised the age-limit from 16 to 18 (and of which *Taste the Blood of Dracula* had taken full advantage), would be removed in the States to avoid the dreaded 'R' rating and risk losing the biggest audience for horror: children.

Controversy aside, *Taste the Blood of Dracula* embodies a fascinating premise: Hinds was at his best when taking pot-shots at Victorian sensibilities, and much of the film is an indictment of the double standards which were prevalent in Victorian society. Whereas *Risen from the Grave* almost enshrined 'conservative' values, *Taste the Blood* lifts the lid on what those same values often concealed. It is as though in the gap between the two films, Hinds had discovered the truth behind what he had advocated before—which in his dealings with Hammer over his 'resignation', to some degree, he had.

Taste the Blood of Dracula (Christopher Lee, Anthony Corlan, Linda Hayden)

30037-45

Hargood (Keen), Paxton (Sallis) and Secker (Carson) are a trio of upstanding gentlemen, respectable and worthy, and strict disciplinarians so far as their families are concerned—but night finds them sex- and sensation-seeking in the lowest dives of London's East End. When Lord Courtley invites them to participate in a black magic rite with the promise of a new thrill, they eagerly agree. But the ritual goes wrong and they collude in his murder. So far so conventional. But Courtley's resurrection in the form of Dracula moves the film into allegorical territory, as the count enacts his predictable 'revenge' through the proxies of the various children and, in so doing, becomes a metaphor for teenage rebellion against an older generation whose hypocritical values are no longer of any relevance. As an overt statement on the politics of the 'generation gap', which had become such a feature of the 1960s, Sasdy's film is unique in Hammer's vampire canon.

For all that, the climax is quite bizarre and harks back to that deployed in *Risen from the Grave*. If the vampirism in *Taste the Blood of Dracula* is representative of youth in revolt and the destruction of the (albeit dysfunctional) family, then all it takes to restore 'order' is once again a return to the old values of Church and State. In the gospel according to Hinds, the land has been corrupted by 'foreign' agitators and the only way to end such defilement is to re-consecrate the soil. This is accomplished in the film by the laying-down of the sacrament and the lighting of candles, which restores the derelict church in which Dracula has been secreted to its former condition as a House of God. The count is suddenly confounded by the religious artefacts with which he is surrounded, and with his powers gradually sapping, he falls onto the altar where he is once more reduced to ash by Les Bowie's special effects.

***Taste the Blood of Dracula* (Christopher Lee, Isla Blair)**

On a purely pedantic level, the question might be asked as to why Dracula is out to avenge the death of his servant, Courtley, when the latter's demise was the key to his own revival. The answer, of course, is that Courtley was meant to be the vampire in the original draft and, as Lee rightly complained, the count was merely added as an afterthought.

This was now the problem with the Hammer vampire. Isla Blair may have been chosen to continue the tradition of the vampiric *femme fatale* in *Taste the Blood of Dracula*, but Hammer's reliance on the character of the count to move the series forward had blunted the edge of the films and left the way open for others to fill the gap in the evolution of the genre, where Hammer had once been the front-runners. If Lee was tiring of the role, so audiences and distributors alike were tiring of the character as he was now being represented on screen. Fresh blood was called for, and while Hammer was indeed to heed the call, others were to heed it also.

As for Lee himself, one can understand his view that *Taste the Blood of Dracula* was simply part of a 'progressive deterioration of the series'. From his stand-point, it was exactly that; he had even less to do than in the two previous productions. But in terms of the allegory, Dracula presides over the abused children in the film like a Charles Manson figure, exhorting them to kill society's corrupt elders. What lay implicit in Stoker's novel had finally featured in a Hammer film: the dark wind of change from the 'land beyond the forest' had taken root in English soil, whereas previous Dracula adventures had always been set in some *mittel*-European/English-Victorian hinterland. For the first time in what was now five films, the Hammer vampire had truly been invested with the figurative dimension to which he (or she) had always adhered. Freed from the constraints of novel and archetype, it would now begin to take on the aspect of cultural icon—resonant of sex and death, and anarchy and rebellion.

While other producers sharpened their stakes in readiness to enter the game, Hammer panicked in the face of a number of corporate setbacks and rushed yet another Dracula film into production.

Taste the Blood of Dracula had only just opened in theatres when Lee wrote a letter to Lillibridge concerning the *next* Dracula film: 'We come to the old familiar scene now—Hammer Films, and another Dracula. Think of it! Another Dracula! This is titled *The Scars of Dracula*, another subtle and intelligent title. I've read the script. I must admit it isn't bad at all. It's considerably better than the last one, but there's one extraordinary element in it and that is that no attempt is made at resuscitation. You remember that in all the previous pictures he has been revived in various weird and wonderful ways after being, so to speak, destroyed in previous episodes. In this one there's no attempt at resuscitation/resurrection, none whatever. I think I know the reason for this. Hammer have approached my agent and asked if I'd be interested in doing this picture. They've also said for the umpteenth time (I think this is my seventeenth or eighteenth film for them) that they can't possibly pay my salary, the same as they paid last year in the other Dracula, whereupon I lose interest, as I'm getting rather bored with this attitude of mind.. The reason they have brought the character back without accounting for his sudden appearance is, I'm quite certain, deliberately contrived in case I should say no and they can put in another actor.. in which case there is no need for any further continuity. They can start all over again with a completely new actor playing the part.'

By now, this dance between Lee and Hammer was almost becoming a ritual; it had been but a few months since he had played the role. The bottom line, as Lee noted in his missive, was that he could not afford to 'turn down the money'. Lee saw

the writing on the wall, however: Hammer's glory days were coming to an end, and the newly-knighted Sir James Carreras appeared to feel that Lee and Cushing were no longer important to the company's success. The latter had already been replaced by Ralph Bates in *The Horror of Frankenstein*, a thinly disguised remake of *The Curse of Frankenstein*, the company's original Gothic success—but the new version had been aimed at a younger, hipper audience. Now, a script that Tony Hinds had written *before Taste the Blood of Dracula* had been dusted off and spiced up with sex, some nudity, and a good deal more gore. *Scars of Dracula* (now without the pronoun) was pretty much a remake of Hammer's original *Dracula*, in the manner of its companion-piece, *The Horror of Frankenstein*. There was nothing new in the story, save for the fact that the antagonists were a pair of pretty young things, standing in for the more mature Van Helsings of yesteryear.

For the third time in a row, the lead is a character named Paul. In an interview I conducted with Hinds for *Fangoria* magazine in 1988, I asked why so many of his heroes were called Paul; he gave a self-effacing answer: 'It's easy to type! I'll tell you another thing. Generally, in my scripts, everybody's initialled. So everybody's name starts out with a different initial. So when you're writing for the director it's easy to type because all you have to do is write the character's initials down.' Thus is 'art' born.

Scars of Dracula, as one of the first pictures in Hammer's new deal with ABC-EMI, was saddled with a shorter-than-usual production schedule. Aida Young, who was once again producer, noted later, 'It was really the beginning of the end for Hammer. And everybody knew it. We went about it as if it were any other film—but I remember at the time we were all rather despondent at the terrible schedule we were given. Other than that, I've really blotted that picture from my memory.' Young could be a hard task-master, as Baker noted for *Fangoria*: 'I knew that things were very tight. The producer.. was a bit of a slave driver. She forced the picture through at a tremendous pace, with no hanging about. God help us all if we hadn't come in on time.'

Principal photography on the film commenced on May 7, 1970. Naturally, it was shot at Elstree, with some location filming in the nearby Scratchwood area. As it was scheduled for release only five months later, Hammer assigned a fast and efficient director to the project: Roy Ward Baker, who had just directed *The Vampire Lovers* for the company—a more significant pointer of the direction that Hammer's vampire films were now to take (see next chapter).

When Baker signed on for the project, he discovered that the script was little more than a flimsy first draft. In a search for inspiration, he went back to the novel. 'I realised when I re-read *Dracula* that there was a gripping description of Dracula climbing down the tower wall, crawling down face-first, and that no one had attempted to film it before,' he recalled, and he decided to append a similar scene to Hinds's screenplay. 'Unfortunately, it was slightly underdone,' he explained subsequently to *Fangoria*, 'because there wasn't enough money to do it properly. We shot it on a sloping set, with a black backing for night, and used an angled camera. I felt there was a certain amount of constraint when I asked for it. Hammer reluctantly agreed to construct the set. It was built for nine-pence, and could have been much bigger, but we pulled it off.'

Hammer had assembled an adequate cast, though cost-cutting was now the order of the day and more experienced actors were noticeable by their absence. The accent was on youth, and Dennis Waterman, the face of 'Just William' on British television, was hired to play the male lead. Jenny Hanley, daughter of Jimmy (who

Scars of Dracula (inset: Anouska Hempel, Christopher Matthews)

had starred for Hammer in *Room To Let* back in 1950), was cast in the role of the nubile young thing in peril of her virtue. Sexy newcomer Anouska Hempel was the count's latest 'bride', and Christopher Matthews, who had sprung from nowhere the year before to star in the AIP-Amicus film *Scream and Scream Again* alongside Cushing, Lee *and* Vincent Price, was the new film's 'Paul'.

A couple of Hammer veterans made what were token appearances: Michael Ripper reprised his innkeeper role from *Dracula Has Risen from the Grave*, and Michael Gwynne, Frankenstein's monster in 1958's *The Revenge of Frankenstein*, turned up briefly as a priest. The character of Klove also made his return, but he was not quite himself: Patrick Troughton, TV's 'Dr Who' to BBC viewers in the mid-sixties, replaced Philip Latham from *Prince of Darkness* and played the part as a seedy, whimpering, masochist.

There had been ample room in the storyline for Baker to flesh things out: basically the story came down to one brother, Paul, finding himself at Castle Dracula and disappearing, and the other brother, Simon, going in search of him. The count makes his 'presence' felt in the local village after the villagers storm the castle, and when Simon returns to it once more in search of his beloved, Dracula is struck by lightning and topples from the battlements into the valley below; much movement

Scars of Dracula (Dennis Waterman, Christopher Matthews)

to and from the keep offered plenty of opportunity for gruesome scenes to be added to the mix, ad hoc.

Les Bowie, who had done sterling work disintegrating Dracula in previous films, was replaced on *Scars* by Roger Dicken, an effects artist from Gerry Anderson's *Thunderbirds*. Dracula had met the same demise in both *Risen from the Grave* and *Taste the Blood*, so the new film sought to ring the changes by making him subject to a *deus ex machina* at the climax, as a bolt of lightning strikes a railing that he has grasped to use as a makeshift spear. Lee's stand-in Eddie Powell had to burst into flames for the scene, but Powell was an old hand at that sort of thing; Jenny Hanley recalled the shooting in *Little Shoppe of Horrors*: 'He was such a wonderful stunt man,' she said. 'I had to be around because I was in the shot. Some awful sticky substances were plastered on him and set fire to. It wasn't so much that he would burn—that was the main drama—but that the fire, being so near his face, would stop the oxygen from getting to him..' Dicken had also to create a model of Dracula for the fall off the castle wall.

Fortunately for all concerned (if Baker is to be believed!), shooting on *Scars of Dracula* wrapped on June 23, exactly as scheduled. MGM-EMI released the film in the UK, while a company called American Continental picked it up for US release. Warners had taken one look at *Scars* and passed. The box office was poor in both territories by Hammer standards, but neither did Continental (which was actually to go out of business after releasing Hammer's later *Lust for a Vampire*) have the advertising budget to create sufficient awareness among American audiences. *The New York Times* gave high marks to co-feature *The Horror of Frankenstein*, praising the performance of Ralph Bates as the Baron, but its critique of *Scars of Dracula* consisted of a single line: 'Avoid the Dracula film like the plague; it's garish, gory junk.'

Time has been kinder to the film. In their book *In Search of Dracula*, Raymond

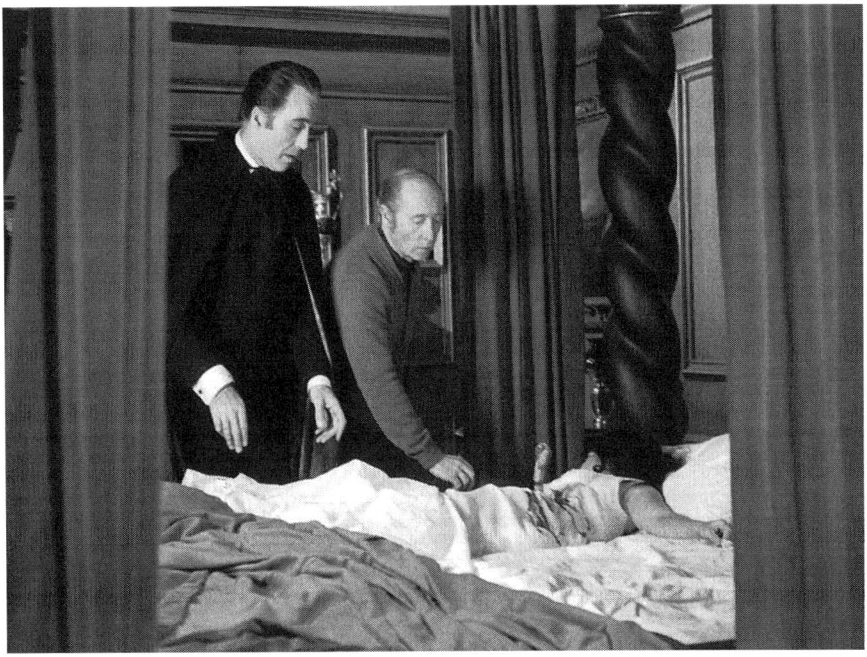

Scars of Dracula: Christopher Lee and Roy Ward Baker on set

McNally and Radu Florescu said of *Scars of Dracula* that it was 'particularly good', while David Pirie noted that the count was 'still recognisably a swash-buckling, arrogant aristocrat' in his seminal *A Heritage of Horror*. Roy Ward Baker himself has been quoted as saying that French critics love the film—though he also thought that they were all quite mad. Lee, too, has professed his dislike of the film time and again, deeming it 'probably the poorest of the whole lot', but when he and Baker were called upon to add commentary to the American DVD release, Lee stated that he was pretty sure that he had never seen it before!

Scars of Dracula has the feel of one of Universal's 'monster rallies' of the forties—fast-paced and action-packed. Baker has said that as it was the first full-fledged Gothic horror film that he had been given to direct (not counting Hammer's *The Vampire Lovers* of four months before, which he considered conversely to have been 'exploitation'), then he was 'bloody well' going to make a real horror film. No overt religious motifs or generation gap allegories for him; he was asked to make a full-blooded Gothic horror, and that was what he tried to do.

It certainly seemed as though Hammer were attempting to 'reboot' the dual franchises of Dracula and Frankenstein. It was noted at the time in Calvin Beck's *Castle of Frankenstein* magazine that *Scars of Dracula* had 'warmed-over (*Horror of*) *Dracula* situations'. The first third of the film is more or less a reprise of the latter, but with Christopher Matthews's Paul standing in for John Van Eyssen's Harker—the only difference being his 'swinging sixties' predilection for attempting to bed every woman he meets, including Anouska Hempel's vampiric Valerie Gaunt clone, Tania.

Paul's first (and last!) night at the castle is straight from the pages of Sangster's script for the first film: Dracula is the consummate host, offering Paul a glass of blood-red wine and even uttering a few of the same lines ('Sleep well..'). The scene with the vampire woman is also almost identical to that between Van Eyssen and Gaunt, with Hempel mooning about how Dracula keeps her a prisoner in the castle;

the difference here is that they end up in bed together before she tries to bite him, but again, in echo of the famous library scene from the original, the count suddenly bursts into the room and stabs his erstwhile 'bride' to death. The remainder of the film amounts to little more than a game of ping-pong between the residents of the village and the occupant of the castle, as they weave back and forth in search of a good line of dialogue or simply a means to bring the undisciplined proceedings to an end.

If *Scars of Dracula* is notable for anything, it is a sense of *excess*. Even Dracula's relationship with Klove is imbued with a homosexual sub-text, and the count 'branding' his servant with a red-hot sword is probably the most gratuitous scene in any Hammer film. Klove seems all too eager to be the subject of Dracula's sadistic impulses, as he whimpers in barely-concealed anticipation, 'I am ready, master', and Lee was moved to point out in his commentary for the DVD that the scene was an example of a 'perfect S&M relationship'. In a strange sexual inversion of the whole vampire ethos, it is the marks on Klove's back, rather than the bites on his victims necks, that are the 'scars' of Dracula here.

Scars of Dracula (Patrick Troughton, Jenny Hanley)

Having been given a perfunctory script to begin with, Baker opted to turn it into a 'penny dreadful' in the style of *Varney the Vampyre*, all bared fangs and heaving bosoms. When I asked Hinds why his script for *Scars* was so sadistic, he was defensive: 'By whose standards?' he bristled. Baker's view was equally down-to-earth: 'The scene where Dracula brands his servant was in the script, so I did it. You know, everything I do—it's likely to be slightly more vivid because I don't do things trivially. If a fellow is going to take a bloody great sword and heat it up in the fire and stick it on somebody's back, then that is what you see.' The unnamed French critics to whom Baker alluded may have seen the film as an allegory of aristocracy literally sucking the peasants dry, but one has really to look very sympathetically at *Scars of Dracula* to discern that.

What you see is what you get, then—although the undercurrent of religious allegory is still present: Dracula is the Antichrist. When the priest is confronted by carnage in his church after Dracula's bat has wreaked havoc on the wives and families of the villagers who had absented themselves in order to burn his castle down, he states solemnly, 'The Devil has won.' And Hammer's conflicted sense of prurience and Puritanism is also on display: after spending an impassioned night with the vampire woman (who has crooned, 'Love me!—Love me!' to him), Paul winds up impaled on a meat-hook in Dracula's crypt. It is one of the first examples in a horror film of a character being 'punished' for having illicit sex, a theme which would feature strongly in many a 'slasher' movie of the late seventies and eighties, beginning with John Carpenter's *Halloween* (1978).

In the final analysis, Baker's film is like Fisher's *Dracula* on steroids, as though

Scars of Dracula (Christopher Lee, Jenny Hanley)

he (and to a lesser degree, Hinds) had decided to pull out all the stops for a thrill-seeking audience that was demanding ever more graphic scenes of sex and violence. To an extent, it was true. The British film industry had been in trouble for some time, and Hammer was not immune to the twin pressures of rising costs and dwindling box-office returns, as well as the pressure of increased competition from the likes of Tigon, Amicus and American International, many of whose films were now out-grossing Hammer's (in both senses of the term). In the face of falling receipts, producers had begun to rely more on increased doses of nudity and gore to assure them of commercial success, and more independent producers were turning to horror in general as a safer bet in difficult times. This further increased competition, and the Hammer vampire was now to come under concerted attack from a number of other directions—some of which would take the genre on into new territory. For all its injections of sex and sadism, *Scars of Dracula* showed that there was little mileage left in Hammer's Dracula series, but the company still had a couple of tricks up its corporate sleeve.

All afternoon he made stakes.

He lathed them out of thick doweling, band-sawed into nine-inch lengths. These he held against the whirling emery stone until they were as sharp as daggers..

From four o'clock on, his gaze kept shifting to the clock on the wall. He worked in silence, lips pressed into a hard line, a cigarette in the corner of his mouth, his eyes staring at the bit as it gnawed away the wood and sent floury dust filtering down to the floor.

Four-fifteen. Four-thirty. It was a quarter to five.

In another hour they'd be at the house again, the filthy bastards. As soon as the light was gone.

—Richard Matheson, *I Am Legend* (1954)

Dracula (Peter Cushing/below: Christopher Lee)

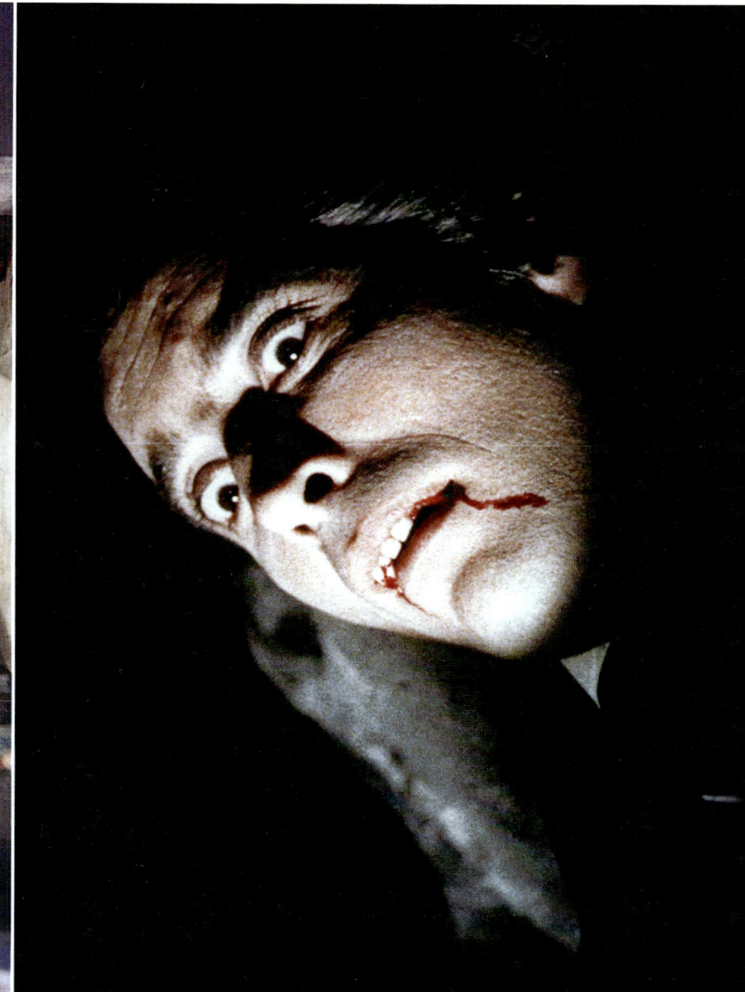

Dracula—Prince of Darkness (Francis Matthews, Christopher Lee)

The Brides of Dracula (Peter Cushing, Martita Hunt)

Dracula has Risen from the Grave (Veronica Carlson, Christopher Lee)

Taste the Blood of Dracula (Christopher Lee, Linda Hayden)

Scars of Dracula (Christopher Lee/above: Christopher Lee, Dennis Waterman, Jenny Hanley)

The Vampire Lovers (Kate O'Mara, Kirsten Betts, Madeline Smith, Ingrid Pitt, Pippa Steele)

Lust for a Vampire (Yutte Stensgaard)

Vampire Circus (Serena)

Dracula AD 1972 (Peter Cushing, Stephanie Beacham)

The Satanic Rites of Dracula (Christopher Lee, Joanna Lumley)

The Legend of the 7 Golden Vampires (above and right: John Forbes-Robertson)

The Satanic Rites of Draculs (Pauline Peart)

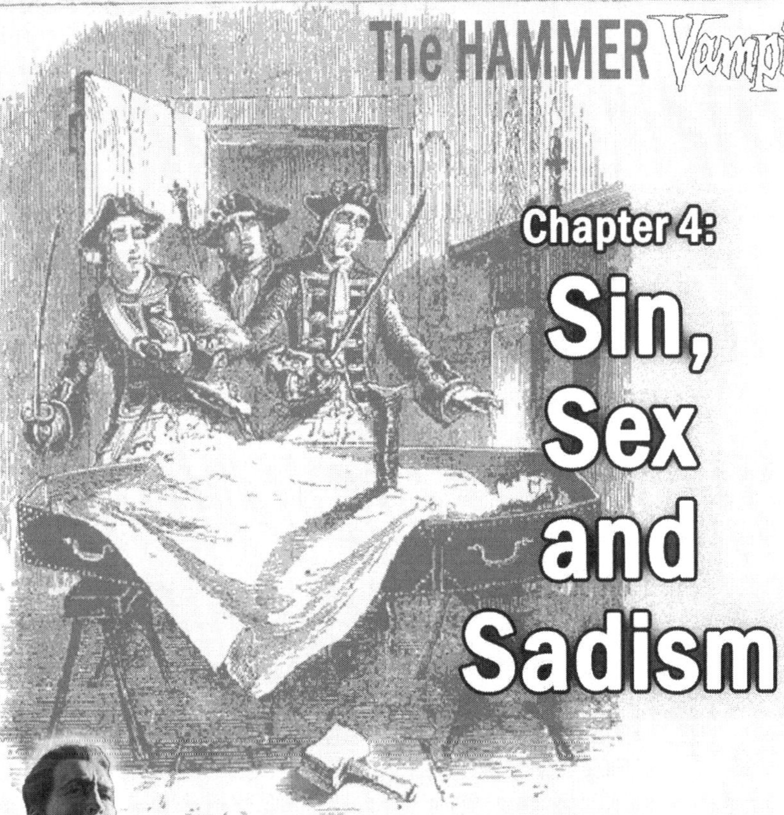

Chapter 4: Sin, Sex and Sadism

Certain vague and strange sensations visited me in my sleep. The prevailing one was of that pleasant, peculiar cold thrill which we feel in bathing, when we move against the current of a river.. Sometimes there came a sensation as if a hand was drawn softly along my cheek and neck. Sometimes it was as if warm lips kissed me, and longer and more lovingly as they reached my throat, but there the caress fixed itself. My heart beat faster, my breathing rose and fell rapidly and full drawn; a sobbing, that rose into a sense of strangulation, supervened, and turned into a dreadful convulsion, in which my senses left me, and I became unconscious.

—J Sheridan Le Fanu, 'Carmilla'/ *In a Glass Darkly* (1872)

The Vampire Lovers

The author and occultist Montague Summers, an early 20th century 'self-styled' expert on all things supernatural in legend and literature, considered Sheridan Le Fanu's novella 'Carmilla' to be 'the best of the English vampire stories'. While such an accolade is usually reserved for *Dracula*, Le Fanu's story predated Stoker's by 26 years. There is no doubt that 'Carmilla' influenced Stoker; both tales take place in central Europe and both use traditional vampire lore to advance their plots. However, Le Fanu's tale was as much Victorian erotica as it was Gothic horror.

Woven into its dream-like fabric of two households in thrall to the baleful influence of a female vampire is a mesmerising tale of lesbian love; Carmilla is a strange and sensuous creature of the night, who exerts a languorous hold over her female victims. Le Fanu's influential novella is not the only Victorian vampire tale aside from *Dracula* to have been adapted for the screen, but it is the only one apart from Stoker's to have furnished a number of different adaptations, as well as a *series* of films.

Dreyer's *Vampyr* was too obscure in its treatment of the story to satisfy audiences in the thirties, and 'Carmilla' was not adapted again until 1960, as Roger Vadim's *Blood and Roses*. Vadim hinted at the lesbian angle quite overtly in his version, and scenes involving the relationship between Elsa Martinelli and Annette Vadim were undeniably imbued with an erotic undercurrent. *Blood and Roses* set the tone for more explicit takes on the tale. The next adaptation was Camillo Mastrocinque's *La cripta e l'incubo* (*Terror in the Crypt*), an Italian-Spanish co-production that featured Hammer's own Christopher Lee as Count Ludwig Karnstein. The lesbian overtures were even more pronounced in this 1964 version, but curiously there was no vampirism; Scirra/Ljuba (Ursula Davis), the 'Carmilla' character in the film, is a voluptuous witch and not a seductive vampire.

The definitive version of 'Carmilla' remained to be made, and the task was left to Hammer Films.

One day late in 1969, ex-theatre manager and one-time actor Harry Fine, who was to become co-producer (along with Michael Style) on what would be known as Hammer's 'Karnstein Trilogy', was leafing through the pages of a scrapbook from his days with Edward Pakenham, the

Earl of Longford, at Dublin's Gate Theatre, when he chanced upon some photographs from a play that the Earl had adapted from 'Carmilla' for his 'Longford Players', with Coralie Carmichael in the lead. Fine recalled the production from May of 1932, and he decided to trace the source for it; now a producer of sexploitation subjects like *The Pleasure Girls* (1965), *The Penthouse* (1967) and *Up the Junction* (1968), what had caught his attention was the implicit lesbianism in the tale. He then asked Tudor Gates—a writer who had helped to script English versions of Mario Bava's *Danger:Diabolik* and Vadim's *Barbarella* (both 1968) and the third partner in his Fantale Films—to read the story and to pen a screen treatment.

Fine, Style (who was himself the producer of *Monique*; 1969) and Gates decided to pitch the idea to James Carreras. Their treatment, entitled simply *Vampire Lovers*, immediately made the Hammer boss sit up and take notice. When Style pointed out subsequently that they did not yet have a script, Carreras told them that it was not a problem—he already had an American distributor lined up, and a start-date had been pencilled at Elstree for January 1970! If nothing else, *Vampire Lovers* exemplified the change of direction on which Hammer had embarked by the turn of the decade. 'I hated the tits-and-bums films that Jim (Carreras) was keen to make and did not want to be involved,' Tony Hinds told Mike Murphy of *Dark Terrors* magazine. With Hinds gone, Carreras was now free to do exactly as he pleased.

The storyline concocted by Gates, Fine and Style (with final screenplay credit going to Gates alone) followed Le Fanu's more closely than previous screen versions. The novella tells of a Styrian family's encounter with the young, beautiful but somewhat mysterious Carmilla Karnstein, who is foisted upon them as a house-guest after a coaching accident. Laura, the daughter of the house, finds herself strangely attracted to Carmilla, and she to her; Carmilla even comes to Laura in her sleep, invading her dreams and seeming to suck the life-force out of her. Several fatalities occur in the nearby village. An old friend of Laura's father arrives: he is General Spielsdorf, and he is looking for the tomb of Countess Mircalla Karnstein, who reputedly was a vampire. The general explains that he, too, had a recent house-guest by name of Millarca, and that she had caused the death of his ward. When he is confronted by Carmilla, the general recognises her as Millarca—and reveals the two to be the centuries-old Mircalla Karnstein. With the help of Baron Vordenburg, he uncovers the tomb and decapitates the vampire.

In sixteen chapters, Sheridan Le Fanu created in 'Carmilla' a monster worthy of standing alongside Stoker's famous count—though her influence on the genre was to be almost forgotten in the wake of the phenomenal success of the latter (and later) novel, until Cambridge academic and ghost story writer M R James took it upon himself to revive Le Fanu's flagging reputation as a master of supernatural fiction. Were it not for Dracula, Carmilla would have remained the archetypal vampire of Gothic literature—a spectral terror of the most devilish kind: sweet, sensual and seductive by day, but insidious, dangerous and life-draining by night.

> ..To this hour, the image of Carmilla returns to memory with ambiguous alternations—sometimes the playful, languid, beautiful girl; sometimes the writhing fiend I saw in the ruined church; and often from a reverie I have started, fancying I heard the light step of Carmilla at the drawing-room door.
>
> **—J Sheridan Le Fanu, *Carmilla* (1871)**

Gates finished his screenplay and, by November 25, the three business partners had finalised their deal with Hammer; AIP was dismayed by the (lack of) quality of Gates's script, as was the British censor, but the production went ahead as planned

The Vampire Lovers

after a number of rewrites. Carreras, in turn, had arranged co-financing for the film with American-International Pictures, which had kept a production arm in the UK since 1964 and Roger Corman's *The Masque of the Red Death*. In Johnson and Del Vecchio's book, *Hammer Films: An Exhaustive Filmography*, AIP Vice-President Sam Arkoff is quoted as saying, 'We finally joined together [with Hammer] with *The Vampire Lovers*—which Jimmy sold to us over a meal!' With AIP putting up $400,000 and Hammer guaranteeing any over-budget expenses, Fantale Films was accorded a 25% profit participation in return for producing *Vampire Lovers*.

While negotiations continued with Christopher Lee for what would become *Scars of Dracula*, (*The*) *Vampire Lovers* went before the cameras at Elstree on January 19. Hammer had suggested Roy Ward Baker as director, who proved to be more than acceptable to AIP and Fantale, and a strong supporting cast was assembled. Peter Cushing played the role of General Spielsdorf, now Laura's father, while the role of Laura herself went to newcomer Pippa Steele. Other cast members included British film and television stalwart George Cole, Hammer veterans Dawn Addams and Ferdy Mayne ('Count Krolock' in Polanski's *Dance of the Vampires*), Douglas Wilmer as Baron 'Hartog', and John Forbes Robertson as the mysterious Man in Black. The dashing young hero was to be played by Jon Finch, who would make more of a mark in Polanski's *Macbeth* in 1971 and in Alfred Hitchcock's *Frenzy* the year after.

But the most important role was that of Carmilla herself. Agent John Redway had recommended former Rank starlet Shirley Eaton, the 'golden girl' from *Goldfinger* (1964), who had just played Sax Rohmer's fiendish female Fu Manchu, Sumuru, in a pair of exploitation thrillers for Harry Alan Towers. Carreras, however, felt that

***The Vampire Lovers* (Ingrid Pitt)**

Eaton was too old for the role at 32. Ironically, the actress who *was* cast was also 32 and, unlike Eaton, she had only a limited command of the English language.

Polish-born Ingrid Pitt (real name Ingoushka Petrov, though she recently suggested an alternative to author Marcus Hearn), a child victim of Nazi persecution and minor European actress who previously had been seen in the West in only a small role in the Clint Eastwood/Richard Burton/Alistair Maclean World War 2 action spectacular *Where Eagles Dare* (1968), had been introduced to Carreras at a party. Pitt was currently 'on the arm' of Rank Bookings Manager George Pinches (whom she was briefly to wed in a marriage of convenience), and Carreras was no sloth when it came to swapping favours; Hammer would sign a four-picture deal with Rank not long after he signed her for the film. *The Vampire Lovers* would introduce Pitt to a whole new genre audience, and she would never look back.

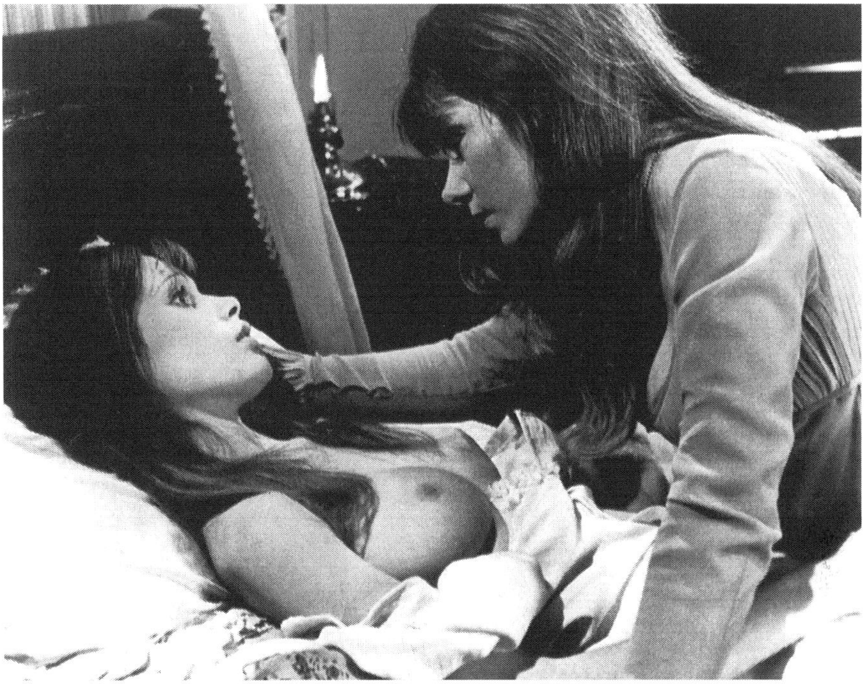

The Vampire Lovers (Madeline Smith, Ingrid Pitt)

When I interviewed writer Tudor Gates for *Little Shoppe of Horrors*, he told me, 'I read 'Carmilla' and on first reading, I didn't see where it had a lot to offer in cinematic terms. Then, reading it again, I realised that if the story had been written today, it would have been more overtly lesbian, rather than just lesbian overtones. It occurred to me to create the first lesbian vampire series, and I suppose that's my main claim to fame.' Although Laura is the heroine of the novella, *The Vampire Lovers* was to relegate her to secondary status; she is only Carmilla's first victim. There would be several others, thus giving the film the opportunity to 'expose' more nubile young flesh to the vampire's Sapphic embrace.

Fine felt that the explicit lesbian angle was what had attracted AIP to the subject in the first place. As far as the nudity was concerned, Pitt had no problems with it. But BBFC Secretary John Trevelyan had written a letter to Fine expressing his concerns about the 'dangerous cocktail of sex and horror', and he urged James Carreras to use his influence to keep the film 'within reasonable bounds'.

In her autobiography, *Life's a Scream* (republished as *Darkness Before Dawn*), Pitt recalled, 'I'd never done the full-frontal bit before but I was proud of my body and not too reluctant to show it. Madeline Smith, who played my second victim, had also kept her gear on in front of the cameras so far. She was a little more apprehensive but saw the relevance and agreed to get it off. Nevertheless we both had reservations, especially as we weren't too familiar with the producers.' It was a view with which Smith concurred, as she told me herself in another interview for *Little Shoppe of Horrors*, 'I can't say I was over the moon about it. I was very naive and innocent, I really was.. But I had a lot of fun on the film. Roy Ward Baker was very patient and understanding, and working with Peter Cushing—he was a most lovely man.'

Both stars were eventually put at their ease. 'I discovered that when you're naked on set everyone is terribly nice to you and looks after you beyond the call of duty,'

***The Vampire Lovers* (Ingrid Pitt, Madeline Smith)**

Pitt added. 'This is particularly the case when you're doing a bath scene.. Jimmy [Carreras] had sent champagne to the set, and Madeline and I indulged ourselves.'

Baker tried hard not to let the film become too exploitative. In his autobiography, *The Director's Cut*, he wrote in his defence, '[*Vampire Lovers*] was obviously intended by the producers to be a sensational exploitation picture. Strictly speaking, this was not the Hammer style. Still, all was not lost. First of all, I had an excellent cast.. They all followed my line, which was to play the thing simply and literally

The Vampire Lovers (Ingrid Pitt, Madeline Smith)

according to script, without camping it up or deriding the characters. If we had gone over the top, the result would have been merely risible and might even have been offensive to some.'

But intentionally or not, vampirism would now become more of a metaphor for 'abnormal sex' than Hammer had ever suggested before. It may have been a sign of the times—with likes of *The Killing of Sister George* (1969), homosexuality was coming out of the cinematic closet for the first time in history—but with an Un-dead creature of the night as fictional substitute for this new threat against 'normality', instinctive homophobia could be couched within the allegory of a Victorian vampire tale made flesh.

Shooting wrapped on March 4, 1970, and the film was under budget. Composer Harry Robinson (real name Robertson) had associations with both Hammer and AIP; he had written the music for Hammer's *Journey to the Unknown* TV series and AIP's *The Oblong Box* (1969), and he had been suggested to Fine and Style by producer Frank Godwin, who would soon make a Hammer horror of his own. '*The Vampire Lovers* was a brutal score to write,' he told me in 1980. 'If I remember right, there was about 75 minutes of music in the movie, and I did it in ten days.. Harry Fine was an extremely irascible man. He and Michael Style were challenging to work for, because if one of them said, "I like it," the other would say, "It's awful".'

What became in release '*The*' *Vampire Lovers* had been something of an experiment on Hammer's part. Although the sex in its vampire films had slowly been moving to the forefront, it was something of a leap to take a more-or-less traditional vampire story and append to it such sexploitational elements as full-frontal nudity and overt lesbianism. As it transpired, Hammer had nothing to fear: *The Vampire Lovers* 'tipped the velvet' at just the right moment: it made a star of Ingrid Pitt and blazed the trail for every horror film thereafter to feature sex and nudity, both of

which are now accepted elements of the genre. It also inspired a wave of 'lesbian vampire films' that continues to this day.

Baker's full-on approach to the subject proved too much for the tender sensibilities of schlock-*meisters* AIP, however. No hint of lesbianism appeared in the film's American publicity campaign, despite an 'R' (for Restricted)-rating first for a horror film, and the company sold it in the States with a typically lurid catch-line: 'A whisper of warm desire becomes a shriek of chilling terror in the embrace of the blood-nymphs!' But no more 'G' ratings would be given to horror films in the wake of *The Vampire Lovers*. This new and more startling approach to the myth did not pass unnoticed in mainstream media: Arthur Knight and Hollis Alpert wrote in *Playboy's Sex in Cinema 2* how the British film industry was once again being saved by American companies(!): 'The English studios were in such deep trouble.. that virtually any picture of interest—*The Music Lovers, Get Carter, The Devils*—was made for, and paid by, an American company,' they boasted, neatly forgetting in the process that American producers had only gone to the UK in the first place because it was *cheaper*, and not for any reasons of artistic endeavour. 'One of the kinkier of these, produced by fun-loving American-International, was *The Vampire Lovers*, a rather skilful interlacing of sex and horror,' they continued. 'Instead of the familiar Lugosi-style vampire, we see the living dead represented by curvaceous Ingrid Pitt, a sultry brunette fatally drawn to creatures of her own sex (although the fatality is unfailingly theirs). Miss Pitt, who recurs in the film as Carmilla, Mircalla and Marcilla, also departs from the vampire norm by nipping her victims not on the neck but on the breast, which adds not only a touch of lesbianism but also a *frisson* of voyeurism whenever the doctor must examine a shapely female corpse for the telltale marks..'

Le Fanu's literary Carmilla is not a creature of night (a feature of the vampire that would enter the mythology with the later *Dracula*) but of overcast *day*, like Polidori's Lord Ruthven, and this and other aspects of the tale are faithfully adhered to in Baker's film:

> She used to come down very late, generally not till one o'clock, she would then take a cup of chocolate, but eat nothing; we then went out for a walk, which was a mere saunter, and she seemed, almost immediately, exhausted, and either returned to the schloss or sat on one of the benches which were placed, here and there, among the trees..
>
> **—J Sheridan Le Fanu, *Carmilla* (1871)**

In this respect, *The Vampire Lovers* resembles *The Kiss of the Vampire* in its treatment of the Un-dead rather than any of Hammer's Draculas, and this subtle recasting of the myth gave some welcome relief to those who were becoming just a little too familiar with the rules and regulations that governed the company's vampire king. Instead of having to seek sanctuary in the nearest coffin at the first sign of daylight, the Karnsteins only rest when they are sated with the blood of their victims, as did Dr Ravna in *Kiss*. ('Open the curtains—it is daylight; she is dead,' Carmilla says to General Spielsdorf on the death of his daughter in an interesting reversal of *Dracula*'s final scene, where Van Helsing did just that in order to *destroy* the count.) If Hinds and Sharp treated vampirism as a social disease, Gates and Baker make it seem more like a real physical illness, its female victims gradually wasting away, in the style of the Romantics and their obsession with 'consumption'; they could as easily be dying of a bout of anaemia brought on by bad diet as by the onslaught of a vampire.

The vampire sequences themselves are equally original, and a far cry from

The Vampire Lovers (Jill Easter)

The Vampire Lovers: Cushing, Wilmer and Roy Ward Baker on set

the more formulaic strictures of the Hinds days. The prologue of the film, in which Baron Hartog lies in wait in a castle corridor for a Karnstein vampire to disgorge itself, ghost-like, from its grave, throw off its mouldering shroud and make its approach in the guise of a beautiful blonde, is one of the high-points of Hammer Gothic and one of the eeriest and most atmospheric sequences in the company's entire *oeuvre*—as much resembling a Roger Corman-AIP Poe film (*The Haunted Palace*, 1963) as it does a Hammer horror. (The baron's subsequent decapitation of said 'blonde' by means of a sword is the one scene more than any other that seemed to launch Hammer into a new era of graphic gore; the makers of *The Vampire Lovers* appeared to appreciate this also, as the scene is then repeated endlessly in flashback throughout the remainder of the film.)

Although considerably older than Le Fanu's Carmilla (who is notioned to be around 19 years of age by the story's narrator), Pitt makes a good fist of a role that requires her to be confidante and *amour fou* of the girls in her charge one minute, and feline fiend the next (the film provides an almost too-literal take on the cat-like creature that Carmilla is perceived to be by her victims in the novella; '..*I soon saw that it was a sooty-black animal that resembled a monstrous cat*'). Her husky voice and phonetic reading of the lines contribute strongly to the feeling of lassitude that pervades the character; where Lee's Dracula is forever leaping about, Pitt's Carmilla glides dreamily, wearing nothing but the allure of the grave beneath her diaphanous nightgown. She is a ghost in the flesh, a sensuous walking nightmare, and Gates's script supplies her with some memorable asides: 'Red or white?' the butler asks as he offers her wine. 'Red,' she replies with a wry smile.

Ingrid Pitt denies to this day that *The Vampire Lovers* has a lesbian bent; her view was—and is—that Un-dead, supernatural creatures have no sexual impulses. In her commentary for the American DVD release of the film, she states, 'I was quite upset when people started calling *The Vampire Lovers* a lesbian film.' Baker, who also commentated, diplomatically disagreed: 'There is an element of lesbianism in the film if you care to see it,' he suggests.

While Pitt may not have been able to 'see' the lesbian overtones in *The Vampire Lovers*, others had seen the exploitation possibilities of a more liberal mixing of sex and horror, especially when it came to vampire films.

One such was Bob Kelljan, a 39-year-old former actor in second-feature schlock and now producer of sexploitation movies like *Flesh of My Flesh* (1969). Kelljan and his partner Michael Macready (son of veteran actor George) had got together with a minor television performer and Angeleno neighbour of theirs named Robert Walter Quarry to make a softcore vampire film, which they had entitled *The Loves*

The Vampire Lovers (Douglas Wilmer, George Cole, Peter Cushing/Peter Cushing, Ingrid Pitt)

of Count Iorga, Vampire! The film was conceived on the cheap, with Quarry's role as 'Iorga' deployed largely tongue-in-cheek to justify an array of scantily-clad vampire 'brides' and some girl-on-girl action among the count's army of concubines in the cellar of his mansion. But after viewing what all three of them considered to be surprisingly good rushes, Quarry convinced Kelljan that he could play the role straight and suggested that instead they shoot the film as low-budget horror. The script was rewritten and the budget upped to $64,000, and the retitled *Count Yorga—Vampire!* became a 'sleeper' success when it was released on the American drive-in circuit by AIP in June, 1970.

Much of the erotic content of the original version had been left in *Count Yorga—Vampire!* to hedge the bets of its producers, but MPAA (Motion Picture Association of America) and BBFC censors reduced it to a minimum on release; busty Marsha Jordan, who had appeared in previous softcore productions like *The Ramrodder* and *Marsha, the Erotic Housewife*, was heavily featured as one of Yorga's 'loves', but the lesbian interlude over which Yorga presides in the crypt of his castle was left to the imagination of the alert viewer.

Count Yorga—Vampire! was basically the *Dracula* plot transposed to modern-day Los Angeles but, as directed by Kelljan, the film managed to give Hammer a run for its money. *Yorga* breathed new life into the formula, and among the novelties on display were mouths *filled* with fangs in the style of Lon Chaney in *London After Midnight*, vampire brides who owed more to the zombies in Romero's *Night of the Living Dead* than the Un-dead beauties of Bray, a knowing approach to the subject and refreshingly wry attitude to the conventions of the genre, and some sprightly action by Yorga himself, whose sudden, full-tilt attacks on trespassers upon his domain were shorn of any possible comedic aspect by being shot in unnerving slow motion. Although filmed on a derisory budget, the film has many effective moments and navigates its slow spots entirely on the strength of Quarry's intelligent performance as a suave and urbane count, very much in tune with the cynical times. It was also one of the first of the 'new' vampire films to feature a downbeat finale, end-titles rolling over the bloodied body of its dead hero-figure.

***House of Dark Shadows* (Jonathan Frid)**

So successful did the film prove to be in release that a follow-up was demanded by AIP and *The Return of Count Yorga* appeared the following year. Again written and directed by Kelljan, what was less of a sequel and more the first film simply remade on a bigger budget added a 'beauty and the beast' romance to the mix and procured Mariette Hartley from Alfred Hitchcock's *Marnie* (1964) and John Sturges's *Marooned* (1969) to bring a little classier light into the suave count's nocturnal love-life. But significant among its many sideswipes at traditional vampire lore—such as Yorga's sneering disdain for anyone who dares to brandish a cross in his face, foolishly imagining it to have power over him—is a scene in which the count is shown watching *The Vampire Lovers* (to which AIP owned the rights) on late-night television; this blatant 'who's the daddy?' dig at the genre's mainstream was a warning shot across Hammer's bows, and it was the Quarry character of Count Yorga who was

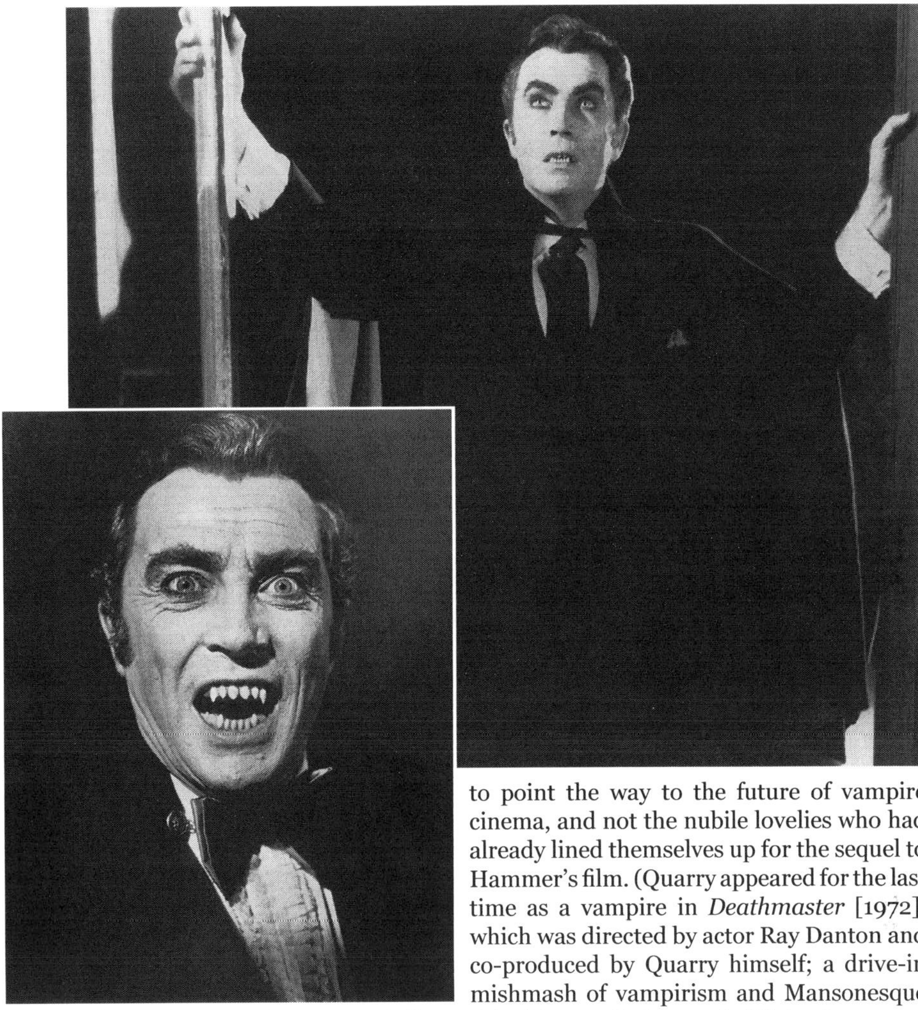

Count Yorga—Vampire/The Return of Count Yorga (Robert Quarry)

to point the way to the future of vampire cinema, and not the nubile lovelies who had already lined themselves up for the sequel to Hammer's film. (Quarry appeared for the last time as a vampire in *Deathmaster* [1972], which was directed by actor Ray Danton and co-produced by Quarry himself; a drive-in mishmash of vampirism and Mansonesque cult murders, *Deathmaster* quickly vanished into well-deserved oblivion.)

M-G-M also got in on the act in 1970 with *House of Dark Shadows*, a feature-length spin-off of the long-running daytime soap opera *Dark Shadows*, which it released in time for Halloween. The TV version had been on air for eighteen months before anyone dared to use the word 'vampire' in context, but as directed by former NBC salesman and the show's executive producer Dan Curtis, the feature quickly made up for lost time. Reuniting all of the cast members from the ABC series, notably Jonathan Frid as 150-year-old vampire Barnabas Collins, *House of Dark Shadows* was shot in six weeks on a budget of $750,000—double that which Hammer usually had to work with. Freed from the constraints of network censors, Curtis's film was able to indulge in the kind of graphic violence that Hammer had pioneered but on which it no longer held exclusive rights, and its climax is a veritable orgy of stakings, impalements and spurting blood—so much so that *Cinefantastique* magazine opined at the time that *House of Dark Shadows* had beaten the British company at its own game. (A semi-sequel, *Night of Dark Shadows*, followed soon after, but that had nothing to do with vampires.)

The Hammer Vampire

House of Dark Shadows made little impact in the UK, where it went out with a curiosity called *The Travelling Executioner* starring Stacey Keach, but Dan Curtis's excursions into the world of vampires were not to end there, and his future endeavours were to have more effect on ending the supremacy of the Hammer vampire.

Oblivious to the growing trend for a more sophisticated take on the myth which also incorporated elements culled from radical 'modern' horrors like *Night of the Living Dead*, Hammer ploughed ahead with its own 't-and-a' variant and sanctioned a sequel to *The Vampire Lovers*, provisionally entitled 'To Love a Vampire', a mere two days after the first film had gone into production and without the financial participation of AIP, which had now got cold feet about the explicit lesbianism of the former.

Years later, Fine admitted that it might have been a mistake to set up the deal so quickly; as a result of AIP's departure, Gates's draft screenplay, dated April 6, 1970, was shorn of references to *The Vampire Lovers*—such as a book in a schoolmaster's study titled *The Karnsteins: A History of Evil* by the first film's Baron Hartog—and 'To Love a Vampire' soon evolved to become more of a generic 'follow-up' than a direct sequel.

Pre-production took place throughout May and June, with Terence Fisher again slated to direct. Again, it was not to be: Fisher was the victim of a *second* road accident and was once more forced to bow out of a film. Fine briefly considered taking over the directing reins himself, but he had other projects in development with Fantale and the reins were handed instead to Jimmy Sangster, who had just helmed *The Horror of Frankenstein* for Hammer.

Sangster had spent much of the late sixties in Los Angeles, as a 'script doctor' for US television, but he had returned to the Hammer fold to produce and first-time direct *The Horror of Frankenstein*, which was currently in post-production, and was therefore available; Sangster was quickly signed to direct 'To Love a Vampire' also, but the film continued to be plagued with problems. Hanging his new story on the old Hammer staple of a 'girl's school' for maximum fleshly opportunity, Gates had written the role of schoolmaster Giles Barton for Peter Cushing, in an attempt to re-engage the new, sexier Hammer with its glorious Gothic past. Days before production began, however, Cushing's wife Helen became seriously ill and he, too, was forced to withdraw. Sangster quickly replaced Cushing with *Frankenstein*'s Ralph Bates. In *Bizarre* magazine, Bates recalled, 'Peter's wife was very ill and he backed out of the production just as it was about to roll. Jim rang me up one afternoon and I was filming the next day. I did it as a favour to him.'

While several cast-members from *The Vampire Lovers* returned for the sequel, albeit in different roles, the starring line-up was all-new: Dawn Addams, Countess Karnstein in the first film, was replaced by Barbara Jefford, best known for her starring role in the film version of James Joyce's *Ulysses* (1967), and Mike Raven, a BBC Radio 1 disc jockey who had featured in Amicus's *I, Monster* alongside Lee and Cushing replaced John Forbes Robertson as Count Karnstein, aka the 'Man in Black'.

(Raven was something of a Lee lookalike and one of the few British actors of the time who actually *wanted* to be a horror star; he would go on to write, co-produce and star in *Crucible of Terror* (1971) and *Disciple of Death* (1972), two very low-budget but not entirely uninteresting films, before retiring from the public eye to pursue the life of a sculptor in rural Cornwall.)

But the key change in 'To Love a Vampire' was in the character of Carmilla. After a lengthy prologue in which she is revived by black magic and the blood of

Lust for a Vampire (Ralph Bates, Yutte Stensgaard)

an innocent peasant-girl—a scene that borrows heavily from Lee's own resurrection in *Prince of Darkness*—she is self-evidently *not* her former self: blonde, younger, and sporting a Danish accent (though she would ultimately be dubbed in the film), Carmilla was now to be played by the 24-year-old Scandinavian wife of Amicus art director Tony Curtis, Yutte Stensgaard, a bit-part actress from Tigon's *Zeta One* and Amicus's *Scream and Scream Again* (both 1969). Ingrid Pitt, meanwhile, had been shunted into *Countess Dracula* for Rank.

When principal photography began on July 6, problems continued with tension between Sangster and his producers. 'Harry Fine and Michael Style [had] already shot *The Vampire Lovers*,' Sangster recalled in his book, *Do You Want It Good or Tuesday?* 'Roy Ward Baker had directed *The Vampire Lovers* for them. I never asked him how well he got on with Fine and Style. I also never asked why he didn't do this, their second movie for Hammer. Maybe he'd got lucky and was working on something else.. Example. First day's shooting. Interior set at Elstree Studios. The coach drawn by four horses is driven into the schoolyard where it pulls up. "Cut!" says I. "Print it. Next set-up!" "We can do better than that," came a voice from the back. It was Michael Style, trying to behave the way he thought a producer should. "You can do better than that? Then you shoot the fucking picture," says I, heading for the nearest exit.. Michael Style went back to his office to sulk and I got on with the next shot.'

A similar incident occurred over a Grecian dance sequence on the school lawn: 'The producers told me I wasn't moving the camera enough,' Sangster explained. 'So I shot it again, moving the camera so much nobody knew where the hell they were. End result, we used the original version, which was what I intended.'

Hammer's sudden proclivity for sex and nudity in its films was less erotic for those concerned than it was for the intended audience. Michael Johnson, who played in Byronic mould as Richard LeStrange, a writer of Gothic horror stories, was quoted in Tim Greaves's booklet *Yutte Stensgaard: Memories of a Vampire* as

Lust for a Vampire

Lust for a Vampire (Mike Raven, Barbara Jefford)

saying, 'Yutte was a very sweet girl. My most vivid memory is of the vampire "love scene", which was added on later to supposedly make the film more erotic! I was paranoid about being too thin to expose my body and insisted on keeping my shirt on, which of course looked ridiculous, and I remember my dear friend the late Ralph Bates feeding me with red wine to get me "in the mood".'

Stensgaard, of course, had to perform with her 'shirt' *off* for much of the time. 'The film was shot in less than six weeks, and we definitely felt the pressure,' she said. 'We filmed in and around a beautiful old country house, which was the perfect setting for the period. Unfortunately I didn't get to know the rest of the cast very well as it was a fast shoot, and everybody was busy. I did get to know the crew, however, as they were always standing around when I was doing a scene. This made some of the partial nude scenes rather embarrassing, but it was a lot more embarrassing when I finally saw the movie.. I feel that I was used for my looks and body. Obviously they thought I wasn't good enough or they would not have put another actress's voice over mine.'

Actress Suzanna Leigh, who played schoolteacher Janet Playfair, had similar reservations: 'The first scene I did, I was going into a dormitory clapping my hands and saying, "Come along, girls", or something like that, and there were all these girls with no clothes on. I was so shocked, and I rushed off and said, "I can't do this picture." So Jimmy said to me, "Oh, that's alright, dear. Don't worry; this is for the Swedish version." I said, "What do you mean, the Swedish version?" He told me, "Unless you're going to Sweden, nobody you know will see it." And I'm amazed that

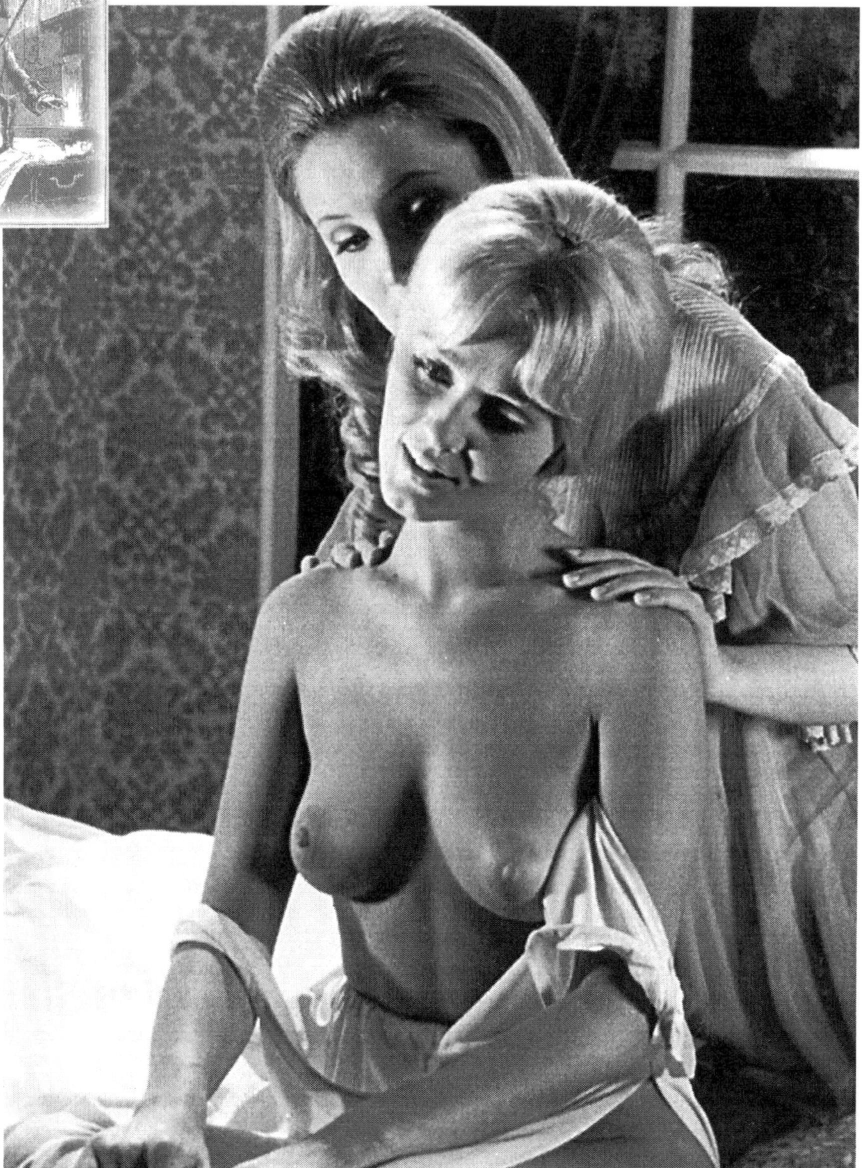

***Lust for a Vampire* (Yutte Stensgaard, Pippa Steel)**

I fell for it! There were Swedish versions made for movies in those days, but this wasn't one of them..'

Shooting wrapped on schedule on August 18, but more controversy was already on the way.

Hammer had been in the habit of dubbing actors and actresses to remove any trace of awkward or regional accents since its days of American co-productions in the fifties, when 'Americanising' a film for US release was the norm. Nothing had changed in the intervening years—if anything, overdubbing had increased throughout the 1960s, as in the case of Ewan Hooper in *Dracula Has Risen from the*

Grave. Sundry players who had been cast on the basis of looks alone were routinely dubbed, but so were stars like Ingrid Pitt and Jenny Hanley (*Scars of Dracula*). *Lust for a Vampire* was no exception, and not only Yutte Stensgaard was to find herself dubbed; Mike Raven's familiar *sotto voce* from his Radio 1 'Rhythm 'n' Blues' show was replaced by that of Valentine Dyall, steam radio's original 'Man in Black'. Raven also had to put up with close-ups of Christopher Lee's bloodshot eyes from *Risen from the Grave* inserted into the film in place of his own, and the rift that resulted led to his swift departure from the Hammer fold. The next film in the trilogy would yield yet another 'Count Karnstein'.

One of the most contentious aspects of what came to be released as *Lust for a Vampire* was the inclusion of a pop song called 'Strange Love', at the request of producer Harry Fine. Composer Harry Robinson penned the tune, to lyrics by Frank Godwin, and found a young singer named Tracy to record it. When Sangster and Bates attended a screening of the finished film, they were less than impressed: 'I consider it to be one of the worst films ever made,' Bates said later.

Lust for a Vampire has been as much maligned over the years, yet there is much to recommend it. 'I think it was a very good script,' Tudor Gates told me. 'I think, in a way, it was the better of the first two.' The plot of the film is actually a reworking of *The Brides of Dracula*—both are set in a girls' school, a mere stone's throw away from a vampire's castle; the difference in this instance is that Carmilla is the one to wreak havoc in the dormitories rather than Baron Meinster. The Gothic setting is ably evoked, and the vampire sequences are imbued with a certain dream-like ambience. Hammer had not entirely lost its way with the tools at its disposal, and while *Lust* must remain one of the more minor horrors in its vast *oeuvre*, it still seemed determined to go down fighting.

Sangster lacked the stylistic flair of Baker, but as one of the architects of Hammer Horror, he knew what he was about and adopted a functional approach to the narrative; the nudity is full-on, although blood and horror are somewhat

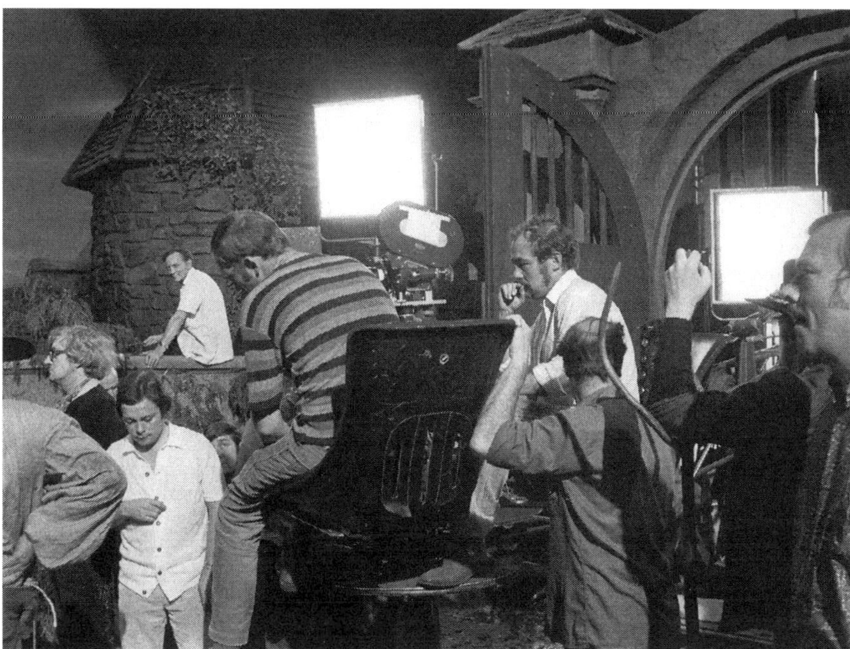

Lust for a Vampire: Jimmy Sangster on set

muted— apart from the oft-quoted scene of Carmilla's resurrection and the demise of Harvey Hall's police inspector, who is unlucky enough to be climbing out of a well just as the Man in Black whips out a knife, cuts through the rope by which he is suspended, and sends him plummeting back into the darkness.

Surprisingly, the film received some favourable reviews in the American press (unlike those in its home territory), such as that by Roger Greenspun in *The New York Times*, who opined, 'Despite many obvious lunacies, *Lust for a Vampire* is not unaware of its conventional sources of vitality, the nice tension between desire and decomposition, the bracelet of bright flesh around the bone..' In *A Heritage of Horror*, David Pirie put it another way in retrospect: 'Sangster seized wholeheartedly on all the more decadent elements in the new genre.. using all the visual devices at his disposal to convey an aura of potent cloying sensuality.' But the film was released in the US by Continental, the same company that had failed to adequately promote Hammer's *Scars of Dracula/The Horror of Frankenstein* double-bill, and it promptly disappeared from sight. The Continental trailer did furnish it with one memorable line, however: 'The finishing school.. where they really do finish you!'

By now, with Hinds and Fisher gone to pastures new and straight commercialism calling the tune, any pretext of subtext was long gone. The 'lesbian' element in this supposed sequel to *The Vampire Lovers* is merely an excuse for some gratuitous nudity, as Carmilla becomes romantically attached to Richard LeStrange rather than any of the adolescent 'tottie' on offer, while the Church in the form of a token priest supplies only grudging support at the climax, when the villagers once again burn Elstree's paste-and-cardboard Gothic castle set to the ground. Hammer may have gone further than ever before in exploiting John Trevelyan's 'dangerous cocktail' of sex and horror, but so had every other desperate producer in the face of falling ticket-sales. The subliminal messages that Trevelyan was concerned with in such exploitation are nowhere in evidence, and *Lust for a Vampire* was now no more subversive in truth than the parade of topless models that featured daily in the nation's tabloid newspapers.

Mary and Madeleine Collinson

Still intent on draining the last drop of blood (and cash) out of his now-ailing company before himself departing for the greener pastures of EMI, James Carreras had set up a deal with Rank for four features, one of which was to be the third in the 'Karnstein trilogy': *Twins of Evil*. Gates had already written a script called *Vampire Virgins*, which he intended as a fourth instalment in the series, but the new film was to provide Hammer with two of those, in any event.

John Hough, another television director who had distinguished himself through his work on *The Avengers* and *The Saint*, was chosen to helm the project; Hough had written a newspaper article critical of the current batch of horror films and Fine felt that he might be just the man to bring a fresh approach to *Twins of Evil*. Hough's feature-film debut was *Eyewitness* (1970), which had been made in Malta, and a Maltese connection was to figure in *Twins of Evil* in the form of the 'twins' themselves—former topless *Playboy* models Mary and Madeleine Collinson, who were natives of the island.

Hough brought with him several of the actors whom he had recently directed in a TV pilot called *Wolfshead: The Legend of Robin Hood*, such as David Warbeck and Kathleen Byron, but the starring role in *Twins of Evil*—that of Gustav Weil, head of a Puritanical witch-hunting organisation called 'The Brotherhood'—once again went to Peter Cushing, in order to show that despite its devotion to plucking starlets from the pages of *Playboy*, rather than the ranks of RADA, Hammer had not yet lost all pretence to respectability. But Cushing's wife had died only two months before, and the actor was now intent on throwing himself into anything that came along as a way of salving his grief. '*Twins of Evil* was the first time I worked with Peter Cushing,' Hough recalled. 'He wore a white glove when not on camera—he was a smoker and he wore the gloves to prevent nicotine stains showing on his fingers.'

The deal with Rank having transplanted the third Karnstein film from Elstree to Pinewood allowed Hammer to construct some of its most sumptuous sets for *Twins of Evil* since the great days of Bernard Robinson. As designed by Roy Stannard, the interior of *schloss* Karnstein is a magnificent construct, as are the extensive village exteriors, which had only just been built for *Countess Dracula* (they would be revamped again for *Vampire Circus* later the same year).

Twins of Evil went into production on March 24, 1971. Although it was Cushing who headed up the cast of the film, studio publicity concentrated on the 'charms' of the Collinson twins, who had honed their craft by posing for softcore pornographer Harrison Marks before featuring as *Playboy*'s 'Playmates of the Month' in 1970. The revolving-door role of Count Karnstein had gone to Egyptian-born Damien Thomas, another television actor who previously had been seen in an episode of Hammer's *Journey to the Unknown*. 'I took a screen test, and I thought I was just being given this screen test to act opposite the others who were taking screen tests,' Thomas told me in 1980. 'I had no idea I was actually in the running for the principal role.'

The special effects were handled by Albert Luxford, who had worked on *Chitty Chitty Bang Bang* (1966) and several of the Bond films. In his autobiography, *Albert J Luxford, the Gimmick Man*, he explained how he accomplished a particular trick on *Twins of Evil*: 'One of the scenes I had to work on with Peter was the decapitation of one of the twins.. It had to look realistic, and also have blood pumping out all over the place, naturally.. So I needed to make a new neck for the victim that I could shoot blood out of. Initially, I decided to use a huge piece of Spam, but that did not work.. Next I tried—at the suggestion of the director—a marrow. We had to have two pipes channelling the blood through the neck, and the marrow just did not support them effectively. I tried one or two other things, to no avail, before I picked up a huge sausage from the butcher—it was a German one, and about four inches in

diameter.. John Hough was adamant that I should perform the severing of the head. I told him that the only way I'd do it is if he shot half of it in reverse, limiting any potential danger to the actress. I put the machete to her neck and pulled it away; they shot it backwards so it looked like I was actually swinging it in to the neck. For the next half of the shot, I substituted my sausage for the neck. We had a little man who was about four feet high, dressed in the girl's costume, with this huge sausage on his head! I then laid into the meat and the machete came away with blood gushing everywhere. If you see the film, it is my hand in Peter Cushing's glove. It wasn't an easy scene, nor particularly satisfactory from my point of view, but it served its purpose.'

'The budget for the film was relatively low, and all the special effects were achieved by the camera during filming—a far cry from the extensive array of computer-generated imagery now available to the filmmaker,' Hough concurred. 'I am still proud of the shots where the vampires and their victims walk in front of mirrors, but only the victim is reflected. I had seen Roman Polanski achieve the same effect in *Dance of the Vampires*, so I went to Paris to ask him how he did it. There is no trick photography in this shot, and enthusiasts are still puzzled as to how I did it.'

Twins of Evil finished shooting on May 8, at a cost of just over £205,000. The film opened as the top half of a double-bill with the Rank-Hammer *Hands of the Ripper* at London's New Victoria theatre and did respectable business; it went on release in Britain in October and in the US in June the following year, where it was heavily cut to obtain an 'R' rating. The days of West End premieres and countrywide American distribution for Hammer's films were well and truly over.

Released in America by Universal, *Twins of Evil* suffered the same fate as the

***Twins of Evil* (Katya Wyeth)**

Twins of Evil (Damien Thomas)

The Vampire Lovers, only more so. AIP had cut around three minutes of footage from the former for its Stateside release, but Universal made cuts to the latter that totalled more than five minutes and included most of the film's sex scenes and nearly all of its graphic violence! Hammer's goriest vampire saga to date was turned into a tame costume melodrama. A total of thirty-four cuts were made at the behest of the MPAA.

With all the exploitative elements of the film removed, the notion of subtext could still be discerned in what remained—at least by American audiences. Whereas *Lust for a Vampire* had relatively little by way of text, let alone subtext, Hough's histrionic direction of *Twins of Evil* ensured that it operated on several levels, even if only the obvious one was intentional.

The evolution of the Hammer vampire had entered a new phase; in the previous films, there was never any question as to who was good and who evil. By the time of *Taste the Blood of Dracula*, the theme of hypocrisy had introduced a disturbing shade of grey, with upright Victorian 'gents' frequenting brothels and participating in devilish rites while maintaining the veneer of respectability. But nowhere in the Hammer canon is this creeping sense of moral ambiguity made more apparent than in *Twins of Evil*.

The relationship between *Twins of Evil* and the previous entries in the so-called 'Karnstein trilogy' is tenuous at best: early in the film, Mircalla Karnstein (Katya Wieth) appears to the jaded and dissolute count as a beauteous spectre, turns him into a vampire, and just as quickly disappears from whence she came. The character serves as little more than a plot device to kick-start the main narrative and, given the fact that Karnstein is *not* a vampire at the outset, *Twins* has to be seen as more of a prequel to *The Vampire Lovers* than a second sequel.

At its heart, *Twins of Evil* is a right-wing rant, railing against the permissive society and lashing out indiscriminately at perceived wrongs, many of which were of its creators' own making in the first place. It is a film of mixed messages: prurient on the one hand, puritanical (literally) on the other—a film that despises its own

undisciplined lurches towards excess. During the course of the story, and encouraged by the successful box-office antics of Cromwellian witchfinder Matthew Hopkins in Michael Reeves's *Witchfinder General* (1968), Weil and his fanatical followers burn to death three innocent women in the name of righteousness. He is unfettered authoritarianism, parental repression and religious intolerance all rolled into one; his sadistic compulsion, and that of his kindred in The Brotherhood, is to destroy whatever it is that he considers to be 'ungodly', whether it be a woman who 'takes many husbands' or a man who simply fails to conform to his own rigid set of beliefs. But in the end, he fails in his climactic bid to exterminate the 'evil' of Count Karnstein, and it is left to David Warbeck's pacifist schoolteacher to strike the fatal blow.

It is clear from the impotent rage embodied by Weil's Brotherhood in *Twins of Evil* that Hammer (and by implication the Christian Right) had no answers to the problems that its vampires had come to represent; it could only illustrate their effect. The Hammer vampire had gone about as far as it could go. Throughout the sixties, the voluptuous female 'vampire' had gradually emerged from beneath the cloak of Fisher's (and Stoker's) virile seducer to become a potent force in her own right, in line with the rise of feminism during the same period and culminating in the character of Carmilla Karnstein. But no one yet knew where such 'girl-power' was to lead, so that road was closed off for now. The metaphor had to be modified in order to survive, and others were seeing opportunities within it to explore a more political agenda, such as the role of the state (*The Night Stalker*) or racial inequality (*Blacula*). The sexual politics of the Hammer vampire were becoming passé; sexual liberation had not only come to pass, it had prevailed. Bob Kelljan's *Yorga* films had given the vampire new 'teeth' and an air of contemporary sophistication; *Dark Shadows* producer Dan Curtis and *Night Stalker* writer Richard Matheson were soon to empower him in a way that Hammer and Bram Stoker could hardly even have imagined.

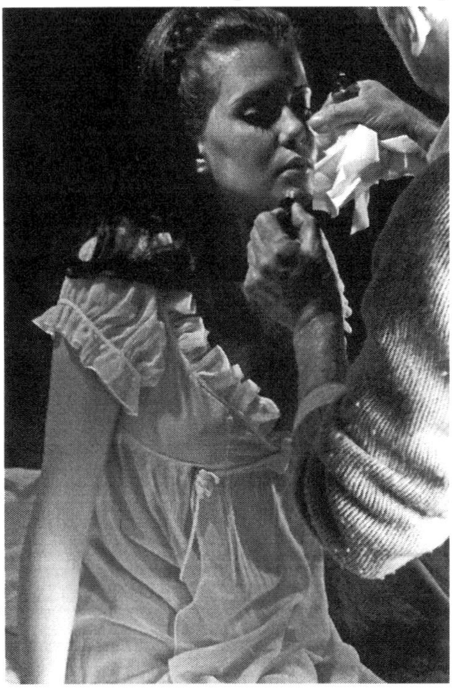

***Twins of Evil*: Mary Collinson on set**

The operatic madness all-too apparent in *Twins of Evil* is the paradoxical argument of another age consumed by its own fatuous reasoning. When Weil's wife persuades him that The Brotherhood should lay siege to the Karnstein keep and cut out the source of the 'satanic' plague that threatens to devour the countryside, Weil and his band of zealots are themselves immolated in the carnage that is the result. The film plays like an ultra-violent vigilante western—a notion underlined by Harry Robinson's rabble-rousing, *Dollars*-composer Ennio Morricone-inspired score—and self-destruction is written into the tapestry of its moral ambiguities from the start. (Hammer's next vampire Gothic, *Vampire Circus*, would take this notion of thematic implosion to its logical conclusion.)

In terms of typical production values and sheer directorial verve, Hammer's 'Karnstein trilogy' ended on a high note, with the best-looking and most thematically

Twins of Evil (Mary Collinson)

Vampyres (*Marianne Morris, Anulka Dziubinska*)

intriguing of the three films. But *Twins of Evil* is Hammer's *mea culpa*: a rabid example of puritanical backlash against the sins of the flesh for which it was itself partly responsible, but in which the flesh self-evidently has won.

The influence of the 'Karnstein' films would continue to be felt throughout the seventies, in the likes of Stephanie Rothman's *The Velvet Vampire* (1971), in which lesbian vampire Diane *Le Fanu* (Celeste Yarnall) entices a young couple to her desert ranch and proceeds to seduce them both, the low-budget Spanish productions *Count Dracula's Great Love* (1972, starring Paul Naschy) and *The Vampire's Night Orgy* (1973), and José Larraz's British-made sexploitation sensation *Vampyres* (1974), in which two bisexual female vampires also lure victims to their doom on the promise of sexual favours.

Hammer had revolutionised the vampire film and had single-handedly created the template by which all screen vampires—male or female— now operated, but it would soon be for other producers to take the myth on and remodel it in their own individual images.

> The grave of the Countess Mircalla was opened; and the General and my father recognised each his perfidious and beautiful guest, in the face now disclosed to view.. The limbs were perfectly flexible, the flesh elastic; and the leaden coffin floated with blood, in which to a depth of seven inches, the body lay immersed. Here then, were all the admitted signs and proofs of vampirism. The body, therefore, in accordance with the ancient practice, was raised, and a sharp stake driven through the heart of the vampire, who uttered a piercing shriek at the moment, in all respects such as might escape from a living person in the last agony. Then the head was struck off, and a torrent of blood flowed from the severed neck.
>
> **—J Sheridan Le Fanu, 'Carmilla'/*In a Glass Darkly* (1872)**

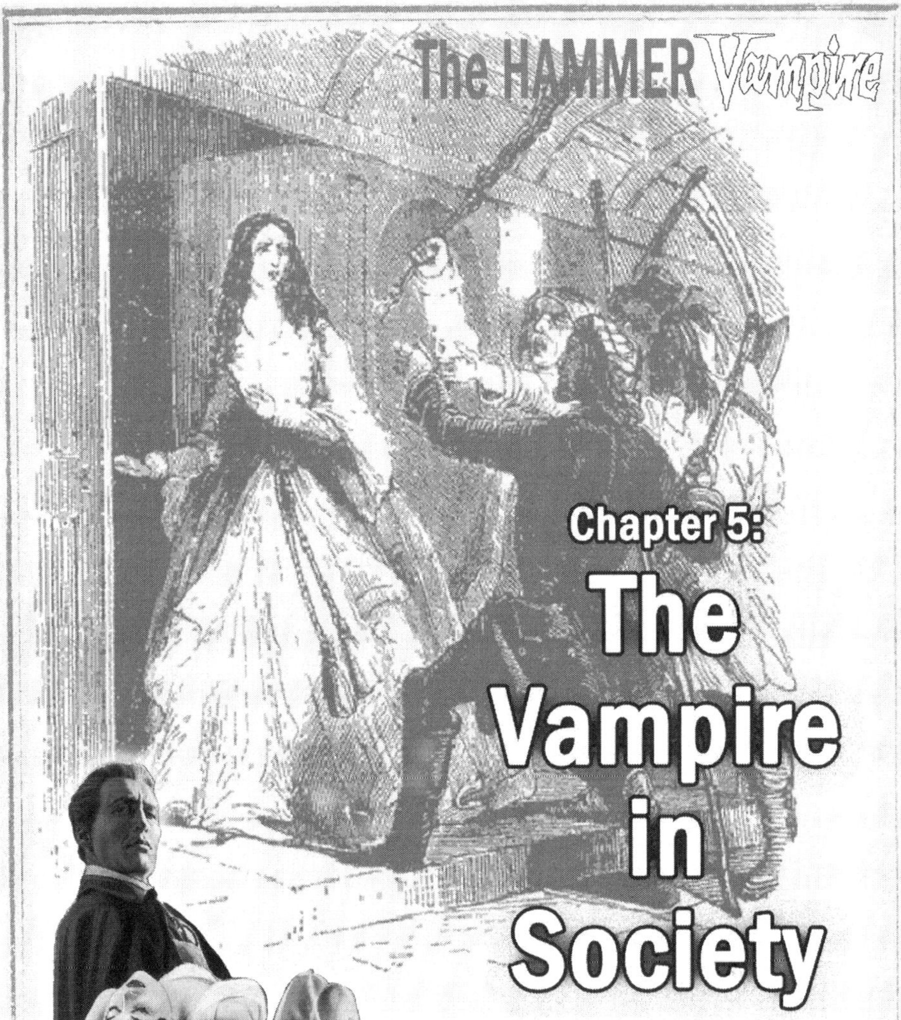

Chapter 5: The Vampire in Society

'Although we hear practically nothing about vampirism nowadays,' he continued, 'that is not to say that ghoulish spirits do not still take up their abode in a living man or woman, thus conferring upon them supernatural powers. What form was the shape you thought you saw?'

'It was like a huge bat,' I replied, shuddering.

'Tomorrow,' said Sanders, determinedly, 'I'm going to London to see Scotland Yard. They may laugh at me at first but—'

—Sydney Horler, 'The Believer'/
The Vampire (1935)

Publicity shot for Dracula AD 1972

After the unspectacular box office returns from *Scars of Dracula*, Hammer was in a quandary as to what to do with what had always been its most successful franchise. Tony Hinds, who was still being called upon to write the occasional screenplay for the company, had come up with an intriguing storyline entitled *Dracula in India* (later revised to become *Kali—Devil Bride of Dracula*), in which the count moved further East, instead of West, in search of victims. In an interview in *Little Shoppe of Horrors*, Hinds was quoted as saying, 'A number of US companies had money frozen in India and one of the only ways they could get it out was by making films there.. Warner Brothers was in that position, so I was asked to come up with something—hence the Dracula/India subject. Michael Carreras tried to set it up when he took over. He rewrote the ending and improved it.. but without success. A pity, as it was one of my favourites. I spent my war career in India and developed the Englishman's inevitable "love-hate" relationship with the place.'

By the turn of 1971, the most successful film

company in Britain had been relieved of its status as a winner of the Queen's Award and the famous insignia no longer flew over Hammer House. Hammer faced increasing competition from all quarters and Sir James Carreras, now nearing 62, had agreed to take a back seat in the company's affairs in return for son Michael's co-operation in helping to steer the business through the troubled waters ahead.

But things were not all bad: the company was sitting on a record number of features either completed, in production, or in the planning, as Michael outlined to Denis Meikle: 'They had a full year; they were heavily ahead. First thing I did was hire a theatre in Wardour Street, and I got prints of all the films that had been made while I'd been away and caught up with that.' *Countess Dracula*, again starring Ingrid Pitt, was already in production at Pinewood; of the horrors to which Hammer was committed but were yet to go into production, two more were vampire films—producer Wilbur Stark's *Village of the Vampires* and Brian Clemens and Albert Fennell's *Kronos*. But there was also another as-yet untitled 'Dracula' sequel for Warners, and attention switched to how to refresh the only subject that was of interest to Hammer's one remaining distribution partner in the US.

The release of Hammer's recent co-production with American-International, *The Vampire Lovers*, had given the company a much-needed shot in the arm. Its opportune mix of horror and lesbian sex had delivered a strong performance on Britain's ABC circuit, but James Carreras's off-hand attitude towards AIP's concerns about the sexual content of the film had nipped the brief alliance in the bud, and what had been trumpeted as a new beginning for both companies at a Savoy Hotel reception on January 13, 1970, was already at an end by the time Michael Carreras had his feet under the desk at Hammer House; the obligatory follow-up, *Lust for a Vampire*, had to be foisted onto EMI instead and consequently was mishandled by Continental for its outing in America.

Hammer's thunder was also being stolen by every horror film release that sought to take advantage of the new 18-X certificate that the BBFC had implemented the previous summer. In a declining market, independent producers were finding it easier than ever before to raise finance for features. In the one field in which its name still meant something, Hammer had now to compete not only against Amicus, Tigon and AIP, but against cheaper, imported horrors, as well as exploitation offerings from the likes of Peter Newbrook (*The Asphyx*; *Incense for the Damned*), Pete Walker (*Frightmare et al*), Anthony Balch (*Horror Hospital*) and others—all of whom had films awaiting release or planned for production.

Michael was only too aware of the danger this posed and he had cancelled a number of projects as a result, losing producer Aida Young in the process. But there remained the matter of the company's contractual deal with Warners, and new president Ted Ashley was adamant that only another 'Dracula' would fit the bill. James Carreras once more took upon himself the onerous task of trying to coerce a recalcitrant Christopher Lee to again don the black cloak of the vampire king. The usual pleas were trotted out in personal phone calls, but another increase in his fee did the trick. With Lee persuaded to return to the role, preparations were made to mount the *seventh* film in Hammer's ongoing saga, though in the absence of Hinds, no one could think of a suitable title for a hybrid which, at Michael's instigation (and partly in response to the contemporisation that had proved so successful in AIP's *Yorga* franchise), now proposed to uplift the count from his native soil and transplant him to modern-day London.

To give the film a more up-to-date look, Canadian Alan Gibson was nominated to direct: 'I'd done *Crescendo* with him and I thought he had a lot of potential from

Publicity shot for Dracula AD 1972

that point,' Michael said. 'I didn't like him as a man but I liked him as a director; for a producer, he was a good director because you'd sit down with him and say this is what we've got to do today and he would find a way of doing it. And if he needed something extra, he'd come and discuss it with you. He was a director without arrogance—which doesn't necessarily make him a good director, but it makes him good from a producer's point of view.'

By the time *Dracula Today* (or *Dracula-Chelsea 1971*) went into production, the nation's cinema chains were gearing up to release not only Hammer's entire studio output for the first six months of the year but horror films from AIP (*The Abominable Dr Phibes*; *Murders in the Rue Morgue*), Amicus (*I, Monster*), and a number of others, as well. Unbeknown to his son, Sir James Carreras had seen the writing on the wall. And even as *Dracula Today* went before the camera of Dick Bush on September 27, under the auspices of former BBC-TV producer (and current

Dracula AD 1972: Elstree's 'Cavern' set (inset: Christopher Neame, Marsha Hunt)

Carreras favourite) Josephine Douglas, he was busied in negotiations behind the scenes to rid himself of the encumbrance of Hammer in exchange for a more profitable position at EMI. While Michael battled on in what eventually would be a vain attempt to find a new direction for the company, the once-mighty Hammer Films was being sold out from under his nose by his own father.

The irony of Hammer's 'new direction' for Dracula was self-evident. In the fifties and early sixties, the company had set trends in horror films. Their Eastman Colour Gothic revivals had led to AIP's *I Was a Teenage Frankenstein* (in which Dr Frankenstein's crates containing lab equipment are shown to have Hammer's Wardour Street address!) and helped to inspire the entire Roger Corman cycle of Edgar Allan Poe films, as well as the period thrillers of Amicus and Tigon. Now Hammer was following a trend set by one of its own imitators.

Hinds had no interest in writing a modern-day Dracula and the task went to television writer Don Houghton instead. Houghton had written scripts for popular series such as *Dr Who* and *Emergency Ward 10* and, by May 1971, he had completed a first draft which was then submitted to Warners for approval. Michael felt that it needed a rewrite, but Warners were keen for production to begin and were already planning for a sequel; Houghton was then assigned to the sequel, so Hammer's first contemporary 'Dracula' had to be shot from a draft screenplay!

Most of the film's predictably young cast were to represent members of Chelsea's 'smart set'. Actress Stephanie Beacham had just caused something of a sensation in Michael Winner's *The Nightcomers*, a bizarrre 'prequel' to the Henry James novel *The Turn of the Screw*, and she was signed to play Jessica Van Helsing. (Beacham had achieved considerable 'exposure' due to her nude love scenes with Marlon Brando in *The Nightcomers*—shots of which had ended up in *Playboy*—but oddly, her role in *Dracula Today* was one for which nudity was not required.) Another model-cum-actress making her debut for Hammer was Caroline Munro, fresh from featuring in billboard ads for 'Lamb's Navy Rum'; Sir James Carreras had signed her to a one-year contract on the strength of them. (Munro's previous genre credit had been a non-speaking role in support of Vincent Price in *The Abominable Dr Phibes*, but she would go on to star in the Ray Harryhausen spectacular *The Golden Voyage of Sinbad*.) Dracula's protégé in this instance would be the anagramatically-named Johnny Alucard, a cheap trick which previously had seen service in Universal's *Son of Dracula*; Alucard was to be played by Christopher Neame, one of the torch-wielding villagers in *Lust for a Vampire*. Alongside him was Marsha Hunt, former girlfriend of Rolling Stone Mick Jagger, and Michael Coles, as the Establishment figure of Inspector Murray.

In the midst of all the pretty young things who were now to greet Count Dracula on his arrival in 'swinging' London, one piece of casting really caught the attention of the fans—Peter Cushing's return to the role of Van Helsing, which he had not played since *The Brides of Dracula* in 1960. Cushing had just given one of his best performances in the Amicus omnibus film *Tales from the Crypt*, and he was now to reprise one of his most memorable turns for Hammer, albeit more than a decade older and in the guise of his own great-grandson.

With a production budget set at £220,000, *Dracula Today* went before the cameras at Elstree. The company's new approach to its most famous trademark still seemed somewhat uncertain, however, as Michael Carreras outlined to Alan Frank in *Little Shoppe of Horrors*: 'When we got down to the modern sequences, we had battles galore. I would have liked the whole concept of the modern Dracula to take place in a churchyard at midnight, since then you don't know where the

Dracula AD 1972 (Caroline Munro, Christopher Neame)

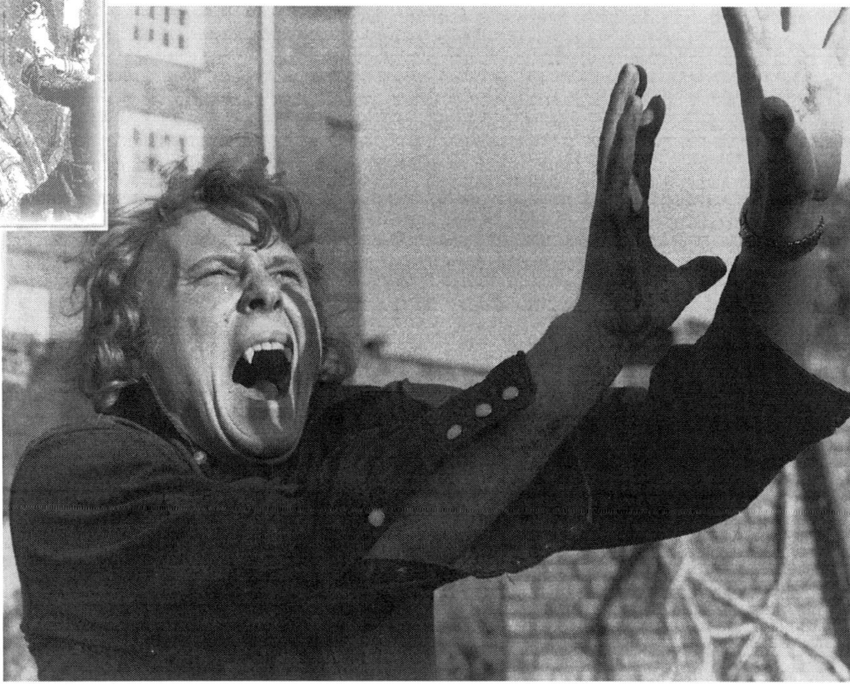

***Dracula AD 1972* (Philip Miller)**

devil you are. Unfortunately you could not do that for a long time. But I was very strong in dragging in a deserted and empty churchyard as much as possible, to give a midnight flavour, even though it was modern.' Don Mingaye, who was the production designer on *Lust for a Vampire*, was thus instructed to mix the old with the new. The 'old' was to be the Gothic interior of St Bartolph's Church, Dracula's 'hangout' in the film, while 'new' would come in the 'Goth' form of The Cavern, the nightclub hangout for almost everyone else in the cast of what was now to be known as *Dracula AD 1971*, before quickly becoming *Dracula AD 1972*.

One thing was certain: Hammer's Dracula would never be the same again.

Lee, as ever, had problems with the screenplay. Rather than speak the lines that Houghton had written ('I am Dracula, Lord of Darkness, Master of the Walking Dead!'), he again inserted some dialogue from Stoker's novel ('You dare play your wits against mine?—I, who have commanded nations!'). Lee had just returned from Transylvania, where he had gone to appear in the feature-length documentary *In Search of Dracula*; there, he had trod the very ground on which Vlad Tepes, the real-life model for the count, had commanded his armies in the 15th century, and he was intent on maintaining the credibility of the character despite the anomalous circumstances in which he now found himself. 'I can assure you that Vlad Tepes Dracula *did* exist,' he sombrely informed another documentary crew which had taken to tailing him for promotional purposes during the filming of *AD 1972*.

By all accounts, the other cast members had a better time of it. 'That was one of the ones I really, really did enjoy,' Caroline Munro told me. 'I had done a few parts before, but this was the first time I felt that acting was what I really wanted to do. I quite believed in what I was doing. I got hooked on it after that.' Munro's role in the film was not a large one, but she left her mark—or rather, Lee left *his* on her: 'In the first reel, I think, he bit my neck and that was it.. well, he was pretty frightening because he was so believable as Dracula. Once he put those great red eyeballs in..

and he's such a tall man. I'm quite tall, but he's six foot four; he really towers above you. Very, very professional and very good. So I really didn't have to do a lot, just look a bit scared, and I felt it too!'

Lee may have taken matters seriously on set, but the same could not be said of Beacham, who later confessed to *Little Shoppe of Horrors*, 'I was laughing with Marsha at just about everything. One of the things that made me laugh more than anything was the fact that she had to be blacked up; she wasn't dark enough.. I thought Caroline was one of the sweetest girls ever. I couldn't believe that anybody so pretty—so beautiful, for Heaven's sake—could possibly be so nice, but she was.. far too lovely hair, it was just immaculate all the time, and she used to look disgustingly good at six o'clock in the morning.'

Cushing put his usual positive spin on things during production, remarking to the press, 'This has been a particularly happy picture. I think we have a great director in Alan Gibson, who has wonderful ideas, and Dick Bush is doing a magnificent job, and Don Mingaye's sets all round are beautiful, and such a lovely cast, all the young people are so marvellous'. Lee, on the other hand, had one of his usual Hammer accidents, as he explained to author Mark Miller, 'They wanted a smoke effect when I touched Stephanie Beacham's crucifix around her neck. The only way they could do this was to put acetic acid, which is like vinegar, onto my fingertips and blow a fan on them from behind the camera. Apparently if you blow air onto something that has acetic acid on it, it smokes. It smoked all right. I lost the skin on my fingertips!'

While the film may have been something of a light-hearted romp for most of the cast, Gibson and producer Josephine Douglas often found themselves at odds with each other. By all accounts, Douglas was a very 'hands-on' producer and Gibson resented her interference. There were problems with the music score as well, which ultimately was credited to former Manfred Mann guitarist Michael Vickers. Gibson had fought for Vickers, who had never written a film score before, and he had been given the job. But Hammer musical director Philip Martell called him a 'crazy, lazy man' and ended up hiring veteran Don Banks to redo some of the track and pad out the rest with library music, such as cues from his own score for the *The Evil of Frankenstein* (1964).

Shooting of *Dracula AD 1972* wrapped on November 5, 1971. In the UK, the film was released on September 28, 1972, on a double-bill with the Freddie Francis-directed *Trog*, a dreadful piece of horror hokum starring Joan Crawford and a tame Neanderthal. In the US, the main feature was preceded by a three-minute short called *Horror Ritual*, a gimmick-piece starring Barry Atwater, who had just played a vampire on American television in a film that was to herald the end of the Hammer variety; essentially a promotional plug for the company's so-called new approach to Dracula, *Horror Ritual* is now a quaint piece of Hammer trivia.

Variety found *Dracula AD 1972* enjoyable: 'Under Josephine Douglas' producer helming and Alan Gibson's direction of the mostly slick script, action travels at a fast pace,' the reviewer noted. A few of the mainstream critics were also impressed, such as Felix Barker of *The Evening News* who called it 'a clear winner,' and Eric Braun of *Films and Filming* who wrote, 'The casting.. gives freshness to the theme, with some interesting new faces among the young people. Christopher Lee and Peter Cushing play with their customary air of dedication which has always given a background of quality to even the least successful of Hammer's blood and thunder penny dreadfuls.' However, most observers were typically unmoved by the film on its release. In the BFI's *Monthly Film Bulletin*, Clyde Jeavons wrote, 'Not even the presence of Cushing and Lee can add conviction to Hammer's latest "batpic", an abortive and totally unimaginative attempt to update the Bram Stoker legend to

present-day Chelsea.' And even the US fan magazine *Cinefantastique*, ordinarily Hammer-friendly, did not take kindly to Hammer's new Dracula. Lee M Kaplan considered it to be 'a mediocre rock-culture drama rammed head-first into a traditional equally mediocre period horror film'.

Perhaps the fairest appraisal came from Nicholas Morgan in the fan-magazine *Castle of Frankenstein*, who opined: 'Though excitement and suspense aren't spared, some fans of the genre may have trouble from flinching at a number of enormous liberties taken to provide this latest vehicle for Count Dracula.. Undoubtedly slick, good entertainment all the way through—but impaired by a lack of those sensitive touches employed by the late Seth Holt in creating *Blood From the Mummy's Tomb*, which retained a powerful and classic period flavour though in modern setting. Les Bowie's special effects are good and Stephanie Beacham in the femme lead has already won fame for beauty and her role opposite Marlon Brando in *The Nightcomers*.'

The plot of the film is perfunctory. After a novel prologue set a century before in which Dracula and Van Helsing grapple in a fight to the death atop a runaway coach in London's Hyde Park, the action moves to the present day and a group of bored twenty-somethings looking for cheap thrills to relieve the monotony of their louche existences; notional leader of the group Johnny Alucard (Neame) suggests a black magic ritual in a desancitified church in the manner of that in *Taste the Blood of Dracula*—but Alucard has a hidden agenda: he plans to use the ceremony to raise Count Dracula from the dead. This he does and, beginning with those in Alucard's jaded circle, the king of the vampires embarks on a new campaign of terror in the very heart of the metropolis.

Unlike most of Hammer's period pictures, *Dracula AD 1972* has not travelled well. There are fans who find that to be part of its charm but although the film is fast-paced, nicely photographed and often captivating in its sheer cheek, it is also Hammer's weakest Dracula, entirely due to the 'new' approach to the subject; even *Scars of Dracula* had moments which harked back to the great days of Hammer's

***Dracula AD 1972* (Peter Cushing)**

Dracula AD 1972 (Stephanie Beacham, Christopher Lee)

1958 original. *AD 1972* offers few of the usual elegant Hammer *frissons*; it may have been better produced than its immediate predecessor, but dialogue and plotting range from the mediocre to the downright dreadful.

The film's biggest error has to do with Michael Carreras's conviction that Dracula should stay nestled within the ruins of a Gothic church. While these scenes feature some of Dick Bush's most evocative images, they also reflect a timidity on the part of the filmmakers over bringing Dracula more determinedly into the modern era, as had AIP with its *Yorga* franchise, in which Robert Quarry's count not only watched television but cruised the LA night in a station-wagon. In *AD 1972*, Hammer's count seemed as ill-at-ease with modern life as Lee now felt in the role itself. Lee invests the part with his usual gravitas, and he is as potent as ever in his climactic scenes with Cushing's 'Lorrimer' Van Helsing, but the old magic is temporal at best. In line with Hammer's recent more graphic approach to its horror films, Dracula's death scene is the best in the series since the original film: he falls onto a stake that Van Helsing has placed, upturned, in an open grave, and his nemesis prods a shovel into his prostrate form, pushing down on it until the stake is forced through Dracula's torso to protrude out of his back, to the accompaniment of a fountain of blood; the predictable Les Bowie disintegration follows swiftly.

The best thing about the film is Cushing's return as Van Helsing. Playing against Lee as Dracula for the first time since 1958, his earnest professor is as elegant and coolly intelligent as ever, if somewhat bemused by the antics of the young generation by whom he now finds himself surrounded. But even his 'scientific' approach to the role is made to appear ridiculous in a scene in which he writes down the name 'Alucard' letter by letter, before realising that it is actually Dracula spelled backwards! (For the sake of an audience also considered by Universal to be slow on the uptake, *Son of Dracula*'s Frank Craven had to do a similar thing and trace out the letters with his finger.)

Johnny Alucard's Christopher Neame does his best with a poorly-written role that includes lines like 'Master!—I did it! I summoned you!'; in the sequence where he resurrects the count, he urges the others in the group to 'Dig the music, kids!' Perhaps his most notable contribution to the series comes in the scene in which Dracula inflicts the bite of the vampire upon him—an oddly homoerotic interlude for the count, who previously had only been seen fanging the females in his entourage. Dracula's off-screen induction of Jonathan Harker in 1958's *Dracula* seemed to be wholly devoid of any such sub-text, but the orgasmic expression on Neame's face as Dracula 'goes down' on him invests the scene with an erotic charge rivalling that of the Karnstein films.

In the same way that the trio of Victorian hedonists in *Taste the Blood of Dracula* represented the unbridled excesses of the swinging sixties, so too do the pot-smoking youths of *AD 1972* represent those same 'dangers' to society. Once again, Hammer tried to have its cake and eat it—on the one hand, appealing to the 'counter-culture' audience, the disaffected youth of the day; on the other, condemning that same audience for its wayward lifestyle and apparent lack of purpose and moral values. Jessica Van Helsing is fascinated by the supernatural, stating to her grandfather's dismay that she finds it 'Weird, man—way out. I mean: spooks, hobgoblins, black magic, all that sort of stuff..' And yet Hammer itself had built a multi-million pound business from that self-same fascination.

Michael Carreras's edict that Dracula should remain in period does provide the film with an interesting undertow, however. The count seems unwilling to leave his

Dracula AD 1972 (Christopher Lee)

Gothic surroundings, as though he is afraid of the new world that he finds around him—how can he strike terror into the hearts of those to whom he is only marginally more terrifying than a bad acid trip? A pity that Houghton and Carreras did not grasp the potential in this conflict more fully and try to integrate the count more comprehensively into '1972'; he could have strode the length of Chelsea's King's Road looking for victims without anyone giving him so much as a second glance, red-lined cloak and all.

As expected of a film made by a team of individuals who knew nothing of the generation to whom they pandered and which they pretended to reflect onscreen, it is left to the older and wiser heads of Van Helsing and the dedicated minions of the Metropolitan police to save London from the 'depravity' of vampirism. *Dracula Ad 1972* is really only notable for its opening, set in the safer Hammer territory of 1872, in which Cushing's 'original' professor dies destroying Dracula once more. It is the best sequence in the film, recapturing as it does—if only for a fleeting moment—the glory days of old. It is the footage that follows which is lacking in credibibility; the curious mixture of styles never really coheres, but there was worse to come.

While Hammer piled on the sex and gore, thinking excess to be the solution to dwindling audiences and diminishing returns, others had different and more original ideas on how to refresh the genre of the vampire film.

In January 1972, a 74-minute ABC made-for-television special became the most widely-watched TV movie of all time on the US airwaves. Written by *I Am Legend*'s Richard Matheson and produced by Dan Curtis of *Dark Shadows*, *The Night Stalker* featured Darren McGavin as hard-bitten newspaper reporter Carl Kolchak and Barry Atwater as vampire Janos Skorzeny. The plot was a typical Matheson tease on genre conventions—if a vampire was actually on the loose in modern-day Las Vegas, who would believe it? The cynical Kolchak is soon convinced, but like believers in UFOs, he finds it impossible to obtain the hard evidence necessary to substantiate

The Night Stalker (Darren McGavin, Barry Atwater)

his theory and convince others likewise; the story then becomes a parable of how contemporary society would react to the idea of a mythical monster in its midst.

Unlike the Gothic vampires of Hammer's films, who were becoming tired and predictable through repetition, *The Night Stalker* had *immediacy*; it had currency. And it had something new and dynamic to add to the mix in terms of its vampire: superhuman strength. Hammer's Dracula may have been physically more powerful than an ordinary mortal, but he was hardly superhuman—witness his struggle with Charles Kent at the climax of *Prince of Darkness*. Van Helsing spoke of the count's 'preternatural strength' in *Dracula*, and it was sufficient to toss his bride aside like a rag-doll or subdue Jonathan Harker and others who came against him, but his real power in Stoker's novel lay in his supernatural ability to change into a wolf, or a mist, and to elude his pursuers that way. Vampire Janos Skorzeny in *The Night Stalker* was not only immortal, he was well-nigh *invincible*.

Directed by John Llewellyn Moxey with a sense of documentary urgency, *The Night Stalker* was as ground-breaking in the Nixonian pre-Watergate period of early 1972 as Hammer's Dracula had been in 1958; as ever, Matheson was ahead of the game, and his tale of a vampire loose in the modern world enabled him to protest the idea of (local) governmental cover-up, while dressing his grievance in the clothes of fantasy. At the end of the film, Kolchak is separated from his girlfriend and both are driven out of town—she to an unknown future; he to blackmailed silence for his part in saving the authorities from themselves. In *The Night Stalker*, the vampire as metaphor was alive and well, but no longer was it in the hands of Hammer.

The Night Stalker led to a second TV movie-cum-pilot—*The Night Strangler*— the following year, which was also scripted by Matheson, as well as a full-fledged series, *Kolchak: The Night Stalker* (one of whose episodes was penned by Jimmy Sangster). Other Dan Curtis productions featured similar 'invincible', juggernaut-like monsters, such as the demonic zombie of *The Norliss Tapes* (1972), but of more concern to Hammer would be the film that Curtis asked Matheson to write when he had done with Kolchak.

Bram Stoker's Dracula was also made for American television, but it would be released theatrically in the UK in 1973. With veteran actor Jack Palance in the lead, and Simon Ward (from *Frankenstein Must Be Destroyed*) as one of his several adversaries, the film trod familiar Hammer territory—literally. Curtis's version not only featured a more ferocious count, who was able to fling his enemies through windows with a single sweep of his arm, but it pitched his Carpathian tent in Oakley Court, scene of many a classic Hammer horror. (When *Vampyres* sought to further exploit the lesbian vampire angle that Hammer had set in train with its 'Karnstein trilogy', it also had the audacity to ensconce its fanged *femme fatales* in Oakley Court!)

What had started with Lee and a renegade production for Harry Alan Towers, and continued through the *Count Yorga* films and their blaxploitation counterparts, *Blacula* and *Scream, Blacula, Scream* (1972 and 1973 respectively, both with William Marshall), now had Jack Palance offering his take on Stoker's famous villain. By 1974, Hammer would have lost all hold on the character of Count Dracula, and with its one remaining cash-cow now effectively a public domain property that any independent producer could plunder, there was nowhere left for the character to go but further East than even Tony Hinds had envisaged in *Dracula in India*, to try to find a new genre into which he could slip unnoticed. By then, however, the image of the Hammer vampire would be so completely absorbed into the films of others that it would also lose its unique identity, and Hammer its edge in the process.

Having failed in his quest to sell Hammer in the meanwhile (first to utilities company Studio Film Labs and then to Tony Tenser's Tigon Pictures), Sir James Carreras had finally been presented with an offer from son Michael that he decided he could hardly refuse. With Michael now occupied on his takeover of Hammer Films, it came time for the company to again fulfil its obligation to Warners and provide it with yet another Dracula. *Dracula AD 1972* had opened inauspiciously in the UK

Bram Stoker's Dracula (Jack Palance)

The Satanic Rites of Dracula

at selected ABC 'first-run' theatres in place of a premiere engagement in London's West End. No sooner was it out of circulation, however, than the comically-titled *Dracula is Dead.. and Well and Living in London* moved onto Elstree's stages.

Jimmy Sangster had worked on a treatment for Hammer's eighth Dracula as early as March 1972, but it was left to Don Houghton to provide the screenplay. In August, coincidentally the same month that Michael Carreras finalised his purchase of Hammer, Houghton delivered his first draft of *Dracula is Dead..* based on Sangster's outline. Houghton's script picked up where *AD 1972* had ended, with the count assuming the identity of a Howard Hughes-style industrial magnate named David Danielovitch Denham, or 'DD' Denham for short. The building that houses the Denham Group of Companies has supposedly been built on the site of St Bartolph's Church, Dracula's previous base of operations, and the science fiction-style scenario involved Dracula and his followers attempting to unleash a strain of bubonic plague upon the world, annihilating whole populations and depriving the count of further victims. It was certainly a curious concept—almost a death-wish on Dracula's part, and perhaps even on the part of Hammer itself?

This time, there was to be no shooting from a first draft. The script was altered considerably prior to production; Houghton's original draft had Dracula present at the black mass which opens the film (he is absent in the event), and Van Helsing observed at one juncture that the count was 'capable of taking on many guises'. There was also a sub-plot involving the assassination of the Bishop of Sandavia, whoever he might have been. It was more Bond than bloodsucker, more fiendish Fu Manchu than frightening. In the rewrites, Houghton eliminated the assassination plot and reduced the billionaire industrialist angle to make the film more of a traditional vampire yarn. The notion of Dracula being able to transform himself into 'one of us' was also discarded, as were a number of other key scenes.

With Sir James literally out of the picture, so was producer Josephine Douglas. Michael installed Houghton as associate producer, a move calculated to avoid the confrontations which had strained the production of *Dracula AD 1972*. Alan Gibson

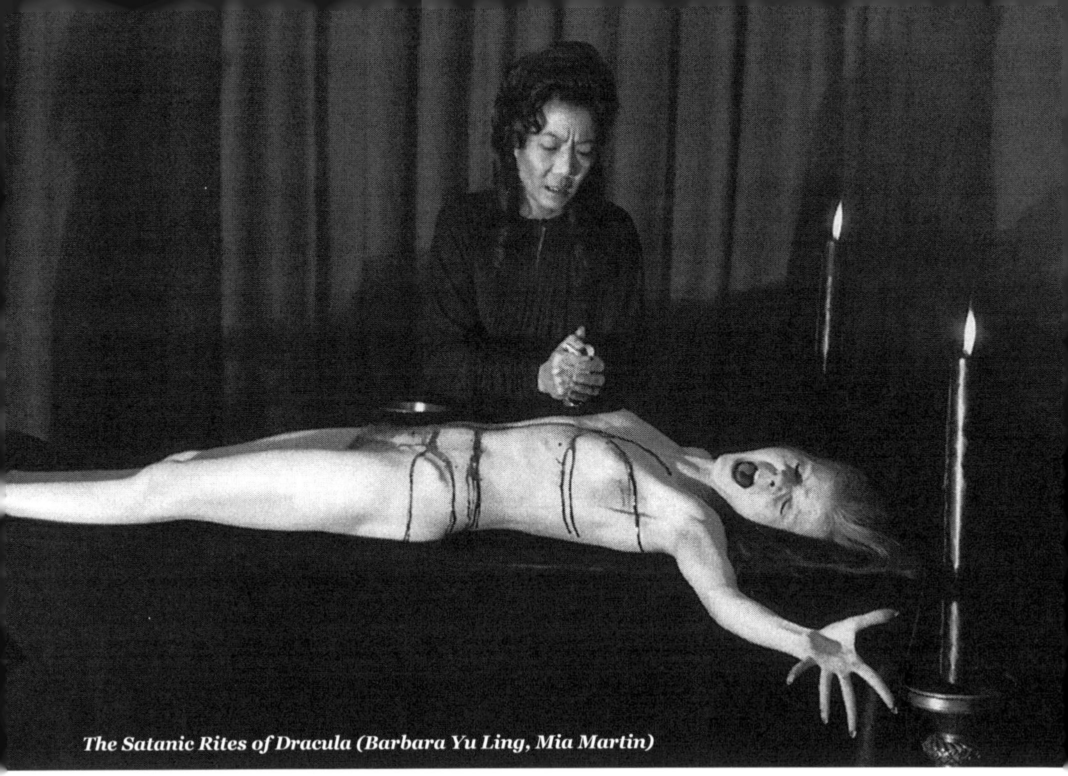
The Satanic Rites of Dracula (Barbara Yu Ling, Mia Martin)

was invited back to the director's chair, thereby becoming the first director since Terence Fisher to helm two Hammer vampire films in a row. Peter Cushing and Michael Coles also returned, as did Lee—under protest, as ever—though his rant to Don Glut in the magazine *Monsters of the Movies* was excessive even for him: 'I just think it's fatuous. I can think of twenty adjectives—fatuous, pointless, absurd. It's not a comedy. At least with me it's not a comedy. But it's a comic title. I don't see the point. I don't see what they hope to achieve. I think it's playing down to people. I don't think people like it. I don't think people appreciate it either, because people who go to see a character like this go to see him seriously. They don't laugh at him. That I know. They may laugh at some of the things in the pictures, but they'll never laugh at me to my knowledge.'

Lee's complaints were equally fatuous, however. When he originally agreed to lend his name and talents to *AD 1972*, he also agreed to a sequel. He was therefore contractually obliged and it would have been no news to him that a sequel was forthcoming. Perhaps he felt that he had to perform this ritual protest in order to maintain his dignity; in any event, it would be the last time he would be required to protest. *Dracula is Dead..* was to be his swan-song in the role.

Despite the presence of various returnees, continuity between the two modern-day Draculas could not be maintained for the role of Jessica Van Helsing. Declaring the new script to be 'very funny', Stephanie Beacham found that she was otherwise engaged (or at least she said she was) and declined to appear again. She was replaced by Joanna Lumley, another model-turned-actress who had featured briefly as a Bond girl in *On Her Majesty's Secret Service* (1969); Lumley was the physical antithesis of the buxom Beacham, willowy and svelte, and her approach to the part would be as diverse as her looks, making Jessica more intelligent and much less 'hip'.

In addition to *AD 1972*'s Michael Coles, William Franklyn joined the cast as agent Peter Torrence of MI7, an organisation apparently one notch higher in secrecy than James Bond's MI6. Franklyn had been one of the many actors considered to play Bond before Sean Connery signed on for *Dr No* in 1962, but he had also appeared in

Hammer's *Quatermass 2* (1957) and *The Snorkel* (1958), though he was currently better known for a long-running series of British television commercials for Schweppes mineral waters. Freddie Jones and Patrick Barr, both also Hammer veterans of note, lent further distinguished weight to the proceedings.

Ex-Hammer company accountant Roy Skeggs was promoted from production supervisor on the previous film to producer on the new, and Dick Bush was replaced as lighting cameraman by Brian Probyn, who had just photographed Fisher and Cushing's final Frankenstein film for Hammer, *Frankenstein and the Monster from Hell*.

Budgeted at roughly the same £220,000 as *Dracula AD 1972*, despite a year of increasing inflation between the two, *Dracula is Dead..* went onto the floor at Elstree on November 13, but it would be the very last time that a Hammer Dracula would tread the boards of a British film studio.

Away from the Elstree stages, there were some interesting locations on display. A house called High Canons on an estate in Hertfordshire doubled for 'Pelham House' in the film, the country retreat of Count Dracula himself, while Queen's Gate Lodge in thc London borough of Kensington became The Keeley Foundation, where Freddie Jones's Professor Keeley creates the strain of bubonic plague that the count is intent on inflicting on humankind. Hammer effects maestro Les Bowie came up with something new in the staking department as well: Former 'Carry On' starlet Valerie Van Ost was staked *topless*—another first for a British horror. In her 1989 autobiography, *Stare Back and Smile*, Joanna Lumley revealed how the effect was achieved: 'A metal brace encircled her chest, with an indentation in front of which was inserted one end of the stake. The stake was telescopic like a stage dagger; as it drove in a blood bag filled with Kensington Gore burst and she howled like a wolf. A visitor on the set had to be helped away, it looked so realistic.' Lumley also recalled how Lee had three sets of contact lenses: 'Prepare to bite (a few veins), ready to bite (riddled with red squiggles) and bite (blood red).'

Cushing, as was his wont, rewrote many of his lines. Concerned about how the mythic aspects of the story were being treated, he scribbled his misgivings over Dracula's alleged fear of silver in the margins of his script: 'This bothers me because of the silver ring Dracula wears..' Evidently he was overruled on that matter by Gibson, as the offending lines remain in the finished film. Freddie Jones, conversely, took a more light-hearted view of things, telling journalist Colin Beardmore, 'I do recall rather distinguished actors and me, ritually garbed, awaiting a set-up. There was a naked girl (virgin?) laying on an altar, a Chinese lady waiting to anoint her with the blood of a live cockerel—all rather comical. I couldn't resist it. I said, "Doubtless, you're all wondering why I called you here today!"'

In an interview for *The House That Hammer Built* magazine, assistant director Derek Whitehurst revealed that he and Gibson did not always see eye to eye: 'Alan was a very nice person, but communication between us was a problem, and a lot of it was shooting on the end of a zoom lens. I think we all knew it was the last one, really. We all felt it was scraping the bottom of the barrel, and the idea of making it in present day I didn't think was too good. I just didn't think it worked well at all.'

Even Christopher Lee, an actor not best known for his sense of humour on set, was moved to adopt an ersatz Bela Lugosi accent during the scene in which Van Helsing is summoned to meet DD Denham, unaware that he is actually Count Dracula. But true to form, Lee also took to carrying around a copy of Stoker's novel as shooting progressed, and he insisted on using another paraphrased quote from the book in the film: 'My revenge has spread over centuries and has just begun!' And

The Satanic Rites of Dracula (Christopher Lee, Peter Cushing)

there was the inevitable 'accident': a prop 'hawthorn' bush did not arrive on time for Dracula's fatal encounter with it at the climax, so Lee had to crawl his way through a real one, thorns and all. In Mark Miller's *Christopher Lee and Peter Cushing and Horror Cinema: A Filmography of their 22 Collaborations*, he recounted the outcome: 'I had on these awful contact lenses, but I would have put them in anyway because it (the thorns) could have gone in my eyes. What did happen, of course, is that I got quite cut up. A lot of that blood is real. Easy job, being an actor!'

On January 3, 1973—fifteen years to the day since Fisher's 1958 *Dracula* wrapped in production—principal photography on *Dracula is Dead..* was completed. An omen, perhaps, but not a good one. The end of an era was at hand.

The film was still known as *Dracula is Dead.. and Living in London* as late as February 13, and all through the editing process, which was supervised by Hammer veteran Chris Barnes. By the time it was finally released in the UK to little fanfare on January 13, 1974 (on a double-bill with AIP's *Blacula*), it had been given the more Hammer-typical title of *The Satanic Rites of Dracula*.

The Satanic Rites of Dracula (William Franklyn, Peter Cushing)

Only a few years before, a new Dracula film from the Hammer 'studio' would have been heralded as something of an event. Times had changed, however, and Warner Brothers, flushed with the recent success of William Friedkin's adaptation of best-selling horror novel *The Exorcist*, had lost interest in its Dracula franchise. Suddenly, there was more money to be made from one *Exorcist*-type blockbuster than from a dozen Draculas, and now Warners, who had been instrumental in giving Hammer its first truly international hit with *The Curse of Frankenstein* in 1957, became party to the company's declining fortunes. At the *Famous Monsters of Filmland* Hammer Convention in New York in November 1975, Michael Carreras seemed to be at a loss to know what to do with the company that he had now inherited. 'We can't go on remaking *Dracula* over and over,' he told an audience of fans, thinly-disguised exasperation in his voice.

Reviews for the film were typically mixed, although not as harsh as they were for the previous entry. David Pirie, writing for *Time Out*, noted the contemporary subtext: 'The beguiling message underlying Hammer's latest modern-dress Dracula movie is that the real vampires of modern London are property speculators. The idea is amazing (after all, Dracula started out as a subversive myth), but inevitably it tends to get lost.. still a vast improvement on the last in the series.'

Warners decided against releasing *The Satanic Rites of Dracula* in the US; it no longer had any need for Hammer Horror. The film was not released Stateside until the end of 1978, by which time Dracula had made an unexpected comeback via, of all places, Broadway. With striking set designs by Edward Gorey and a stunning star-turn by the classically-trained Frank Langella, the original Hamilton Deane adaptation of Bram Stoker's novel which had made a star of Bela Lugosi in 1927 became a Broadway smash all over again after fifty years. The inevitable film version followed, predictably produced by Universal, in which Langella reprised the role opposite Laurence Olivier's Van Helsing. As a direct consequence of this resurgence of interest in the character, German director Werner Herzog remade Murnau's *Nosferatu* shot-for-shot as *Nosferatu the Vampyre*—although the most financially

The Satanic Rites of Dracula (Valerie Van Ost)

successful film in the new cycle would turn out to be the AIP spoof *Love at First Bite*, starring George Hamilton as a count with his fangs firmly in his cheek.

In the midst of all this Dracula mania, *The Satanic Rites of Dracula* slipped into American theatres under the radar. Early in 1979, the title was changed to *Count Dracula and His Vampire Bride* and the film was paired with Hammer's final 'Dracula' effort, 1974's *The Legend of the 7 Golden Vampires* (see Chapter 6), which also suffered the indignity of a title-change to the moronic *The Seven Brothers Meet Dracula*. The saving grace of this ignominious end to Hammer's best-known film franchise was that *Satanic Rites* was not shorn of twenty minutes running time, as was *7 Golden Vampires*.

The *auteur* of this distribution disaster was none other than Max Rosenberg, formerly the business half of the duo behind Amicus Productions. By this time, Rosenberg's partnership with Milton Subotsky had been acrimoniously dissolved and each had gone their separate ways—Rosenberg to a distribution outfit called Dynamite Entertainment, which then released the Hammer double-feature. But Dynamite was seriously under-funded and could in no way compete in advertising acumen or marketing dollars with companies like Universal, Fox or AIP (the latter of which would become Orion Pictures). The US release of Hammer's last Dracula film was correspondingly low-key and unsuccessful, and Dynamite Entertainment itself imploded not long afterwards.

As a result, *The Satanic Rites of Dracula* ironically has become one of the most widely-seen and easily available of the Hammer Draculas because the copyright in it was thus allowed to lapse. It turns up (under its Rosenberg-imposed title) on every cheesy cable channel with a supernatural bent, and it features regularly on public domain download sites and on all manner of DVD horror compilations.

As with *Dracula AD 1972*, the passage of time has served to add a patina of nostalgia to *The Satanic Rites of Dracula*. There is an air of melancholy about the film, as though all concerned with it did indeed know that the end of the road was

The Satanic Rites of Dracula (Christopher Lee)

nigh—a sense of finality to the proceedings that echoes Michael Carreras's wish to see the Dracula series brought to some sort of conclusion, a notion made all the more tangible by Dracula's own 'death wish' in the film.

This atmosphere of impending doom is beautifully captured in Brian Probyn's autumnal cinematography. Many of the film's interiors are shot using blue and amber gels and with a great deal of side-lighting, in some ways similar to Jack Asher's lighting scheme for Fisher's 1958 *Dracula*, while the countryside exteriors in the late autumn/early winter often look as though they were lit with a tallow candle. Hammer's Dracula franchise was burning down to its last, sputtering flame.

And beyond the visuals, subtext looms larger in *Satanic Rites* than in any other film in the series. The count is now a reclusive billionaire, a concept borrowed by Houghton from 1971's Bond film *Diamonds are Forever*, in which Spectre supremo Ernst Stavro Blofeld (Charles Gray) impersonates reclusive industrialist Willard Whyte, another Howard Hughes clone. In developing their theme, Houghton and Gibson turned Hammer's traditional conservatism in on itself: Dracula's acolytes are no longer bored Victorians but jaded captains of British industry in search of salacious thrills in a world already full to bursting with sensory pleasures for the rich and decadent. In this male-dominated world of politicians and financiers who fund human sacrifice on a whim for their own depraved ends or engage in corrupt conspiracies to bring about the downfall of civilisation for their own gain, women are kept in chains and in basements, literally and figuratively—mere vessels for the amusement of those in power above them. In the end, the high-flyers are suitably horrified when they are faced with the consequences of their greed and venality, but by then it is too late. It is remarkable how prescient this scenario has turned out to be with the passing of time!

If nothing else, the metaphor had been given new and vibrant life in *The Satanic Rites of Dracula*. The Hammer vampire was feeding on its own progeny—as it would

The Satanic Rites of Dracula (Christopher Lee)

have had to do if the count's apocalyptic plot had come to fruition. No longer did it represent sexual freedom, libertarian excess or youthful rebellion; now, it was simply big business itself—amoral, acquisitive, beyond the law, and perfectly capable of bringing the roof down on all around it in pursuit of a single mad dream.

Yet when Van Helsing finally despatches Dracula for the last time, it is almost with a sense of regret. This time, there is no battle of wills and worlds; no sadistic dissolution as in *Dracula AD 1972*. Instead, Van Helsing seems somewhat reluctant to drive in the purgative stake, knowing that it means the end for them both. As Dracula lies writhing at his feet, crucified, Christ-like, by the allusive hawthorn bush, Van Helsing looks down on him with a tinge of sadness in his eyes, aware, in the final analysis, that the two of them are inseparable; that neither one can exist without the other.

Or as Lee himself put it to Tom Johnson and Mark Miller in *The Christopher Lee Filmography*, 'I moved on and didn't look back. I'll always be grateful for Dracula and what he did for my career, but everything comes to an end.'

> For when they were yet a few yards from the mound the flickering light of the lantern fell upon Angelo's white face, unconscious as if in sleep, and on his upturned throat, over which a very thin red line of blood trickled down into his collar; and the flickering light of the lantern played upon another face that looked up from the feast—upon two deep, dead eyes that saw in spite of death—upon parted lips redder than life itself—upon two gleaming teeth on which glistened a rosy drop.
>
> **—F Marion Crawford, 'For the Blood is the Life'/**
> ***Wandering Ghosts* (1911)**

Chapter 6:

Variations on the Theme

It was dark in the crypt, and musty. The Count moved about restlessly. His knee grazed the edge of the empty coffin set on a trestle in the tomb. He shuddered involuntarily, loosening his cape at the throat. It would be good to remove it, good to be out of here, good to shed the role of the vampire forever. He'd played it well, but now he was anxious to be gone.

—Robert Bloch, 'The Living Dead' (1967)

Captain Kronos—Vampire Hunter (Horst Janson, John Cater)

Joseph Sheridan Le Fanu's character 'Carmilla' may be the most famous female vampire in fiction and film, but she had a real-life counterpart who resided in Hungary in the 17th century. Countess Elizabeth Báthory was perhaps the most prolific female serial killer in history, reputed to have tortured and murdered over 600 victims, mostly young girls. The fact that she was also said to have bathed in the *blood* of her victims in order to preserve her youth accorded her the title of 'Blood Countess', or 'The Tigress of Csejte' (her castle home). Báthory was never tried for her crimes but, in 1611, her accomplices were and all were executed as a result; witness testimony told of horrors that included the biting of flesh, crude surgery, starvation and sexual abuse. Being of noble blood, Báthory was walled up in a suite of apartments within the castle in order to avoid further scandal. She was found dead in 1614, aged 54.

The sheer scale of the atrocities that purportedly were committed by Elizabeth Báthory and her cohorts has ensured her a place in the hall of infamy alongside 15th century French child-murderer Gilles de Rais and Wallachian *voivode* Vlad III (the 'Impaler'), the partial model for Stoker's Dracula. Surprisingly, no one had thought to use her story as the basis for a horror film. In 1970, while trawling every available avenue left to it in an increasingly desperate attempt to keep the company (and the genre) afloat, Hammer decided to do exactly that.

Countess Dracula, as the project was called, was brought to James Carreras by Hungarian émigré and independent producer Alexander Paal, whose affiliation with Hammer went all the way back to 1952 and the days of its parent company Exclusive, when he made *Mantrap* and *The Four Sided Triangle*. Paal had put together an outline treatment along with fellow Hungarian Peter Sasdy,

who had just directed *Taste the Blood of Dracula*. It had sprung from an idea by another Hungarian, London *Times* journalist Gabriel Ronay, a self-styled authority on the legend of the 'Blood Countess' and other historical 'vampires', who would himself write a book on the subject in 1972, entitled *The Dracula Myth*.

At the time, Carreras was finalising his new deal with Rank, and *Countess Dracula* was appended to the roster as the first of what was to end up as four films for the distributor. Television scriptwriter Jeremy Paul was commissioned to pen the screenplay, but Paul's instructions were to play down the horror and make more of the historical drama. Paal and Sasdy each had their own ideas about how to the character should be depicted; Sasdy, who did not see himself as a 'horror director', sought to reduce the sadistic elements of the tale in favour of a prestige period-piece—despite the film's somewhat misleading title. Paal, on the other hand, wanted an out-and-out Hammer horror film. The two would clash frequently during the production.

Paul's final draft was submitted on June 1, and it opened with the statement: 'The film is based on a true story.' To enliven the proceedings, he had come up with the idea of a countess *literally* rejuvenated by 'bathing' in blood so that she can pretend to her young lover that she is her own daughter—but she has to make herself scarce when the effect begins to wear off, like Cinderella when the clock strikes twelve. Despite this somewhat inane Jekyll-and-Hyde addendum to an already-cluttered legend, the rest of the script was a relatively routine account of court intrigue and tragic romance among the Hungarian nobility, circa 1611. The violence was muted, and sex and nudity were brought more to the fore. Sasdy was hired to direct and, given the title (the relevance of which is non-existent and substantiated in the film only when a peasant incongruously coins the term in respect of the imprisoned countess in its final frames), the obvious choice to star was now Ingrid Pitt, fresh from her success in *The Vampire Lovers*. But *Countess Dracula* was destined to be the first—and only—Hammer vampire film not to feature an actual vampire!

Countess Dracula went into production on July 27 at Pinewood Studios, reusing sets that had been built for Charles Jarrott's *Anne of the Thousand Days* (1969). Art director Philip Harrison redressed the various interiors, giving the film an opulent look that belied its low budget. Hammer's schedule at this time was so crowded that while *Countess Dracula* was being shot at Pinewood, *Lust for a Vampire* was still on the floor at Elstree and *Creatures the World Forgot*, the latest of its 'prehistoric' adventures in the wake of *One Million Years BC* and *When Dinosaurs Ruled the Earth* (1966 and 1969 respectively) was in pre-production in Namibia. At least a dozen more films were in the pipeline, a good many of them in the horror genre. Cracks were beginning to show, but Hammer seemed oblivious to the fact that it was now saturating the market.

In front of the camera, Sandor Elès also returned to Hammer, having played the assistant to Baron Frankenstein in Freddie Francis's *The Evil of Frankenstein*; Elès was also Hungarian and had fled to the UK during the revolution of 1956. He was to play Báthory's lover, Imré Toth. Nigel Green, an imposing baritone-voiced stalwart of British films, well-known for his roles in *Jason and the Argonauts* (1963), Sidney J Furie's *The Ipcress File* (1965) and the Jimmy Sangster-scripted *Deadlier Than the Male* (1967), was cast as Dobi, captain of the palace guard, and Maurice Denham, a veteran of both television and film, including Jacques Tourneur's classic *Night of the Demon* (1957) as well as Hammer psycho-thriller *Paranoiac* (1963), was hired as Master Fabio. Nike Arrighi, the wide-eyed ingénue of Hammer's Dennis Wheatley black magic opus *The Devil Rides Out (1967),* was cast in a small role as an ill-fated

Countess Dracula (Ingrid Pitt)

gypsy girl, while Lesley-Anne Down featured more prominently as the countess's put-upon daughter.

Pitt approached the role of the 'Blood Countess' with commendable seriousness, although she was sometimes non-plussed when Sasdy and Paal shouted at each other in Hungarian. After researching the story herself, she was also surprised at how much the horror was being diluted, complaining to Sasdy about a scene in which she was to be seen bathing in blood; Pitt thought it so anaemic as scripted as to be 'ridiculous'. 'It was a wasted opportunity,' she told Wayne Kinsey in *Hammer Films: the Elstree Studios Years*. 'Elizabeth Báthory was one of the greatest female serial killers of all time. She used to hang her victims up, slit their bellies and sit underneath to shower in their blood. That's what we should have done!'

When production wrapped on September 4, there was a bigger surprise in store for Pitt: her lines were dubbed by another actress, and she only found out when the voice artist concerned sent a 'thank you' note and some flowers. 'I thought it was a case of extreme treason,' she told me when I interviewed her for *Femmes Fatales* magazine. 'I was livid,' she reasserted to Kinsey.

According to Pitt, Sasdy disliked her Polish accent and thought that the countess should speak the Queen's English, despite the fact that she was Hungarian. Pitt claimed that she had gone to some trouble to sound suitably old in the film as her character ages, like Professor Bonner in Hammer's *The Man Who Could Cheat Death* (1959), when she cannot get her 'fix' of blood. 'I had studied my mother's voice and after every take I would rush over to the sound man to listen to it,' she explained to Kinsey. 'It took away my performance and now Sandor Elès is the only one left with an accent.'

Composer Harry Robinson had complaints of his own, as he outlined to Dick Klemensen in *Little Shoppe of Horrors*: 'The shortest scoring time I had for any Hammer movie was 12 days. This was for *Countess Dracula*. The reason was that I

Countess Dracula (Ingrid Pitt)

Countess Dracula (Peter Jeffrey, Sandor Elès, Ingrid Pitt, Nigel Green)

was also doing *Lust for a Vampire* as well as a pile of recording work for a recording company.. The two Hungarians kept hammering on at me that they wanted me to do a historically-correct score. And I followed their instructions by steeping myself in ethnic Hungarian music and using certain instruments—like the cimbalom. In fact they gave me etchings relating to Countess Báthory to "inspire" me.'

Countess Dracula opened at the New Victoria cinema on February 14, 1971, to disappointing takings and an even more disappointed Rank management. In the US, it had to wait to be paired with Hammer's next, *Vampire Circus*. Even the censor had been mildly taken aback by the lack of horror content in the film. Having been long used to inflicting cuts on Hammer's films, BBFC Secretary John Trevelyan had noted with some surprise on December 18: 'Having already seen this film I had expected there would be an "X" without cuts since there was hardly any horror in it.. Indeed I heard that Hammer were disappointed that there wasn't more horror!'

Countess Dracula is unique in the annals of the 'Hammer vampire' for being the only film that is 'vampire' in name only, and that merely by indirect association. Paal wanted to follow it up with another of the same based loosely on the life of Vlad Tepes, the 'real' Dracula, but Christopher Lee had already featured in a documentary on that very subject and the poor returns from *Countess Dracula* inspired little further confidence from Hammer's board. With its pseudo-historical backdrop, its Grimm's plot of a wicked 'queen', conniving courtiers and a young heir in peril, it is a curiosity at best. The link with vampirism is tenuous and wholly commercial, though the countess herself is possibly Hammer's most decadent aristocrat, literally washing her cares (and her wrinkles) away in the blood of the peasants. This is nicely illustrated in an opening scene, echoing that in Corman's *Masque of the Red Death* (1964), in which Báthory's coach runs over a woodsman, whose wife then denounces her as a 'devil woman'; it is she who dubs Báthory 'Countess Dracula' as the end credits roll.

The countess's great sin, at least in Sasdy's film, is not so much that she engages in the torture and slaughter of young girls but that she falls in love with a man half

her age. In this, the moral proprieties of Hammer's horrors come once more to the fore and reveal the same stubbornly conservative streak that would feature even more strongly in the prurient 'slasher' thrillers of the late 1970s, such as *Halloween* and *Friday the 13th*: never mind that the countess cuts up innocent virgins for a hobby—what grates is the fact that she takes a toy-boy for a lover. The naïve storyline and juvenile plotting are ever at odds with the ponderous reconstruction of Hungarian court-life, as though two different films (or rather two different approaches to the same film!) had suddenly found themselves joined at the hip.

Pitt struggles valiantly with a role that could have been the centrepiece of a historical horror made by another company, but the mix of authentic period touches, lush score, elegant cinematography and dull but exquisite art direction (by Philip Harrison) with the jarring insertions of gratuitous nudity and moments of graphic gore make for a curate's egg of a film. In the process, Pitt's performance is all-but overshadowed by that of Nigel Green. Green often liked to chew the scenery and as the countess's would-be suitor, he virtually gobbles it up and spits it back out again. Against his upstaging histrionics, the empathetic roles of Elès and Down pale into the pastel of the backgrounds.

When it was screened for Rank's theatre managers, their response was one of bewilderment: not only was *Countess Dracula* not a vampire film, it was barely even a Hammer film either.

Hammer's brief flirtation with Hungary's 'Blood Countess' and more prolonged fixation with lesbian vampires did, however, inspire others to follow suit. 'Straight' lesbian takes on the myth had begun to emerge in the wake of *The Vampire Lovers*, but Belgian writer-director Harry Kümel went one further and also employed the character of Countess Báthory as an immortal vampire in his *Les lèvres rouges* (UK: *Daughters of Darkness*, 1971), an art-house piece memorable for its austere landscapes of Ostend in the closed season. American actor John Karlen, fresh from Dan Curtis's *House of Dark Shadows*, was cast opposite French film diva Delphine Seyrig—wife of noted director Alain Resnais—as the countess. *Les lèvres rouge* had none of the gloss (and little of the gore) of Hammer's film, but it quickly attained a cult status that it retains to this day.

The vampire as child-molester. If that sounds like a distasteful idea, it was only one of the many in Hammer's *Vampire Circus*, its last outing for Rank and second-to-last Gothic vampire film.

The concept was enticing: a travelling circus populated entirely by vampires who lure their victims to their deaths by using the trickery of the fairground to lull them into a false sense of security. It was a theme which had served author Ray Bradbury well with his 'Dark Carnival' in *Something Wicked This Way Comes*, a novel that Christopher Lee admired so much that he had expressed a desire to play Mr Dark were it to be adapted for the screen (in the event, the role went to Jonathan Pryce in Jack Clayton's film of 1983). Hammer's film had begun life as *Village of the Vampires* when it was submitted to Sir James Carreras in May 1971. But Carreras had reservations: 'Very, very bloody,' he said in a memo to Michael. 'I suppose OK for the rest of the world, but I dread to think what will happen in the USA..'

Carreras had good reason to fear; in recent times, he had seen significant cuts requested in such Hammer horrors as *Taste the Blood of Dracula, The Vampire Lovers, When Dinosaurs Ruled the Earth* and others in the American market, so US distributors would have no problem with the new ratings system. Gone were the

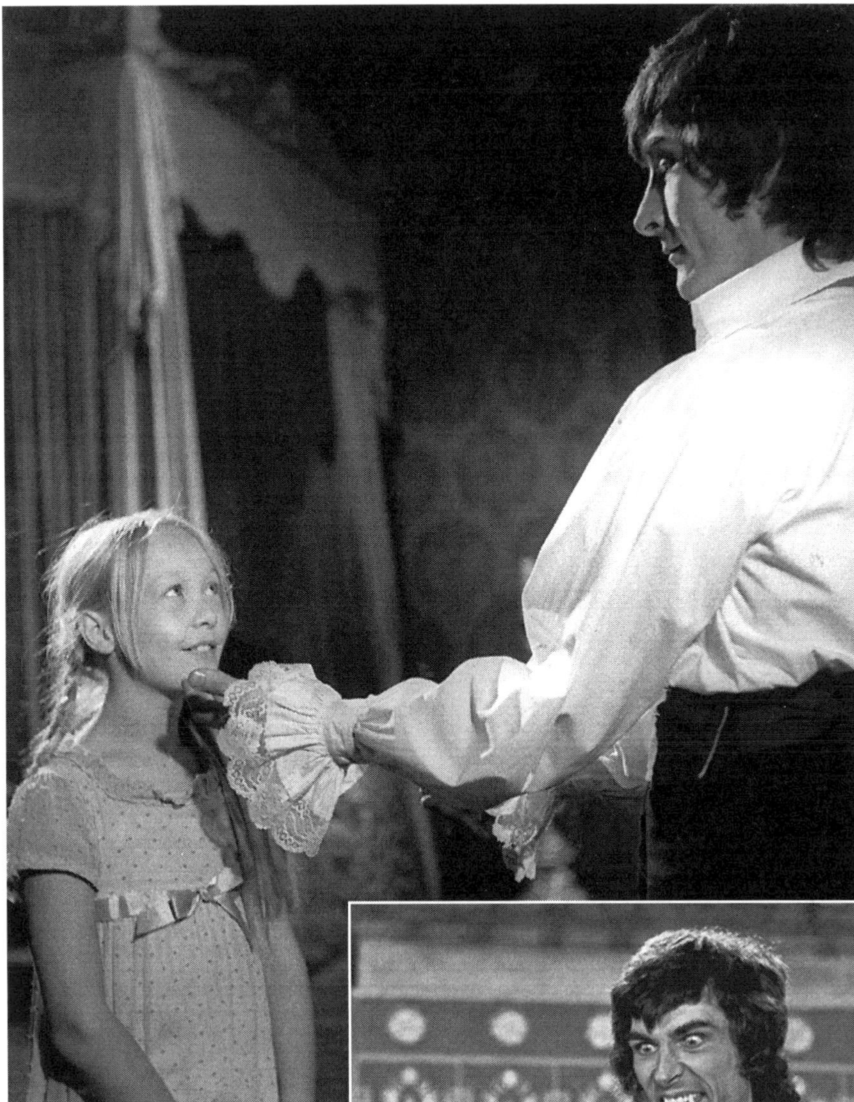

Vampire Circus (Jane Darby, Robert Tayman)

days when American audiences were privy to more gore than their British counterparts; now, due to the more liberal British X certificate, the situation was reversed. In the US, horror films had still to be somewhat 'family friendly'. *The Vampire Lovers* may have been rated 'R' in the States, but it had lost some of its nudity and graphic content to achieve even that.

The new treatment which had given Carreras pause for thought had been concocted by independent producer Wilbur Stark and screenwriter George Baxt.

Vampire Circus (Serena)

Baxt had a bit of a thing about circuses—he had written *Circus of Horrors* for Anglo-Amalgamated, a sex-and-sadism classic that had helped bring an end to the Golden Age of British horror in 1960, along with AIP's *Horrors of the Black Museum* and Michael Powell's *Peeping Tom*. But he was well known to Hammer for having 'Americanised' some of its films under the aegis of Tony Hinds, such as *The Revenge of Frankenstein*, where he adopted the pseudonym of 'Hurford Janes'; he had also written the 1960 suspense-thriller *The Shadow of the Cat*, which was produced on Hammer stages under the direction of John Gilling.

Michael Carreras was more receptive to the Baxt treatment than his father had been. This was still at a time when the company was inundated with outside producers wanting a piece of the action and Michael commissioned a full screenplay from American screenwriter/producer Judson Kinberg (whose credits included William Wyler's *The Collector*; 1965). The script was then sent to AIP 'reader' Nadja Regin, a former Bond girl who had played in both *From Russia with Love* (1963) and *Goldfinger* (1964). Regin registered her concerns in a memo dated July 25, 1971, in which she pointed out the script's 'almost pathological obsession with children victims'. Sir James Carreras took note, observing that, 'If shot as scripted, 50% will end up on the cutting room floor.'

The problem was partly of Hammer's own making: after the departure of Hinds, no one had thought to install an executive producer who would be able to cast a practised eye over its shows before they began; Michael no longer had the time, and those whom he did delegate to supervisory positions lacked the experience. As a result, filmmaking at Hammer was largely a free-for-all. 'There were no restrictions,' Kinberg said in *Little Shoppe of Horrors*. 'Anything you could think up worked because you were in a kind of horror-land.' Kinberg was particularly fascinated by

Vampire Circus (Domini Blythe, Robert Tayman, Anthony Corlan)

the surreal elements of the fairground, such as its 'hall of mirrors': 'The minute you start to deal with mirrors, you're really dealing with a sort of Pirandello kind of world where you don't know what is reality and what is fantasy, or in this case, what is reality and what is horror.'

In Kinberg's scripted delirium, the village of Schtettel finds itself cut off from the outside world—and, by implication, from reality itself—by a virulent plague that seems to be the result of a curse placed on the heads of its elders for having destroyed the vampire Count Mitterhouse in the course of trying to rescue a child from his clutches. Their enforced isolation is partially relieved by the arrival of a strange circus—the 'Circus of Nights'. But all is not as it seems; the circus troupe is comprised of shape-shifting vampires intent on wreaking revenge on the village and resurrecting the count in the process.

With the dangers inherent in its various 'acts' and its culture of disguise, the circus has always lent itself to dark imaginings, from Tod Browning's *Freaks* (1932) to Baxt's own *Circus of Horrors* and the 1967 Joan Crawford vehicle *Berserk*. But *Vampire Circus*, with its intermingling of many perverse and disturbing themes, is one of the most jaundiced and subversive takes on the essential innocence of the carnival ethos. The moral universe of the film is a strangely inverted one: the villagers are not trapped in their predicament over some perceived sin that was committed in the distant past—to the contrary, they had rid the surrounding countryside of a predatory paedophile vampire. And yet, they find themselves 'cursed' and isolated as a result, haunted by horror, and ultimately picked off one-by-one for having had the temerity to confront the evil in their midst; for most of the film, it is the vampires who hold sway—taunting, torturing and eventually killing every inhabitant of Schtettel who has dared to challenge their dominance of the land. In *Vampire Circus*, good has long-since given up the fight, and the viewer was being invited to watch as the last remnants of moral rectitude were chipped away to leave a desolate landscape, piled high with shattered dreams and the bloody corpses of dead children.

Despite his father's increasing concerns, Michael Carreras opted to move ahead with *Vampire Circus*. He felt that the story and screenplay at least showed a fresh approach and he decided to hire another new director to make the film. He had seen 38-year-old ex-theatre director Robert Young's short fantasy film *The Goldfish Bowl* and had initially asked him to helm a feature adapted from ITN newsreader Gordon Honeycombe's novel, *Neither the Sea nor the Sand*. But Hammer ultimately lost the project to Tigon, who produced it (badly) in 1972; Young's consolation prize was the offer to direct *Vampire Circus*.

Vampire Circus went onto the floor at Pinewood on August 9. With a run-up to production of only six weeks, there had been no time to build lavish sets, so many of the sets constructed for Hammer's previous Rank films were re-dressed, notably the village square which had seen service in both *Countess Dracula* and *Twins of Evil*. In a cast devoid of star-names, only Thorley Walters and Adrienne Corri lent familiar faces: Walters from numerous Hammers and many a Rank comedy of the fifties and sixties, and Corri from *The Tell-Tale Heart* (1960), *A Study in Terror* (1965) and more. One-time BBC glamour-boy Laurence Payne (who coincidentally had been Corri's co-star in *The Tell-Tale Heart*) was shoehorned into his role as the father of the murdered child when original choice Anton Rodgers was taken ill. But the casting director missed the film's best commercial opportunity when former *Godspell* cast-member and wannabe rock star David Essex lost out to *Taste the Blood of Dracula*'s Anthony Corlan for the part of a vampire who transforms himself into a black panther.

Nominal lead John Moulder-Brown had appeared with German actress Lilli

Vampire Circus (Serena/Lalla Ward)

Palmer in a Spanish horror film called *La residencia* (UK: *The Boarding School*); playing opposite him was Lynne Frederick, later to become the fifth and final wife of comedian Peter Sellers. Others in the cast included Skip Martin (from *Masque of the Red Death*), David Prowse, who would go on to become Darth Vader (physically, at least) in the first three *Star Wars* films, and Lalla Ward, who would also achieve more lasting fame as an assistant to Dr Who. Even the film's vampire was a relative unknown: television bit-part player Robert Tayman was cast for his supposedly saturnine looks, but his cockney accent was considered at odds with that of a *mittel*-European count; like Mike Raven before him, Tayman would find himself dubbed (by David de Keyser) when the film eventually went into release.

What the film lacked in star-quality, it made up for in quantity: *Vampire Circus* had an unusually large cast by Hammer standards. However, most of Young's problems were with the non-human actors. 'If you're working with a panther, it's quite difficult because they're quite treacherous,' he explained. 'The woman working with it, Mary Chipperfield, had already lost a finger to a lion some time before! When she worked with the panther she was very calm.. so whenever you see the panther out of the cage, it's Mary in the costume with it.' And he had definite ideas about how he wanted to handle the typical elements of Hammer Horror. 'I wanted to have a *real* bat in the film,' he told *Little Shoppe of Horrors*. 'I wanted to get it as close to reality, as opposed to cardboard cut-outs, however well they might be done.' Which was all very well, but as soon as the studio lights were turned on, the bats had a tendency to fly up into the rafters of the sound stages, well away from the 'offending' lights!

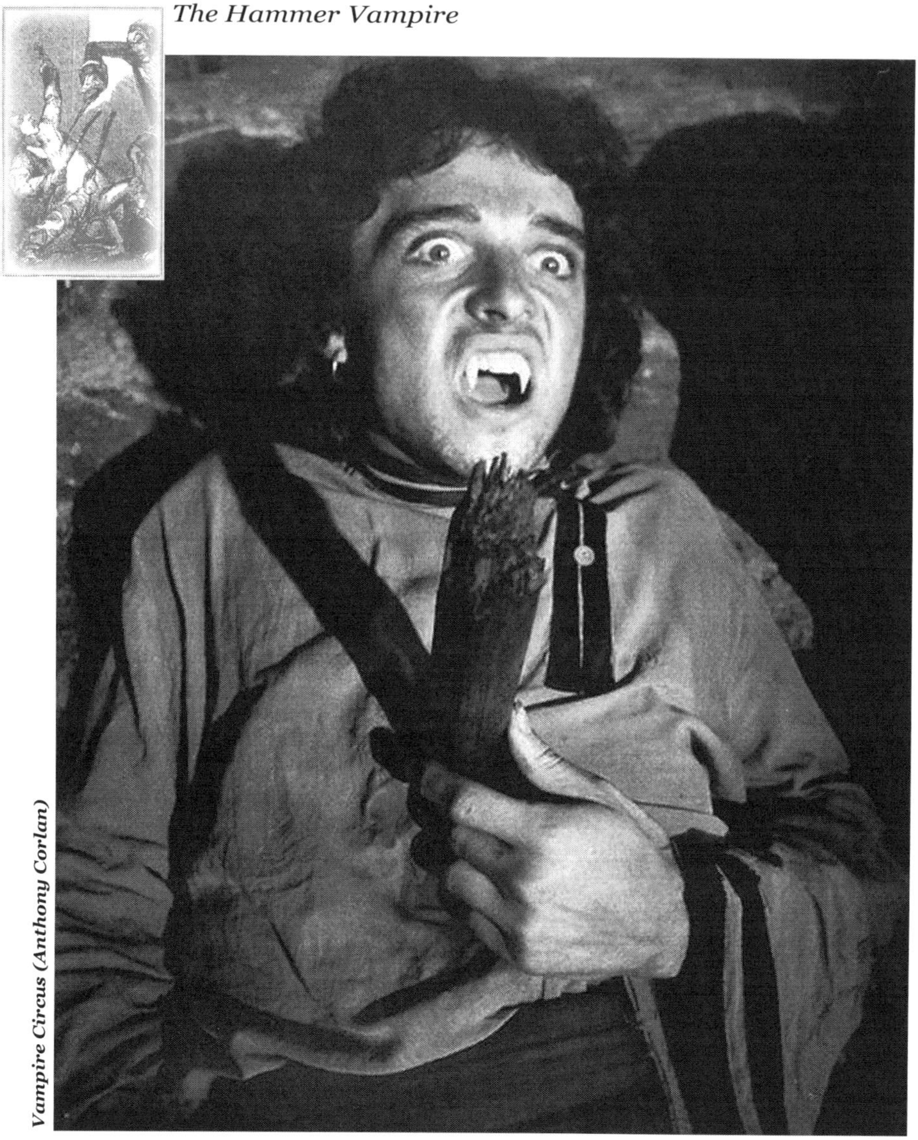

***Vampire Circus* (Anthony Corlan)**

Vampire Circus turned into a baptism of fire for Robert Young. By all accounts, Wilbur Stark was not an easy producer to work for and, in later years, he has tried to take credit for the directing of some of the animal sequences, which Young has always denied. The novice director was also under pressure from Hammer's head office, as he told Sue and Colin Cowie: 'I got a telegram from Michael Carreras which said, "Vampires are silent" and I asked him quite a considerable amount of time later what on earth he meant. He said he really didn't know! Well, that's the sort of pressure which is implied if you're working on something and although you enjoy the people you're working with, you don't have a close relationship with them that allows you to ring up and say, "What the hell do you mean about that?" You have to try and work out from these people above the messages that you're getting. It can be a bit nerve-wracking!'

Young's inexperience showed up further when *Vampire Circus* became one of

Vampire Circus (Adrienne Corri, Anthony Corlan)

the few Hammer horrors to run behind schedule. Despite a large and unwieldy cast of actors *and* animals, he had been allotted the usual six-week schedule and he was forced to drop several scenes that were in the script. 'I reckon I could have done with just half a day more and I couldn't have it,' he complained.

Michael Carreras shut down production on September 21, just two days into what would have been the film's seventh week. Assistant director Derek Whitehurst explained to Wayne Kinsey, 'It was a very difficult picture to do. The animal stuff was extraordinarily difficult, and all the circus stuff, and Robert hadn't really planned anything at all and got carried away with the whole thing. It's a shame, because I think directors should have a chance to exploit their imagination, but unfortunately on Hammer pictures, there has to be a limit.' 'They just pulled the shutters down—no question about it,' Young said. 'There wasn't even an area to negotiate.'

Vampire Circus was released in Britain on April 30, 1972—appropriately enough, May Day Eve, or Beltane to the Celts; *Walpurgisnacht* to the Germans—a time of demons and witches. When the film later made it to the US, it was in somewhat reduced form. Picked up by Fox as a co-feature for *Countess Dracula*, both of these latter-day Hammers were trimmed of their nudity and violence in order to obtain PG ratings! (While *Countess Dracula* is available on DVD in the States in its original X-certificate length, an uncut print of *Vampire Circus* has not been seen in America to this day.)

Notwithstanding its dubious subject-matter and the reservations of its makers, *Vampire Circus* turned out to be one of the best-received Hammer horror films of the 1970s in the US, even in truncated form. *Cinefantastique*'s David Bartholomew gave it a rave review: 'Divertingly entertaining, stylistically fresh if not wholly original, and imaginatively produced.. It is exactly this rapid-fire force, a never lagging, cleverly balanced series of surprises in every aspect of the production, from screenplay to photography to special effects, that makes *Vampire Circus* as consistently good as it is,' he continued, going on to compare it to Ingmar Bergman classics such as *The Seventh Seal* and *The Magician* in its use of surrealism: '*Vampire Circus* is that

rarity of genre films, even for Hammer; it has a firm conception of what it is, where it is going, and how to get there. And it arrives, with us in tow, in fine spirited condition,' he concluded. However, it is difficult to gauge how much merit can be accorded to a review that was based on a *different* version of the film than that which its director intended. *Vampire Circus* was commercially unsuccessful in the UK and was reissued by Rank in 1974 as the supporting feature to Tyburn's *Legend of the Werewolf*, but to no better effect.

Bartholomew's praise for the 'rapid-fire force' of *Vampire Circus* can be justified by the film's prologue alone—a 12-minute pre-credits sequence which is almost a feature in itself. Anna Mueller (Domini Blythe) leads a young girl to the castle of her lover, the vampire Count Mitterhouse; as the count feeds from the throat of the child, Anna watches in voyeuristic ecstasy. 'One lust feeds another,' the count notions, and he and Anna then make love in one of Hammer's most perversely-sensual sex scenes. But the villagers are alert to the probable source of their missing children and they attack the castle, killing Mitterhouse—though not before he has issued his deadly curse. The naked Anna is forced to run a 'gauntlet' of belts and whips, but she escapes from the mob and returns to her dying lover in time to hear his last request, as the castle burns down around them..

The intermingling of vampirism and plague goes back to Murnau's *Nosferatu*, in which the count was followed by a horde of pestilential rats. A similar sense of *ennui* is to be found in *Vampire Circus*: Schtettel is quarantined from the outside world, at least until the 'Circus of Nights' arrives. But these vampires do not bring the plague; they are rat-*exterminators*, and all the 'rats' are to be found within the village, their only sin having been to try to protect their offspring from harm and do what Van Helsing or Father Sandor or Monsignor Muller would have been praised to the heavens for doing in previous Hammer horrors. This theme of role-reversal

Publicity shot for Captain Kronos—Vampire Hunter

continues throughout the film: the villagers are *de facto* innocent parties in the story; the kind of 'purge' that they enact in the prologue had served as a climax to the likes of *Lust for a Vampire* and *Twins of Evil*—yet in *Vampire Circus*, they are portrayed as conniving, guilt-ridden and generally deserving of the various fates that the vengeful vampires see fit to bestow upon them. The casting of the film aids this perceptive paradox: the vampire troupe are mostly 'beautiful people'—young and talented and sexy—whereas the villagers are invariably middle-aged, unattractive and riddled with fears and prejudices. Young's film had turned Hammer's traditional empathies on their head, as though it were made for an *audience* of vampires. And in a way it was. If the metaphor was to be believed, we were all 'vampires' now, and Hammer was playing the last blood-soaked card in its pack, ladling on the gore as though there were no tomorrow. Soon, there would be no tomorrow for Hammer, or for anyone else who tried to peddle a vampire film of the old school in the financial climate of the UK in the mid-seventies.

In many ways, *Vampire Circus* anticipates the premise of Wes Craven's *A Nightmare on Elm Street* (1984), in which a group of parents band together to kill a child-molester who then returns to haunt the children in their dreams. The vampire as paedophile would be a scabrous notion in any film, let alone an exploitation one from a company like Hammer, and it harks back thematically to Fritz Lang's *M* (1930)—although its provenance can actually be traced to the 'bloofer lady' in Stoker's *Dracula*. A scene in which vampire siblings lure two boys to the circus's 'Mirror of Life' is particularly uncomfortable to watch, as the vampires caress the faces of the youngsters before victimising them. Small wonder Nadja Regin felt that parts of Kinberg's script were 'strongly reminiscent of the Moors murders'.

Where *Countess Dracula* had a bath of blood, *Vampire Circus* has a bloodbath; by the end of the film, there are more bodies piled up than at the climax of *Hamlet*. In the time-honoured tradition, the vampires are still ultimately defeated by the power of good, but it is only a temporary respite; a lone bat flies away from the scene of carnage behind the closing credits. True to the period in which it was made, Hammer's penultimate Gothic vampire yarn offered audiences of the seventies as bleak and nihilistic a view of the battle against 'evil' as its makers then had of the state of their own ailing business.

'There are as many species of vampire as there are beasts of prey,' Professor Grost announces in Brian Clemens's *Captain Kronos—Vampire Hunter* (1972), so as to clear the way for his creator to rewrite the rules of the genre, as others were already doing.

After scripting the previous year's *Dr Jekyll and Sister Hyde*, Clemens had pitched a second idea to Hammer, which new Managing Director Michael Carreras had sanctioned for production only because it held the promise of a spin-off series for television, which had been Clemens's home turf as a writer and how he had sold the project to the increasingly-desperate company to begin with. In a *Little Shoppe of Horrors* interview with Al Taylor, Clemens explained how *Kronos* came about: 'To get [the Hammer] style I watched dozens of their movies. It struck me that the vampire movies were all the same—same buildup, same premise, same stake in the heart. I proposed bending the established conventions and establishing my own—also making the lead the hero—till then, the lead in any vampire film was inevitably the villain, the vampire. Hammer bought the idea, but I held back unless I could direct. They agreed.'

As with almost every Hammer production over the previous years, *Kronos* was produced independently, in this case by Clemens and partner Albert Fennell, who

Captain Kronos—Vampire Hunter (Horst Janson)

had worked with him on TV's *The Avengers*. *Kronos* was intended to be the first in a series, 'A bit like a Marvel Comics hero, really,' Clemens noted, and the character was originally intended to be a time traveller—thus the name 'Kronos'—somewhat like Dr Who, who would face many kinds of vampires at different times and in different places. 'I originally wanted Captain Kronos to travel in a kind of golden coach.. and sleep in a golden coffin!' he said. 'But the budget would not run to it—and my maxim is.. if you can't do it right.. then don't do it at all, and find an alternative.'

Clemens wrote the screenplay in a brisk three weeks, and casting began when Michael Carreras accepted the final draft. The director called upon veterans of *The Avengers* to aid him in his task: John Cater as Professor Grost, Kronos's assistant; John Carson in the pivotal role of Dr Marcus; Ian Hendry, the original Dr Keel of *The Avengers*, as a mercenary named Kerro. Hendry had a drink problem and had trouble finding work, and Clemens wrote the part especially for him. Caroline Munro was now under contract to Hammer, having appeared in *Dracula AD 1972*, and she was nominated for the part of the gypsy girl who accompanies Kronos on his quest. 'Hammer insisted I use Caroline,' Clemens recalled in *Fangoria* magazine. 'Everyone said Caroline couldn't act. Well, she could not act the gypsy girl, that's for sure. But I had her read the part quite naturally, in her own soft-spoken voice.. It worked, and so I reconceived her character to fit Caroline, and I think that worked too.'

Clemens was forced to look a little further afield for a suitable actor to play the title-role, however. Pre-publicity described the character of Kronos as 'a hero—a

Captain Kronos—Vampire Hunter (inset: Ian Hendry)

swashbuckling, handsome figure of a man —who sets out to destroy evil wherever and whenever it is to be found'. Clemens eventually settled on German actor Horst Janson, who was currently in England having appeared in the ITV drama series *Upstairs, Downstairs*. Janson had also recently featured in several mainstream British films, including *The McKenzie Break* and *Murphy's War* (both 1970). 'Horst Janson was okay, and probably the best actor I have ever worked with from the point of view of never, *never* bitching,' Clemens said. 'When he said he could fight with the rapier sword, he could. He said he could ride a horse; he could. Many actors admit to doing everything just to get the part—and then, come the day of shooting, you find you have to use a stunt stand-in. Horst did all the work—brilliantly—and never once complained, and some of those locales were tough and cold.'

Other faces were more familiar: 25-year-old Shane Briant, who had made his debut for Hammer in the previous year's *Demons of the Mind* and was also under contract, was added to the cast, as was Lois Daine, who had appeared for Hammer in *Hell is a City* (1960) and *Cash on Demand* (1961), and Wanda Ventham—who had recently played the role of *The Blood Beast Terror* for rivals Tigon.

Before filming began, Clemens wanted to ensure that he was well prepared for his first feature in the director's chair. 'I drew 1300 little drawings before I rolled any film,' he recalled. 'It's the Hitchcock technique. I felt I should steal from the

best. I was with a new crew, a bit wet behind the ears, and I didn't want them to see me hesitating.'

Kronos—which had its title changed to *Captain Kronos—Vampire Hunter* only after the shooting was complete—went before the cameras at Elstree's MGM-EMI Studios on April 10, 1972. The schedule was a slightly more relaxed eight weeks, with five in the studio and three on location. The extra location shooting was dictated by Clemens's desire to make the film 'in the idiom of a western'. Even so, the scope of his vision had to remain somewhat confined: the opening scene of *Kronos*, in which the vampire hunter and his hunch-backed servant Grost gallop across the countryside behind the credits, was shot in Clemens's own 'back yard' of Ampthill Park, Bedfordshire, where the writer had lived for many years; the house that can be glimpsed in the background is his! Other exteriors were filmed in the Hammer 'backlot' of Black Park, behind Pinewood Studios.

In the course of what Clemens described as an 'energetic' shoot, the only concerns that arose had to do with Hendry and Munro. Caroline Munro was averse to doing nude shots, so Clemens hired a body double to perform naked in her stead and to try to convince her otherwise. 'I still did it the way I wanted, rather than how they originally wanted it done, which was to have it all off and show everything,' she recalled for *Fangoria*. 'I did what I felt was right, which was suggestive enough and certainly as far as I would go. I wasn't really nude, because I was wearing thick flesh-coloured bikini pants and Judd [Munro's husband] had stuck my long hair to my chest. They also used "Charley bars", which are great big lighting devices that block off certain sections you don't want shown. So although I had my back, tummy and front bit bare, I felt relaxed. However, it was quite painful getting the glue off afterwards.'

Ian Hendry's scenes in the film were slightly more problematic for Clemens. 'He promised me he wouldn't drink,' Clemens said. 'I went into make-up at 7:15 in the morning and he had a lager can in his hand and I said, "You said you wouldn't drink." And he said, "It's only lager, that's not drinking!" The most challenging scene was the fight in the bar, because I saw it in my mind so clearly, and to get what I wanted, I had to get nearly one hundred set-ups in three days. He was on call for three days. But to give him his due, he hit all his marks. He wasn't drunk on set—it didn't impede him at all. A wonderful talent who ruined his career and eventually lost his life because he couldn't avoid the bottle..'

Professional fight arranger Williams Hobbs did double-duty on *Kronos*; as an actor, he played a vampire named Hagen but he also organised the sword-fights. Hobbs had worked on (and acted in) Polanski's *Macbeth* (1971) and Richard Lester's *The Three Musketeers* (1973) and Clemens knew of his skills in both areas. 'I had never used William Hobbs before.. But because he had been an actor and came in to choreograph the fight, I thought it better that he acted the part. There wasn't a great deal of dialogue—it just saved us doubling him. Horst can fight, so [the climactic sword fight between Kronos and Hagen] is one of the most authentic sword fights you'll see, because there is no doubling.'

Shot on what Clemens referred to as 'the blue set' at Elstree, the sword fight was complicated by the fact that the filming of it was a battle against time. Cast and crew worked on the sequence for three days, and Clemens wanted one more day to ensure himself of the coverage that he felt he needed. But the set was due to be struck to make way for another production; Clemens was given an extra hour, but he has often said over the years that he wished he had been able to get 'those other ten shots'. As things turned out, the set actually went unused for a further six weeks.

Captain Kronos—Vampire Hunter (William Hobbs, Horst Janson)

Captain Kronos—Vampire Hunter (Caroline Munro, Horst Janson)

Kronos wrapped on May 27, on time and on budget, and Clemens hired Laurie Johnson to compose the music; Johnson had scored the theme for *The Avengers*. Again, Hammer opted to re-dub the lead in one of its films: Janson was re-voiced by *Carry On* veteran Julian Holloway, son of musical comedian Stanley Holloway. Clemens has said that he had no problem with Janson's accent, but Hammer thought differently; Michael Carreras was having trouble enough getting Hammer's films distributed in the US and he was acutely aware of the need for the 'transatlantic' accents that had been deemed necessary since the 1950s. Clemens disagreed. 'I think [Janson] was better than the dub.. I lost that one,' he told interviewer Brian Gallagher. Caroline Munro was allowed her own voice, unlike in her later turn in *The Spy Who Loved Me* (1977).

But there was more than Janson's accent to bother Michael about *Kronos*. 'I really don't want to discuss *Kronos*,' he told Dick Klemensen of *Little Shoppe of Horrors*. 'It was so badly mis-handled. The conception was very good but unfortunately it wasn't handled by the Hammer team. The people involved in the making hadn't the Hammer talent but they had the ideas.' And his concerns were proved right, as it turned out. The retitled *Captain Kronos—Vampire Hunter*, to play up the traditional Hammer angle, was passed by the BBFC in September 1972 with a milder

'AA' Certificate (age fourteen and over), the only Hammer horror of the period not to receive an X. The film had been made for Paramount in the US, as was the earlier *Frankenstein and the Monster from Hell*, but it had been put into production with no guarantee of distribution in the UK due to a falling-out between Hammer and EMI when Michael had taken over the company. Consequently, it was allowed to languish on the shelf and was not released in Britain until April 1974, on a double-bill with a Shaw Brothers martial arts production called *The Girl with the Thunderbolt Kick*.

Despite Michael's misgivings, the film received some good pre-release reviews. Marjorie Bilbow, of *Cinema TV Today*, said of it: 'An ingeniously different variation of the many variations on the original, providing scope for some dashing swordplay and quality-raising character acting from John Carson, John Cater and Ian Hendry.' And Richard Combs, in the BFI's *Monthly Film Bulletin*, opined, 'That so much of the character of Brian Clemens' television work should emerge in his debut as feature writer-director is an unexpected pleasure.. If for nothing else, Clemens deserves some credit for sheer cheek.'

Paramount also waited until 1974 to release *Captain Kronos—Vampire Hunter* as support for its previous Hammer film, *Frankenstein and the Monster from Hell*. In *The Hollywood Reporter*, Alan Howard considered it 'a kinky, peculiar, well-made attempt at bringing new life to the vampire genre.' And Vincent Canby of *The New York Times* took the opportunity to admit to a guilty pleasure concerning Hammer's films: 'The new double bill from the Hammer horror film factory in England presents something of a problem. Anyone with a grain of sense shouldn't care less about them, but anyone who has a grain of sense as well as a fondness for horror films, especially the expensive-looking, mostly deadpan Hammer kind, can't afford to miss them.' In *Cinefantastique*, Tim Lucas proclaimed *Captain Kronos* to be one of Hammer's 'all-time greats in the horror genre'.

Viewed from this distance, *Captain Kronos* can be seen as a film that was ahead of its time. It is a 'buff's' movie, in the sense that Quentin Tarantino's films are—a cross-genre piece, containing elements of Kurosawa, John Ford (Clemens nominates Ford as one of his influences) and Gothic horror. It is also a mix that should not work, yet it does. The film is subtle, stylish and witty, and full of splendid touches, not least a scene in which a mysterious, hooded vampire moves through a forest and causes flowers to wilt in its path—and a sequence that I discussed personally with Caroline Munro, in which John Carson rides through the same wood and is attacked by a vampire off-screen, at which point nature itself seems almost to stand still; when he then rides into a clearing, the only evidence of the assault is a single drop of blood on his white glove. Munro called *Captain Kronos* 'romantic horror', which is as apt a description as any for the changes that Clemens tried valiantly to ring on a tired genre.

The fact that much of the film takes place in broad daylight is a clever inversion of the myth of the vampire. The 'creatures of the night' who feature in *Captain Kronos* do not disintegrate into dust in the rays of the sun; to the contrary, they stroll in the dappled light of the forest searching for victims, in the way that Carmilla took the air on an overcast day in *The Vampire Lovers*. This makes for an unsettling mood, as the old rule-book of stakes and crucifixi is torn up in favour of—who knows what can defeat this new breed of Un-dead? Kronos and Grost know, and as the captain rides through the territory like a neo-Gothic 'man with no name', Clemens's direction and Ian Wilson's lush camerawork evoke the feeling of a medieval English western in the idiom of Michael Reeves's *Witchfinder General*.

The sequence in which Kronos and Grost are forced to destroy Dr Marcus (Carson) after he has been turned into a vampire appears to have been inspired by that in Hitchcock's *Torn Curtain* (1966), where Paul Newman and Julie Andrews attempt to kill a German agent with a knife, a frying pan and just about anything else they can lay their hands on, finally pushing him head-first into an oven and turning on the gas. Hitchcock had wanted to illustrate how difficult it could be to kill a man; Clemens wanted to show how difficult it was to kill a certain type of vampire—in the universe of *Captain Kronos*, the type that drains its victims not of blood, but of their very youth. 'What he doesn't know about vampirism wouldn't fill a flea's cod-piece,' Kronos says in reference to Grost, who tries every means in the vampire hunter's handbook to accomplish the deed—including staking and hanging the unfortunate doctor—before he discovers that silver will do the trick. Clemens was having some fun with the well-worn clichés, and the sequence is masterful in its comic timing.

Not surprisingly given its provenance, *Captain Kronos* seems at times like a period episode of *The Avengers*. Eccentric characters abound (including a hunch-back and a pair of androgynous, incestuous twins), the spectre of an eerie old manor-house hovers tantalisingly in the background, and quirky set-pieces are orchestrated to the accompaniment of Laurie Johnson's playful score; the bar-room brawl in which Kronos despatches Kerro and his thugs is a loving *hommage* to all those samurai epics in which the protagonist manages to slice through several opponents without receiving so much as a cut on his finger. In this respect, Clemens's irreverent take on Hammer Horror has much in common with the *Dr Phibes* films of AIP and director Robert Fuest, who also helmed several episodes of *The Avengers* (and whose *Phibes* duo also featured John Cater).

In the same vein, the repartee between the principals is honed from the slicker pace of television: 'I know you've got guts, Kronos. I've seen them,' Marcus observes dryly. In another aside, he turns to Grost and tells him, 'I've been saving a bottle of wine for a rainy day'; the hunch-back gazes up at the clear blue sky, smiles, and retorts, 'It's pouring.'

Brian Clemens had ideas for several sequels to *Captain Kronos—Vampire Hunter*, aside from the TV spin-off that Michael Carreras was himself keen to promote, but Michael's lukewarm attitude to the finished film, EMI's total antipathy, and the fact that it was denied any sort of an audience rained on its parade. Hammer found itself virtually unable to mount another Gothic horror film in Britain. In recent years, there has been talk of reviving the character of Kronos. In an age when popular culture is rife with vampires of all persuasions, we may yet see the return of the doughty captain, who was, after all, always intended to be the Dr Who of vampire-hunting.

The Legend of the 7 Golden Vampires

Time was running out for the Hammer vampire, and for Hammer itself. By 1973, the British film industry had tumbled into its worst-ever slump. American distributors had withdrawn their support and the market for horror, in particular, had been thoroughly saturated. Michael Carreras was running the company at the worst possible time. He had neither the contacts nor the social acumen of his father and if Hammer were to survive, new ideas and new areas of finance had to found. And quickly.

Having taken Hammer back to its roots and produced a series of inexpensive (but commercially successful) comedies based on British television series, Michael picked up on a trend that was sweeping the film world: martial arts films made in Hong Kong. A Chinese-American martial arts instructor and former bit-part actor named Bruce Lee had recently become a superstar in films like *Fists of Fury* (1971) and *The Chinese Connection* (1972) and Warners had just contracted him for his first starring role in an American film, to be titled *Enter the Dragon*. US television had even cashed in on the trend with a series called *Kung Fu*, starring David Carradine. As it happened, Hammer had its own 'chinese connection' in actress Pik-Sen Lim, the wife of screenwriter Don Houghton.

Houghton's father-in-law was a friend of martial arts movie mogul Run Run Shaw, one half of Hong Kong's Shaw Brothers, the owners of the sprawling studio conglomerate whose productions were currently taking the world's cinemas by storm. Michael sent Houghton to the former British colony in February 1973, to meet with the Shaws and pitch an 'East meets West' Dracula film; Houghton was given a grand tour of the studio, and the result of a three-hour meeting with Run Run Shaw himself was a co-production deal between Hammer and the Shaws for a 'kung fu' Dracula which would be shot in Hong Kong. The count, in the green-faced

The Legend of the 7 Golden Vampires (David Chiang, Julie Ege, Peter Cushing)

form of John Forbes Robertson (the Man in Black in *The Vampire Lovers*), was now to pop up, literally, for a final encore that would remove him from his Gothic comfort-zone at Hammer and set him uncomfortably down among the high-kicks and marshal-arts mayhem of *The Legend of the 7 Golden Vampires*.

The deal with the Shaws was for two films: the first to go before the cameras would be Houghton's script for *The Legend of the 7 Golden Vampires*, followed in rapid succession by a second Houghton project, *Shatter*, the latter being a routine cop/kung fu thriller with a Hong Kong setting. A start date of September 3 was pencilled-in on Hammer's not exactly busy schedule.

Pre-production art for *The Legend of the 7 Golden Vampires* made it sound very grandiose indeed. 'In the tradition of *The Seven Samurai* and *The Magnificent Seven*, Hammer now present.. *The Legend of the 7 Golden Vampires*.' But there was a great deal of head-scratching over budgets before the film actually commenced shooting on October 22. Hammer was once again able to cast the ever-willing Peter Cushing in the part of Van Helsing alongside Norwegian sex symbol Julie Ege (who had recently starred for the company in Don Chaffey's *Creatures the World Forgot*). Lee's steadfast refusal to play the count again elevated Forbes Robertson to a role that Mike Raven might have been offered had he not fallen out with Hammer over *Lust for a Vampire*. The Shaw Brothers pitched in with the rest of the cast, including contract players David Chiang (from TV's *The Water Margin*) and Shih Szu.

The experienced and reliable Roy Ward Baker was assigned to direct, but he found the experience a serious case of culture-shock. Despite Houghton's visit to the Shaw studios, no one saw fit to tell Baker that the facilities available were not exactly on a par with those of Pinewood, or even Elstree. For one thing, the stages were not sound-proofed and films were shot silent, so that they could be dubbed

The Legend of the 7 Golden Vampires (John Forbes-Robertson)

into the different Chinese dialects in post-production. Baker explained some of the difficulties involved to Gary Parfitt in *Little Shoppe of Horrors*: 'There was a clash of cultures,' he said. '[The Chinese] shot their pictures like the Italians used to shoot them years ago, fifteen languages at once and put on anything you want afterwards. You see, you've got to look at it from their point of view. When distributing the picture in the Philippines, Korea, India, all those Far Eastern countries, what language are you going to shoot the bloody thing in? There is no point in shooting with direct sound, but in this case it was agreed that we would shoot in our language—English.'

Unfortunately, most of the supporting players could not actually speak English. 'They had to say their words in Chinese,' Baker went on, 'and in any case, there were eighteen barking dogs and two thousand people all working around you on the sets and reconstructing the studio, going to the canteen and all that sort of stuff. It was absolute bedlam and you could not keep them quiet. They had been making pictures the way *they* had been making pictures for all that time, and for us to come into there and think it was all going to work like clockwork, like Pinewood, was cock-cycd.'

In addition to the communication difficulties between the English and Chinese crews, there were also problems in finding suitable locations. A week into the shoot, Run Run Shaw took a look at some of the footage of a kung fu sequence and ordered it to be re-shot by second unit director Chang Cheh, who had helmed many of the studio's own action pictures. This was not agreeable to Baker so a compromise had to be negotiated, as he explained to Parfitt. 'As far as the kung fu was concerned, I said, "I'm going to film it with my unit. You can arrange the fights, sure, but the way they are covered and presented will be my way of doing it, as it is my picture." And the result is that those kung fu sequences are more effective than the average kung fu sequence in the average Chinese picture, because they've been better photographed

The Legend of the 7 Golden Vampires

The Legend of the 7 Golden Vampires (Julie Ege)

and they've been better directed and the camera being in the right place at the right moment, and the cuts are set to a pattern.'

Because of all the production problems, the film went over budget and came in at some $800,000 HKD. Despite everything, Warner-UK was pleased with the finished product and a British premiere was held at the newly-christened Warner Rendezvous in London on August 29, 1974.

However, it was a sign of the times that Warners again opted not to release the film in the United States. It was eventually put out by Dynamite Entertainment in 1979 under the ridiculous title of *The 7 Brothers Meet Dracula* (or, according to the trailer, *The 7 Brothers and Their One Sister Meet Dracula*) on a belated double-bill with *The Satanic Rites of Dracula*. The decision not to accord it a Stateside release effectively killed *The Legend of the 7 Golden Vampires*; the company that had helped to bring Hammer to worldwide prominence in the 1950s was now instrumental in ending its dominance over the horror genre almost two decades later.

To add insult to injury, *7 Golden Vampires* had performed well on its British release, but not well enough to interest Warners sufficiently, which was currently preoccupied with the global phenomenon of *The Exorcist*.

The Legend of the 7 Golden Vampires (Chan Shen, Shih Szu)

The Legend of the 7 Golden Vampires is far from being one of Hammer's best, but it has gained a cult following with the passage of time. It certainly contains its quota of charms. The cinematography of John Wilcox and Roy Ford features some of the most dramatic colour effects since the days of Freddie Francis and *Dracula Has Risen from the Grave*: interiors are bathed in bright primaries of red or green, giving the film a heightened aura of the fantastic. The exotic locales are easy on the eyes, and the whole production crackles with a compulsive energy that makes it watchable almost despite itself. There is a comic-book feel to the proceedings as a whole—a kind of adventurous abandon when it comes to the conventions of Hammer Horror, not unlike the approach that Brian Clemens took to *Captain Kronos—Vampire Hunter*.

But much of the film is uneven at best. Cushing aside, the acting on the whole is indifferent and the Julie Ege character functions merely as window-dressing. As might have been expected of a Hong Kong 'Hammer', John Forbes-Robertson looks more like a drag-queen in pancake makeup than the Prince of Darkness. His performance, which had to be re-voiced by the ubiquitous David De Keyser, is also on the level of a school production but his appearances are so brief—he serves as 'book-ends' to the story—that *7 Golden Vampires* could easily have done without him altogether (which almost came to pass, but the Shaw Brothers insisted that Dracula be in the film).

Worst of all is Houghton's screenplay, which stretches even Peter Cushing's po-faced performance to the limits of conviction with lines such as, 'The horror is real.. and the whispered word is "vampire".' Even allowing for the simplifications in plotting and dialogue that were thought to be necessary to make the production work for both audiences, Eastern martial arts action does not so much meet Western

The Legend of the 7 Golden Vampires

horror in *7 Golden Vampires* as collide with it head-on—though Baker does his best to keep things moving at such a pace that the absurdities of the script are glossed over in favour of some of the best action sequences that Hammer ever produced. (A memorable scene in which the vampires rise from their graves and march, stiff-legged, to attack a village may look somewhat peculiar to Western eyes, but the Chinese legend of *jiang shi* features reanimated corpses who are forced to 'hop' because rigor mortis prevents them from bending their legs!)

The film is notable not only for Peter Cushing's final outing as Van Helsing but for a farewell score by Hammer 'house composer' James Bernard—even though his surname is mis-spelled 'Benard' in the credits. As part of his attempt to break Hammer into other media, as well as markets, Michael Carreras arranged the release of a soundtrack album of the music from the film, with Cushing acting as 'narrator' in the guise of Van Helsing (a similar album had already been released of Bernard's music from *Dracula*, with Christopher Lee doing the narrative honours). Bernard had been given only two weeks to write the score, and he was forced to pad it out with cues from previous scores for *Taste the Blood of Dracula* and *Frankenstein Must Be Destroyed*, but the result was still one of the best things about *The Legend of the 7 Golden Vampires* and a fitting swan-song for a man who had done as much as anyone to formulate the unique identity that was Hammer Films. A decade after the company's incursion into the world of Asian vampires, Chinese producers belatedly latched onto the idea and created a whole new sub-genre in the image of Hammer's film, beginning with Ricky Lau's horror/comedy/martial arts movie, *Geung si sin sang* (US: *Mr Vampire*, 1985), which kicked off an entire franchise.

While it is doubtful that Houghton ever intended his script to have any sort of subtext, some critics will read spurious analogy into *anything*. *The Legend of the 7*

The Hammer Vampire

Golden Vampires inspired Phil Chandler of www.dvdcult.com to opine: 'Now before you think this movie is all blood and guts and no brains, let me say that this is also a lesson in world history! Think about it. The preyed-on villagers seek assistance from foreigner experts. They are victims of Chinese vampires who are under the influence of a European vampire (which can be interpreted as local Chinese feudal lords working for capitalists who are in the service of Western imperialism). The peasants are unable to combat this alliance and turn to a Western intellectual, Van Helsing (playing the Karl Marx role). The new alliance of Western theory and Chinese peasant.. eventually overcomes the dominion of the local allies led by Dracula. Peace and Prosperity [are] restored much like Chairman Mao and the Chinese Communist Party. So there you have it.'

There *he* had it, at any rate. It can certainly be said that *7 Golden Vampires* was almost a metaphor for its own production: Count Dracula appears in Far Eastern guise (in the film, he assumes the form of a vampiric warlord) and calls on Chinese help to restore him to power and dominance, but he is still defeated by the familiar features and formulaic traditions of Hammer Horror. *7 Golden Vampires* and *Shatter* were such problematic productions for Hammer that Michael Carreras wrote to fellow director Brian Lawrence in March, 1974, 'I doubt if I will ever be able to convey to you the frustrations that have occurred here. It is an episode of my life that I wish to forget as soon as possible. I never want to produce or direct another picture again—it's been that bad.' Michael had promoted Don Houghton to the role of associate producer on the first of the two to help smooth its passage, but the pressure proved too much for Houghton and when filming was complete, he never saw his erstwhile screenwriter again.

The Legend of the 7 Golden Vampires was the Hammer vampire's last, brief expiration of breath as the stake was rammed home—one final, defiant effort in a battle that was already lost. Much had been done in the previous two decades to make the myth acceptable to a modern audience and to formulate in the public's mind the image of the vampire as sexy, sophisticated and scare-worthy, all rolled into one. But despite attempts to ring in the changes with the likes of *Captain Kronos* or *7 Golden Vampires*, it would soon be up to someone else to take the struggle forward. Michael would produce only two more features: *To the Devil—a Daughter* (1976) and *The Lady Vanishes* (1979). Hammer Films was put into receivership in 1979 and the horror genre entered a whole new phase with the rise of the 'slasher' film, inaugurated by John Carpenter's *Halloween* (1978).

Other studios were about to take over Hammer's turf. As Michael had confessed four years before, Hammer could not keep on remaking Dracula—but Universal, 20th Century Fox and Columbia Pictures now felt that *they* could.

> The first blow sent the tent peg in three or four inches, and the sound of a snapping rib grated on the clergyman's ear, so that for a moment he turned his head aside in revulsion. Then, as though alarmed lest his resolve weaken, he struck again, and the blood rose up in a scarlet fountain; a cascade of dancing rubies, each one reflecting the room with its starlike lamp, and the dripping, drenched face of a man with a coal hammer. The hammer, like the mailed hand of fate, fell again, and the ruby fountain sank low, then collapsed into a weakly gushing pool. Carola released her life in one long, drawn-out sigh, then became a black and white study in still life.
>
> **—R Chetwynd-Hayes, 'The Werewolf and the Vampire'/ *The Monster Club* (1975)**

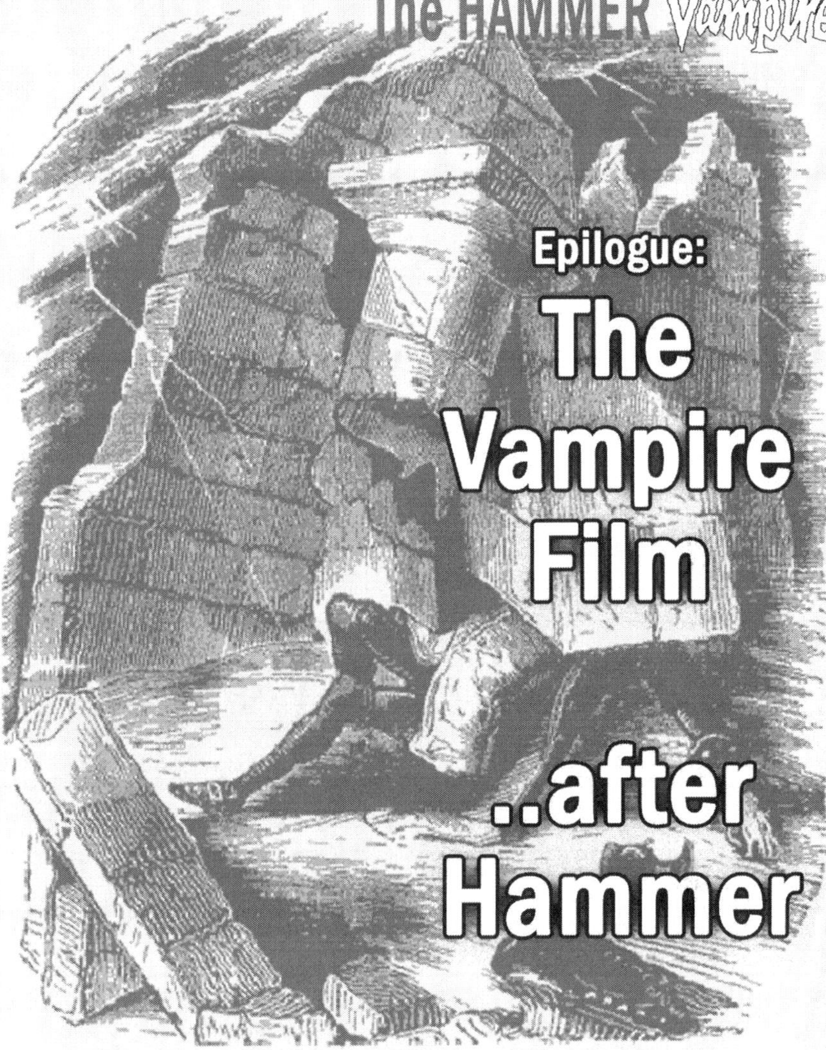

Epilogue: The Vampire Film ..after Hammer

'Now, do you still want the interview?' the vampire asked.

The boy's mouth was open before the sound came out. He was nodding. Then he said, 'Yes.'

The vampire sat down slowly opposite him and, leaning forward, said gently, confidentially, 'Don't be afraid. Just start the tape.'

—Ann Rice, *Interview with the Vampire* (1976)

When he'd caught his breath a second time, he raised his glass in a silent toast. Then he set it down, rose from his chair, and came and stood beside me. He bent forward and gently—very gently—placed his lips against my neck.

—Alan Ryan, 'Following the Way' (1982)

Van Helsing (Hugh Jackman)

By 1974, the first great post-war horror film boom was all-but dead. But like a vampire, it did not die quickly or quietly. There were other disciples tucked away in the darker recesses of the crypt. Clive Donner's British *Vampira* was a supposed horror-comedy starring David Niven as the count, who steals the blood of Playboy bunnies to try to rejuvenate his catatonic bride, but a mix-up with the plasma turns Countess Vampira (Teresa Graves) black and boosts her libido at the same time. This mildly-offensive 'blaxpoitation' caper was released by AIP in the US under the title of *Old Dracula* to cash in on the success of Mel Brooks's *Young Frankenstein*; *Vampira* was written by actor Jeremy Lloyd, but it managed to waste the talents of an excellent cast that included former Hammer stars like Veronica Carlson, Linda Hayden and Freddie Jones. The same year, Udo Kier played the count for director Paul Morrissey and producer Andy Warhol in *Blood for Dracula*, a crassly-amateur take on the myth in which the count restricts himself to the blood of virgins, only to find Warhol 'Factory-stud' Joe Dallesandro getting to his victims before him. Gore and nudity compensated for a lack of virtue in every other department.

By the time burly Ohio-born Michael Pataki got into the act as rapist-vampire Caleb Croft in *Grave of the Vampire* (also 1974) and, later, as Count Dracula himself in *Zoltan, Hound of Dracula* (US: *Dracula's Dog*, 1978), the blood-bank had well and truly run dry.

Vampire cinema had reached something of an impasse.

But within a couple of years, there were the first signs of new blood. Novels like Stephen King's *Count Yorga*-inspired *Salem's Lot* (1975)

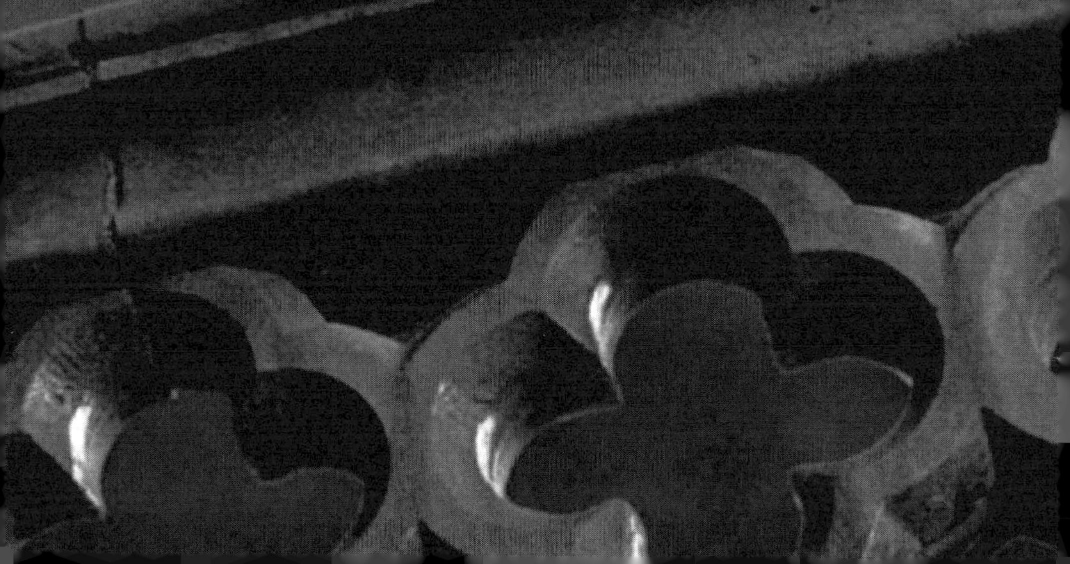

Blood for Dracula (Udo Kier, Joe Dallesandro)

and Anne Rice's more modernist *Interview with the Vampire* (1976) had both been best-sellers and had started readers thinking afresh about nocturnal blood-suckers. The trend continued into 1977, when *Dracula* itself was revived on Broadway with *Diary of a Mad Housewife*'s Frank Langella in the title role. Like Lugosi before him, Langella turned the character into a matinee idol through charm and good looks, and the play became one of the biggest hits of the year.

The inevitable screen version followed in 1979, with Langella reprising his stage-role opposite Laurence Olivier as Van Helsing. Under the stilted direction of John Badham, who previously had helmed the disco-blockbuster *Saturday Night Fever* (1977), the film was a misfire: he and Langella did not get along and the production was compromised as a result. Polanski cinematographer Gil Taylor's lensing was appropriately Gothic but the film as a whole contained little that was new. Badham's *Dracula* was actually a remake of Tod Browning's Universal film of

Dracula (Frank Langella)

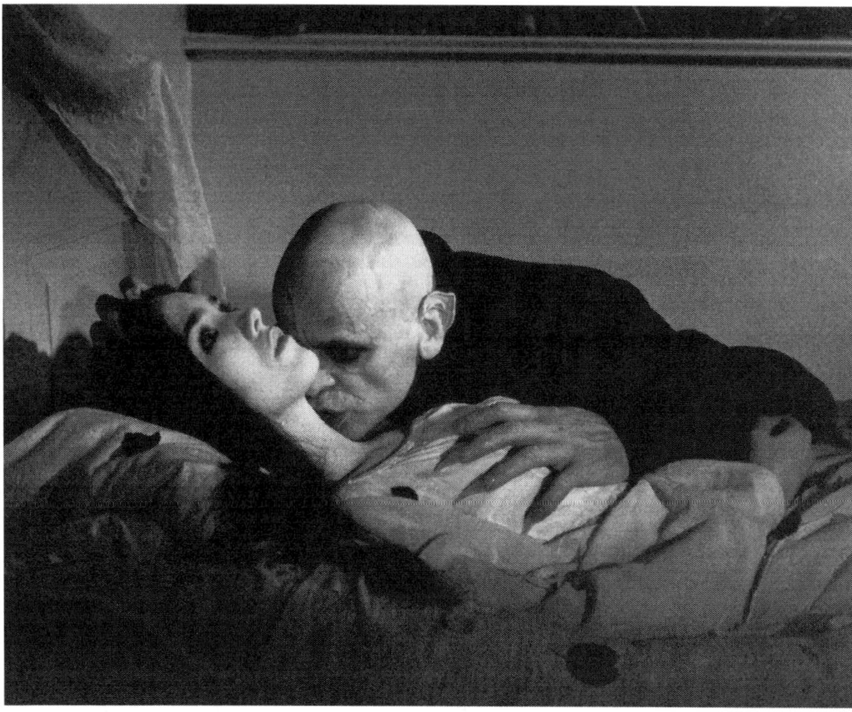

Nosferatu the Vampyre (Isabelle Adjani, Klaus Kinski)

1931, but without its novelty. Langella's refusal to wear fangs ('They're a gimmick,' he was quoted as saying) provided the film with one of its many inconsistencies; Mina not only has fangs but is made up to look like a rotting zombie; when Lucy transforms into a vampire, she also sprouts fangs. Its occasional moments of visual lyricism apart, 1979's *Dracula* was mostly a case of missed opportunity that failed to foster any new franchise.

But a renewed interest in vampires (inspired, in part, by an excellent CBS mini-series adaptation of Stephen King's *Salem's Lot*, directed by *The Texas Chain Saw Massacre*'s Tobe Hooper) encouraged 20th Century Fox to simultaneously finance a reverential remake of *Nosferatu* by German director Werner Hertzog, which was helpfully retitled *Nosferatu the Vampyre*. Herzog cast his friend and collaborator Klaus Kinski as Orlock/Dracula; with his expressive eyes, tortured demeanour and air of barely-contained violence, it was a role that the volatile actor was almost born to play. The film is a visual and aural feast, with music by Wagner and Popol Vuh, but ponderous in the extreme and strictly art-house in approach. Dream-like and surreal it may be but commercial it was not, though it later inspired Augusto Caminito to shoot a sequel of sorts—*Nosferatu a Venezia* (UK: *Vampires in Venice*, 1988)—which returned Kinski to the role but lacked the poetry of its predecessor.

The biggest vampire hit of 1979 was *Love at First Bite*, a broad but affectionate parody of all things Stoker-related with former matinee idol George Hamilton as Dracula, 'Laugh-In' regular Arte Johnson as Renfield, and the amiable Richard Benjamin as a modern-day Van Helsing. The comedy was camp and obvious, but the film proved immensely popular and it seemed for a while as though audiences were still in no mood to take vampires seriously, at least not on the big screen. The count and his cohorts retired to their coffins once more.

In 1983, after several years of gore galore in a hundred 'realistic' horrors from *The*

Omen and *The Amityville Horror* and their various sequels through to the *Friday the 13th* and *Halloween* 'stalk-and-slash' franchises, the screen vampire made a tenuous return in Tony Scott's *The Hunger*, based on Whitley Strieber's best-selling novel. The film featured Catherine Deneuve as a bisexual vampire who seduces both David Bowie and Susan Sarandon. Scott's self-consciously arty direction ensured the film few viewers, however, and the word 'vampire' never crossed the lips of any of the cast, as though the makers of *The Hunger* were embarrassed by the fact that their chic stars and *Vogue*-like visuals were being pimped to the service of a horror film. It was left to Susan Sarandon's husband Chris to raise the genre's game in 1985 and open the way for the vampire film to make the kind of comeback that would so entrench it in the the popular imagination that it would never have to retreat into the dark again.

Released by Columbia Pictures, writer/director Tom Holland's *Fright Night* was a huge success, both critically and financially. Actually a clever reworking of 1958's *The Return of Dracula*, *Fright Night* was a comedy-horror that delivered laughs and scares in equal measure as teen horror film fan William Ragsdale starts to believe that a real-life vampire, in the guise of Sarandon's suave Jerry Dandridge, has moved in next door. *Fright Night* was a conflation of every cinematic trend in vampires from Universal's *Dracula* to *Love at First Bite*, and a lot more besides: Sarandon's saturnine good looks and weary air of sophistication invests Dandridge with the seductive qualities of Lugosi's predatory lounge-lizard; he turns into a bat like John Carradine; his steel-grey leather coat echoes of Baron Meinster's cloak; he sets up shop in a California Gothic mansion like Count Yorga, complete with brutish manservant. The plot of the film borrows heavily from *The Night Stalker*, while comedy is provided with a broad brush by Roddy McDowell's foppish TV host in Vampira mode, 'Peter Vincent (itself a conflation of Peter Cushing and Vincent Price)—vampire killer', and a more subtle one in Ragsdale's attempts to expose Dandridge as a vampire using the 'tried-and-trusted' tests that he has culled from Vincent's TV show. But the real coup of *Fright Night*, apart

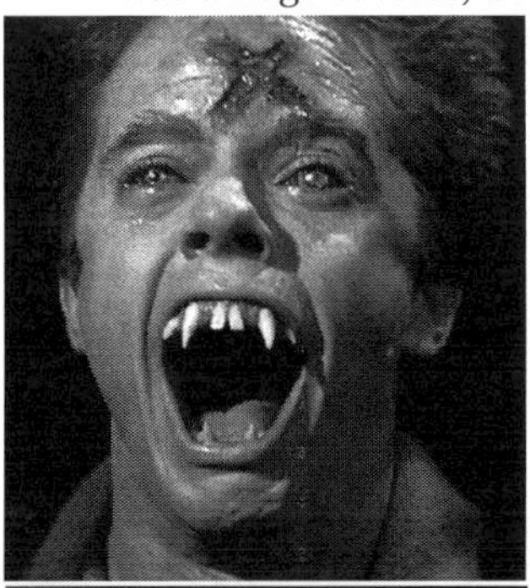

Fright Night (Chris Sarandon)

from its state-of-the-art special effects, was what it brought it to the party from the *oeuvre* of John Badham. Rather than look to the director's version of *Dracula* for inspiration, it made a blatant steal from his *Saturday Night Fever*, so Dandridge the vampire not only charms the ladies with smooth sex-appeal but disco-dances them into his vampiric clutches to the music of Evelyn 'Champagne' King and Sparks.

The vampire, in self-parodying style at least, was back. Now all that remained was for him to return in seriously threatening fashion. Fans of the genre did not have long to wait, as future Oscar-winning director (for *The Hurt Locker* in 2010) Kathryn Bigelow showed only two years later, when she totally reinvented the myth for a more connected audience in her first solo feature, *Near Dark*. Conceived as a modern western but converted to a horror film to increase its pulling power at the box-office, *Near Dark* featured a 'family' of vampires roaming the mid-West in a Winnebago and preying on the inhabitants of outlying towns; en route, they pick up a loner who has fallen for the daughter of the group and he joins them on the journey, little realising the true nature of his fellow-travellers. With its allusions to the Manson gang, its ultra-violence, and Lance Henriksen's typically psychotic turn as vampire patriarch Jesse Hooker, *Near Dark* was a landmark feature in more ways than one, and it was to set a new standard for vampire films. This younger and more dynamic approach to the myth of the vampire was consolidated by *The Lost Boys*, a perverse retelling of *Peter Pan*, with Keifer Sutherland playing the leader of an Un-dead motorcycle gang. *The Lost Boys* became the most financially successful vampire film to date, earning over $30 million for itself in the US alone. Despite indifferent direction by Joel Schumacher, it, too, set a trend in the many 'punk vampires' that have featured in both cinema and television ever since.

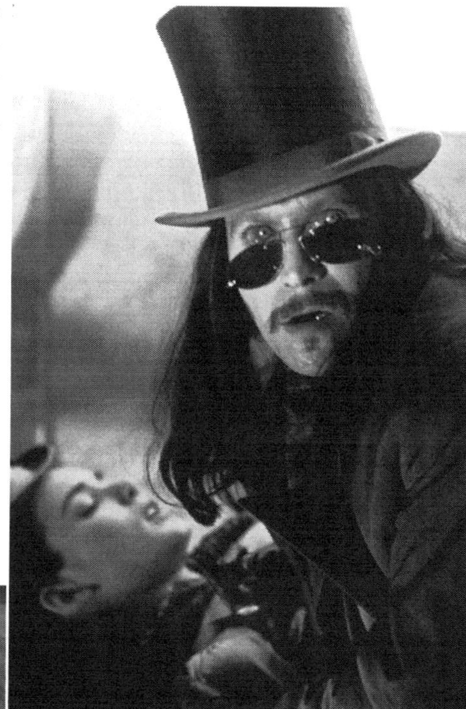

By the early 1990s, the figure of the

Bram Stoker's Dracula (Gary Oldman, Keanu Reeves)

Interview with the Vampire (Tom Cruise, Brad Pitt)

vampire was once again a staple of the horror industry, but his profile had altered to meet the niche-market needs of a fast-fracturing audience who now looked for their jollies not only on the big screen but to graphic novels, to bands, on television and in video games.

As though to celebrate not only the vampire's triumphant return to the screen but also his move from genre films to the cinematic mainstream, Columbia gave *Godfather* director Francis Ford Coppola an unprecedented $40 million to mount yet another big-screen adaptation of Stoker's novel. In 1992, *Bram Stoker's Dracula* brought the original tale to a new audience on the kind of budget that Hammer could only have dreamed of. Visually arresting and extremely bloody, the film's screenplay (by James V Hart) stayed close to the book in terms of incident but was wholly different in tone, and in its treatment of the material; so much so that it is doubtful if the author would have recognised his Count Dracula in Gary Oldman's powdered wig-wearing aristocrat, who looked more like Edith Evans in Thorold Dickinson's *The Queen of Spades* (1949) than a Transylvanian nobleman. Despite some grievous miscasting, such as that of Keanu Reeves as Jonathan Harker (attempting and failing to adopt an Oxbridge accent), and a promotional campaign which also sought to play down its origins in a horror novel in favour of spurious Gothic romance ('Love Never Dies'), *Bram Stoker's Dracula* deservedly won Oscars for Best Costume Design, Best Make-up and Best Sound Editing. The film was hugely successful, taking almost $200 million in ticket-sales, due in no small part to Coppola's grandiloquent, graphic novel-inspired mise en scène, and it set in train a mini Gothic revival which included versions of *Mary Shelley's Frankenstein* (1994, starring and directed by Kenneth Branagh) and *Dr Jekyll and Mr Hyde*, in the guise of Stephen Frears's *Mary Reilly* (1996).

Another high-profile vampire film of the early 1990s was Neil Jordan's 1994 *Interview with the Vampire,* based on the novel of the same name by Anne Rice. The controversial casting of A-lister Tom Cruise as Rice's vampire Lestat proved to be the film's major attraction, and Cruise proved himself to be more than just a pretty face in a ferocious performance, fangs and all. *Interview with the Vampire* took in $220 million against a budget of $60 million.

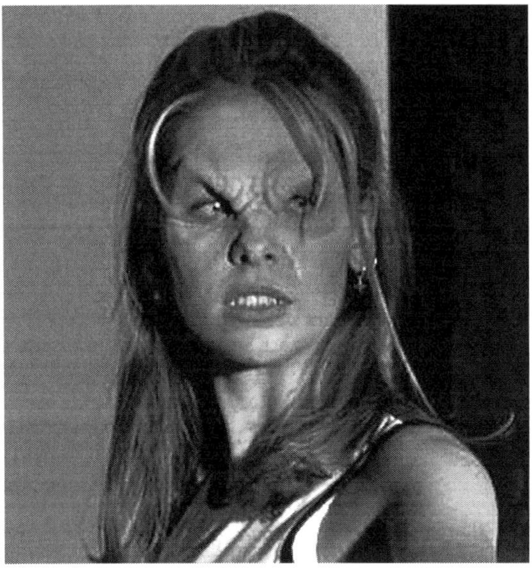

***Buffy the Vampire Slayer* (Sarah Michelle Gellar)**

But the most significant vampire hit of the decade was sired by a film that had been overshadowed at the time of its release by *Bram Stoker's Dracula*. 1992's *Buffy the Vampire Slayer* was a modestly-budgeted horror-comedy starring Kristy Swanson as a high school cheerleader-turned-vampire hunter; five years later, writer Joss Whedon's original script was adapted for television and the resultant series, with Sarah Michelle Gellar taking over the role of 'Buffy', became one of the most successful series ever on the small screen. The show ran for seven years on American television and it inspired a host of imitators, as well as a devoted cult-following.

By the late 1990s, vampires were big business and more variations on the theme were now a matter of course: *From Dusk to Dawn* (1996), directed by Tarantino protégé Robert Rodriguez , was a wild and woolly romp in which George Clooney found himself in a Mexican strip-club filled with vampires, while *Blade* (1998), based on the Marvel comic of that name, was the first in a trio of films to recount the adventures of a half-man, half-vampire who is also adept at the martial arts—shades of *The Legend of the 7 Golden Vampires* perhaps?

News of a Hammer 'revival' also proliferated in the 1990s, as current company owner Roy Skeggs (who along with his co-director Brian Lawrence had prised the business from the hands of the receivers in 1983) sought to maintain franchising interest in the brand by announcing its imminent return to filmmaking at regular intervals, none of which actually came to pass.

The 'humanisation' of the vampire which had begun in the 1980s continued into the new millennium in films like *The League of Extraordinary Gentlemen* (2003), an adaptation of Alan Moore's graphic novel in which a vampiric Mina Harker not only featured as an anti-hero but a superhero to boot, helping to save the world from the dastardly plotting of a Victorian megalomaniac. The wheel was turning full circle and the former fiend was returning to his Romantic roots; in an age of political correctness, the figure of the vampire was now coming to represent the outsider, the social outcast—someone to feel sorry for, to empathise with rather than fear, and whose plight is the solitude of an existence that is dependent on the drinking of blood to survive. This was particularly evident in the *Twilight* novels of Stephenie Meyer, the first of which appeared in 2005. In Meyer's wistful saga, all of

Twilight: New Moon (Robert Pattinson)

the instalments of which are drawn from Romantic literature such as Jane Austin's *Pride and Prejudice* and Emily Bronte's *Wuthering Heights*, a young girl named Bella Swan falls in love with a 104-year-old vampire named Edward Cullen. It was only a matter of time before Meyer's novels found their way to the screen.

Van Helsing (Silvia Colloca, Kate Beckinsale)

Hollywood's intense affair with CGI skewed the trend temporarily, and Dracula continued to show up in more traditional guise in the likes of *Dracula 2000* (2000), in which Gerard Butler played the count in a warm-up for his Phantom in *The Phantom of the Opera* (2004), and Stephen Sommers's mega-budgeted *Van Helsing* (2004), both of which turned out to be multi-million dollar fiascos. Richard Roxburgh's lunatic count in the latter was a Lugosi-accented caricature of his old self, while Hugh Jackman's Van Helsing looked more like Robert E Howard's Solomon Kane and made Bond-style quips every time he despatched one of the film's cartoon creatures with an anachronistic crossbow; the main point of interest in *Van Helsing* was Kate Beckinsale's modishly-corseted vampire-slayer—as it had been also in the previous year's *Underworld*, in which more CGI vampires feuded with CGI werewolves while the intrepid Kate tried to put a stop to the mayhem clad in a skin-tight suit of black leather and wielding a lot of oversized weapons.

Both *Underworld* and *Van Helsing* were out of tune with the public mood, however. The monster of choice in the modern horror film was now the zombie, but exactly half a century after the opening of Hammer's *Dracula*, 2008 was to become the Year of the Vampire. Catherine Hardwicke's *Twilight*, based on the first of Meyer's best-selling novels, grossed more than $300 million worldwide and instantly became the most successful vampire film of all time. On American television, *True Blood*, based on Charlaine Harris's sexier vampire stories, and *The Vampire Diaries*, an edgier version of *Twilight*, went on to take the number one spots on their respective networks. Early in 2009, a Swedish vampire film entitled *Låt den rätte komma in* (UK and US: *Let the Right One In*) was widely welcomed as the most original and inventive vampire film of the decade and was quickly announced for the remake treatment by the newly-invigorated Hammer Film Productions, now a wholly-owned subsidiary of Dutch entrepreneur Jan de Mol's media conglomerate Cyrte Investments. Tomas Alfredsson's stunning feature about a child vampire named Eli who befriends a lonely, victimised little boy was a heart-rending analysis of adolescent angst, and it was hailed by *Newsweek* as 'a vampire tale like no other.. mesmerising'.

But what of the company that started it all? Hammer had been sold into new hands on several occasions since its descent into bankruptcy in 1979, but de Mol's

Let the Right One In (Lina Leandersson)

new acquisition of the company was the first to actively revive Hammer's historic involvement in feature production. The 'new' Hammer, which is effectively a brand-name and not a separate business *per se*, dipped its toes tentatively back into genre waters with a low-budget online serial called *Beyond the Rave*—a vampire film in modern, foul-mouthed dress (and featuring Ingrid Pitt in a small role)—but one that was well enough received to encourage further production. After a false start with witchcraft thriller *The Wake Wood*, which ended up being farmed out to another distributor, Hammer has again announced plans for several films in the horror vein, including a suspense thriller called *The Resident* featuring Christopher Lee, and the aforementioned remake of *Let the Right One In*, to be retitled *Let Me In*.

However things turn out in the future, the influence of the Hammer vampire on the genre as a whole cannot be underestimated. Hammer made the vampire sensual; it removed it from the rigid rules of folklore and turned it into a Romantic icon to be reckoned with, while at the same time investing it with a brute dynamic that gave literal meaning to Shelley's muse on the Medusa as 'the tempestuous loveliness of terror'. In the wake of the Hammer vampire, the screen version of the ancient legend has become sexier (*Embrace of the Vampire*, 1995), more decadent (*The Forsaken*, 2001), more ferocious (*30 Days of Night*, 2007), and more blatantly commercial (*Lesbian Vampire Killers*, 2009). When Hammer remade *Dracula* in 1958, only a relative handful of vampire films had preceded it; since then, and especially in recent years, vampire films are everywhere. The vampire is big business in all media; he inspires a cult following for his various guises like no other monster in history. *Buffy the Vampire Slayer*, *Interview with the Vampire* or even *Twilight* might well have emerged into popular culture without the Hammer vampire as their primary

Lesbian Vampire Killers (Mathew Horne, Vera Vilatova)

influence, but they would likely have emerged in a different form: fangless, sexless and probably quite bloodless too.

The vampire has always exerted a strong pull on the imagination. Vampire films have extended the reach of that fascination to all corners of the globe and to every person on the planet. Their undying appeal was rightly summed up in the American advertising for *Dracula has Risen from the Grave*: 'You just can't keep a good man [or woman] down'. In the case of the Hammer vampire and all that it has inspired, truer words were never spoken.

Filmography

DRACULA
(US: Horror of Dracula)

Cast

Peter Cushing....................Dr Van Helsing
Christopher Lee....................Count Dracula
Michael Gough....................Arthur Holmwood
Melissa Stribling....................Mina Holmwood
Carol Marsh....................Lucy Holmwood
Olga Dickie....................Gerda
John Van Eyssen....................Jonathan Harker
Valerie Gaunt....................Vampire woman
Janine Faye....................Tania
Barbara Archer....................Inga
Charles Lloyd Pack....................Dr Seward
George Merritt....................Policeman
George Woodbridge....................Landlord
George Benson....................Frontier official
Miles Malleson....................Marx, the undertaker
Geoffrey Bayldon....................Porter
Paul Cole....................Lad
Guy Mills....................Coach driver
Dick Morgan....................Driver's companion
John Mossman....................Hearse driver
Judith Nelmes....................Woman in coach
Stedwell Fulcher....................Man in coach
Humphrey Kent....................Fat merchant
William Sherwood....................Priest

Selected Credits

Directed by Terence Fisher
Screenplay by Jimmy Sangster
Based on the novel by Bram Stoker
Produced by Anthony Hinds
Executive Producer Michael Carreras
Associate Producer Anthony Nelson Keys
Music Composed by James Bernard
Music Conducted by John Hollingsworth
Director of Photography Jack Asher BSC
Camera Operator Len Harris
Supervising Editor James Needs
Editor Bill Lenny
Production Designer Bernard Robinson
Sound Recordist Jock May

Production Manager Don Weeks
Makeup Phil Leakey/Roy Ashton
Hairstylist Henry Montsash
Wardrobe Molly Arbuthnot
Continuity Doreen Dearnaley
Special Effects Sydney Pearson/Les Bowie
Stills Cameraman Tom Edwards
Assistant Director Robert Lynn

82 minutes Technicolor
Produced November 11, 1957/
Released June 16, 1958
Rank/Universal-International (US)

THE BRIDES OF DRACULA

Cast
Peter Cushing..............................Dr Van Helsing
Martita Hunt..........................Baroness Meinster
Yvonne Monlaur.....................Marianne Danielle
Freda Jackson..Greta
David Peel..................................Baron Meinster
Miles Malleson......................................Dr Tobler
Henry Oscar...Herr Lang
Mona Washbourne.............................Frau Lang
Andree Melly..Gina
Victor Brooks...Hans
Fred Johnson...The Curé
Michael Ripper...................................Coachman
Norman Pierce.....................................Landlord
Vera Cook..................................Landlord's wife
Marie Devereux...................Village girl/Vampire
Harold Scott...Severin
Michael Mulcaster....................................Latour

Selected Credits
Directed by Terence Fisher
Screenplay by Jimmy Sangster/Peter Bryan/ Edward Percy
Produced by Anthony Hinds
Executive Producer Michael Carreras
Associate Producer Anthony Nelson-Keys
Music Composed by Malcolm Williamson
Musical Supervisor John Hollingsworth
Director of Photography Jack Asher BSC
Camera Operator Len Harris
Supervising Editor James Needs
Editor Alfred Cox
Production Designer Bernard Robinson
Art Director Thomas Goswell
Sound Recordist Jock May
Sound Editor James Groom
Production Manager Don Weeks
Makeup Artist Roy Ashton
Hairstylist Freda Steiger
Wardrobe Mistress Molly Arbuthnot
Continuity Tilly Day
Special Effects Sydney Pearson
Assistant Director John Peverall
Second Asst Director Hugh Harlow

85 minutes Technicolor
Produced January 26, 1960/
Released July 7, 1960
Rank/Universal-International (US)

THE KISS OF THE VAMPIRE

Cast
Clifford Evans..........................Professor Zimmer
Noel Willman...Dr Ravna
Edward de Souza.......................Gerald Harcourt
Jennifer Daniel.....................Marianne Harcourt
Barry Warren.....................................Carl Ravna
Jacquie Wallis...............................Sabena Ravna
Isobel Black..Tania
Peter Madden..Bruno
Vera Cook...Anna
Noel Howlett..................................Father Xavier
Stan Simmons..Hans
Brian Oulton...................................First disciple
John Harvey................................Police sergeant
Olga Dickie..........................Woman at graveyard
Margaret Read..........................First girl disciple
Elizabeth Valentine...............Second girl disciple

Selected Credits
Directed by Don Sharp
Screenplay by John Elder

Produced by Anthony Hinds
Music composed by James Bernard
Musical Supervisor John Hollingsworth
Director of Photography Alan Hume
Camera Operator Moray Grant
Supervising Editor James Needs
Production Designer Bernard Robinson
Art Director Don Mingaye
Sound Recordist Ken Rawkins
Sound Editor James Groom
Production Manager Don Weeks
Makeup Roy Ashton
Hair Stylist Frieda Steiger
Wardrobe Supervisor Molly Arbuthnot
Wardrobe Mistress Rosemary Burrows
Continuity Pauline Wise
Special Effects Les Bowie
Assistant Director Douglas Hermes
Second Asst Director Hugh Harlow

98 minutes Eastmancolor
Produced September 7, 1962/
Released January 26, 1964
Rank/Universal-International (US)

DRACULA—PRINCE OF DARKNESS

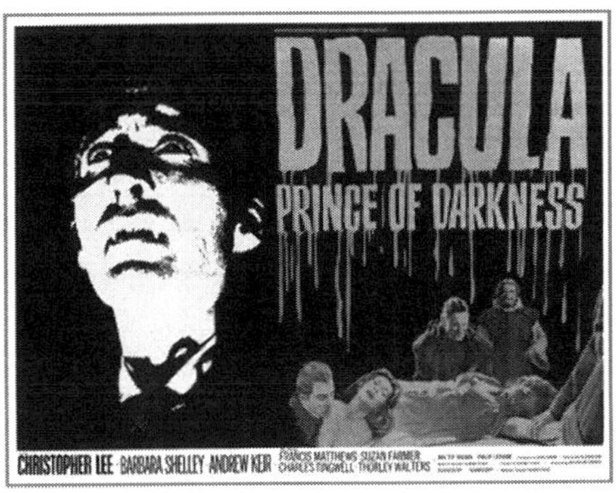

Cast

Christopher Lee	Dracula
Barbara Shelley	Helen Kent
Andrew Keir	Father Sandor
Francis Matthews	Charles Kent
Suzan Farmer	Diana Kent
Charles Tingwell	Alan Kent
Thorley Walters	Ludwig
Philip Latham	Klove
Walter Brown	Brother Mark
George Woodbridge	Landlord
Jack Lambert	Brother Peter
Philip Ray	Priest
Joyce Hemson	Mother
John Maxim	Coach driver
Peter Cushing	Dr Van Helsing

Selected Credits
Directed by Terence Fisher
Screenplay by John Sansom (Jimmy Sangster)
From an idea by John Elder
Based on characters created by Bram Stoker
Produced by Anthony Nelson Keys
Music Composed by James Bernard
Musical Supervisor Philip Martell
Director of Photography Michael Reed
Camera Operator Cece Cooney
Supervising Editor James Needs
Editor Chris Barnes
Production Designer Bernard Robinson
Art Director Don Mingaye
Sound Recordist Ken Rawkins
Sound Editor Roy Baker
Production Manager Ross Mackenzie
Makeup Roy Ashton
Hair Stylist Frieda Steiger
Wardrobe Rosemary Burrows
Continuity Lorna Selwyn
Special Effects Bowie Films Ltd
Assistant Director Bert Batt
Second Asst Director Hugh Harlow

90 minutes Technicolor/Techniscope
Produced April 26, 1965/
Released January 9, 1966
Warner-Pathé/Fox (US)

DRACULA HAS RISEN FROM THE GRAVE

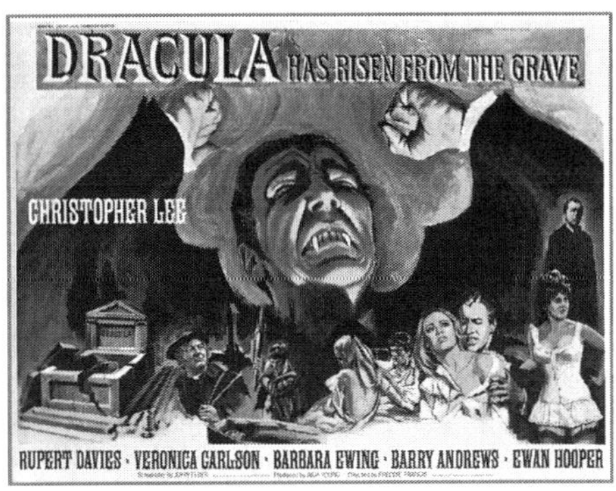

Cast

Christopher Lee	Dracula
Rupert Davies	Monsignor Ernst Muller
Veronica Carlson	Maria
Barbara Ewing	Zena
Barry Andrews	Paul
Ewan Hooper	Priest
Marion Mathie	Anna
Michael Ripper	Max
John D Collins	Student

George A Cooper ... Landlord
Chris Cunningham ... Farmer
Norman Bacon ... Boy
Carrie Baker ... Girl in bell

Selected Credits

Directed by Freddie Francis
Screenplay by John Elder
Based on the character created by Bram Stoker
Produced by Aida Young
Music Composed by James Bernard
Musical Supervisor Philip Martell
Director of Photography Arthur Grant BSC
Camera Operator Moray Grant
Supervising Editor James Needs
Editor Spencer Reeve
Supervising Art Director Bernard Robinson
Sound Recordist Ken Rawkins
Sound Editor Wilfred Thompson
Production Manager Christopher Sutton
Makeup Heather Nurse/
Rosemarie McDonald-Peattie
Hair Stylist Wanda Kelley
Wardrobe Mistress Jill Thompson
Continuity Doris Martin
Special Effects Frank George
Matte Artist Peter Melrose
Construction Manager Arthur Banks
Assistant Director Dennis Robertson
Stunts Peter Diamond/Eddie Powell

92 minutes Technicolor
Produced April 22, 1968/
Released November 7, 1968*
Warner-Pathé/Warner-7-Arts (US)

TASTE THE BLOOD OF DRACULA

Cast

Christopher Lee ... Dracula
Geoffrey Keene ... William Hargood
Gwen Watford ... Martha Hargood
Linda Hayden ... Alice Hargood
Peter Sallis ... Samuel Paxton
Anthony Corlan ... Paul Paxton
Isla Blair ... Lucy Paxton
John Carson ... Jonathon Secker
Martin Jarvis ... Jeremy Secker
Ralph Bates ... Lord Courtley
Roy Kinnear ... Weller
Michael Ripper ... Sergeant Cobb
Russell Hunter ... Felix
Shirley Jaffe ... Hargood's maid
Keith Marsh ... Father
Peter May ... Son
Reginald Barratt ... Vicar
Maddy Smith ... Dolly
Lai Ling ... Chinese girl
Malaika Martin ... Snake girl
with Amber Blare, Vicky Gillespie, June Palmer

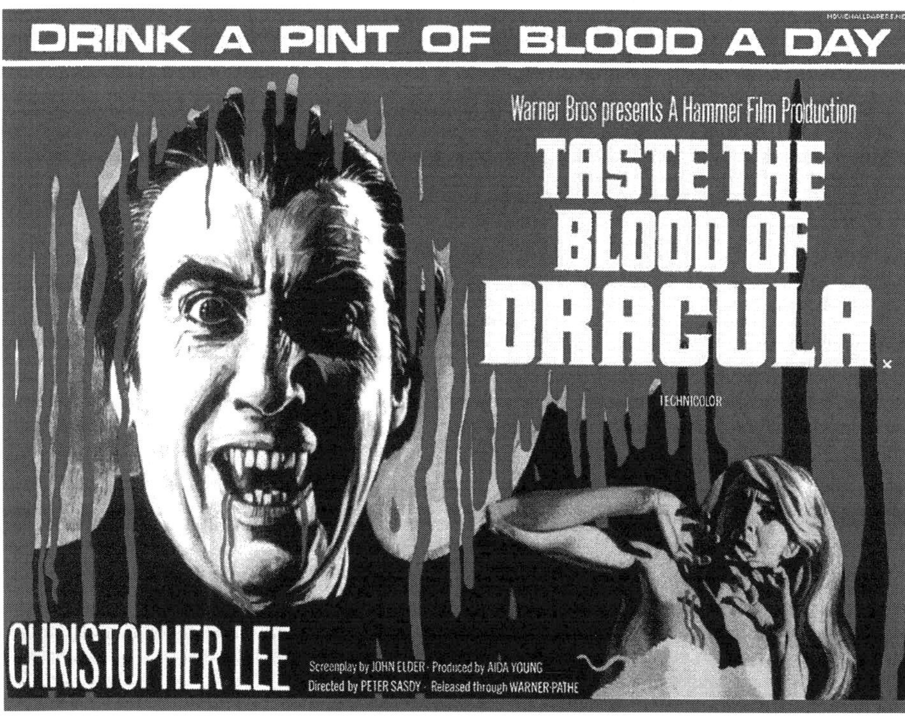

Selected Credits
Directed by Peter Sasdy
Screenplay by John Elder
Based on the character created by Bram Stoker
Produced by Aida Young
Music Composed by James Bernard
Musical Supervisor Philip Martell
Director of Photography Arthur Grant BSC
Editor Chris Barnes
Art Director Scott Macgregor
Sound Recordist Ron Barron
Sound Editor Roy Hyde
Recording Supervisor Tony Lumkin
Dubbing Mixer Dennis Whitlock
Production Manager Christopher Sutton
Makeup Supervisor Gerry Fletcher
Hairdressing Supervisor Mary Bredin
Wardrobe Master Brian Owen-Smith
Continuity Geraldine Lawton
Special Effects Brian Johncock
Construction Manager Arthur Banks
Assistant Director Derek Whitehurst

95 minutes Technicolor
Produced October 27, 1969/
Released May 7, 1970
Warner-Pathé/Warner Bros. (US)

THE VAMPIRE LOVERS

Cast
Ingrid Pitt..............................Carmilla Karnstein
Peter Cushing..........................General Spielsdorf
Pippa Steele..Laura
Madeline Smith...Emma
George Cole....................................Roger Morton
Dawn Addams.................................The Countess
Kate O'Mara...Governess
Douglas Wilmer..............................Baron Hartog
Jon Finch...Carl
Harvey Hall...Renton
Ferdy Mayne..Doctor
Kirsten Betts...................................First vampire
John Forbes Robertson...................Man in black
Janet Key...Gretchen
Charles Farrell.......................................Landlord
Shelagh Wilcocks............................Housekeeper
Graham James...............................1st young man
Tom Browne..................................2nd young man
Joanna Shelley...................Woodman's daughter
Olga James...Village girl
Jill Easter...................................Woodman's wife
Lindsay Kemp...Jester
Sion Probert........................Young man in tavern
Vicki Woolf.........................Landlord's daughter

Selected Credits
Directed by Roy Ward Baker
Screenplay by Tudor Gates
Adapted from J Sheridan Le Fanu's 'Carmilla' e
Produced by Harry Fine/Michael Style
Music Composed by Harry Robinson
Musical Supervisor Philip Martell
Director of Photography Moray Grant
Camera Operator Neil Binney
Editor James Needs
Art Director Scott MacGregor
Sound Recordist Claude Hitchcock
Sound Editor Roy Hyde
Dubbing Mixer Dennis Whitlock
Recording Director Tony Lumkin
Production Manager Tom Sachs
Makeup Supervisor Tom Smith
Hairdressing Supervisor Pearl Tipaldi
Costume Designer Brian Box
Wardrobe Mistress Laura Nightingale
Continuity Betty Harley
Construction Manager Bill Greene
Assistant Director Derek Whitehurst

91 minutes Technicolor
Produced January 19, 1970/
Released September 3, 1970
MGM-EMI/American-International (US)

SCARS OF DRACULA

Cast
Christopher Lee.......................................Dracula
Dennis Waterman.....................................Simon
Jenny Hanley..Sarah
Christopher Matthews..................................Paul
Patrick Troughton..Klove
Michael Gwynn...Priest
Michael Ripper..Landlord
Wendy Hamilton...Julie
Anouska Hempel..Tania
Delia Lindsay...Alice
Bob Todd...Burgomaster
Toke Townley...........................Elderly waggoner
David Leland.....................................First officer
Richard Durden.............................Second officer

Morris Bush....................Farmer
Margo Boht....................Landlord's wife
Clive Barrie....................Fat young man

Selected Credits

Directed by Roy Ward Baker
Screenplay by John Elder
Based on the character created by Bram Stoker
Produced by Aida Young
Music Composed by James Bernard
Musical Supervisor Philip Martell
Director of Photography Moray Grant
Supervising Editor James Needs
Art Director Scott MacGregor
Sound Recordist Ron Barron
Sound Editor Roy Hyde
Recording Supervisor Tony Lumkin
Dubbing Mixer Dennis Whitlock
Production Manager Tom Sachs
Makeup Supervisor Wally Schneidermann
Makeup Assistant Heather Nurse
Hairdressing Supervisor Pearl Tipaldi
Wardrobe Mistress Laura Nightingale
Continuity Betty Harley
Special Effects Roger Dicken/Brian Johncock
Construction Manager Arthur Banks
Assistant Director Derek Whitehurst

96 minutes Technicolor
Produced May 11 7, 1970/
Released October 8, 1970
MGM-EMI/Continental (US)

LUST FOR A VAMPIRE

Cast

Barbara Jefford....................Countess Herritzen
Ralph Bates....................Giles Barton
Suzanna Leigh....................Janet Playfair
Yutte Stensgaard....................Mircalla
Michael Johnson....................Richard Lestrange
Helen Christie....................Miss Simpson
Mike Raven....................Count Karnstein
Christopher Cunningham....................Coachman
Harvey Hall....................Inspector Heinrich
Michael Brennan....................Landlord
Pippa Steele....................Susan Pelley
Judy Matheson....................Amanda
Caryl Little....................Isabel
David Healy....................Raymond Pelley
Jonathan Cecil....................Biggs
Eric Chitty....................Professor Hertz
Jack Melford....................Bishop
Christopher Neame....................Hans
Kirsten Lindholm....................Peasant girl
Luan Peters....................Trudi
Nick Brimble....................First villager
David Richardson....................Second villager
with Melinda Churcher, Melita Clarke, Vivienne Chandler, Erica Beale, Jackie Leapman, Patricia Warner, Sue Longhurst and Christine Smith

Selected Credits

Directed by Jimmy Sangster
Screenplay by Tudor Gates

Based on characters created by J Sheridan Le Fanu
Produced by Harry Fine/Michael Style
Music Composed by Harry Robinson
'Strange Love' sung by Tracy;
lyrics by Frank Godwin
Musical Supervisor Philip Martell
Choreographer Babbie McManus
Director of Photography David Muir
Camera Operator R Anstiss
Editor Spencer Reeve
Art Director Don Mingaye
Sound Recordist Ron Barron
Sound Editor Terry Poulton
Dubbing Mixer Len Abbott
Boom Operator John Hall
Recording Director Tony Lumkin
Production Manager Tom Sachs
Makeup Supervisor George Blackler
Hairdressing Supervisor Pearl Tipaldi
Wardrobe Mistress Laura Nightingale
Continuity Betty Harley
Construction Manager Bill Greene
Assistant Director David Bracknell

95 minutes Technicolor
Produced July 6, 1970/
Released January 17, 1971
MGM-EMI/Continental (US)

COUNTESS DRACULA

Cast

Ingrid Pitt................................Countess Elisabeth
Nigel Green......................................Captain Dobi
Sandor Elès...Imre Toth
Maurice Denham............................Master Fabio
Patience Collier..Julie
Peter Jeffrey...............................Captain Balogh
Lesley-Anne Downe.....................................Ilona
Leon Lissek.................. ....Sergeant of bailiffs
Jessie Evans..Rosa
Andrea Lawrence..Ziza
Susan Brodrick..Teri
Ian Trigger..Clown
Nike Arrighi...Gypsy girl
Peter May..Janco
John Moore...Priest
Joan Haythorne..............................Second cook
Marianne Stone..............................Kitchen maid
Charles Farrell....................................The seller
Sally Adcock...Bertha
Anne Stallybrass......................Pregnant woman
Paddy Ryan...Man
Michael Cadman................................Young man
Hulya Babus....................................Belly dancer
Lesley Anderson/Biddy Hearne/Diana Sawday
....Gypsy dancers
Andrew Burleigh....................................First boy
Gary Rich..Second boy
Albert Wilkinson/Ismed Hassan
....Circus midgets

Selected Credits

Directed by Peter Sasdy
Screenplay by Jeremy Paul
Story by Alexander Paal/Peter Sasdy
Based on an idea by Gabriel Ronay
Produced by Alexander Paal
Music Composed by Harry Robinson
Musical Supervisor Philip Martell
Choreographer Mia Nardi
Director of Photography Ken Talbot BSC
Camera Operator Ken Withers
Editor Henry Richardson
Art Director Philip Harrison
Sound Recordist Kevin Sutton
Sound Editor Al Streeter
Dubbing Mixer Ken Barker
Production manager Christopher Sutton
Makeup Supervisor Tom Smith
Hairdressing Supervisor Pat McDermot
Costume Designer Raymond Hughes
Wardrobe Master Brian Owen-Smith
Continuity Gladys Goldsmith
Special Effects Bert Luxford
Construction Manager Arthur Banks
Assistant Director Ariel Levy

93 minutes Eastmancolor
Produced July 27, 1970/
Released February 14, 1971
Rank/20th Century Fox (US)

TWINS OF EVIL

Cast

Peter Cushing....................................Gustav Weil
Madeleine Collinson...................Frieda Gellhorn
Mary Collinson............................Maria Gellhorn
David Warbeck................................Anton Hoffer
Damien Thomas..........................Count Karnstein
Katya Wyeth............................Countess Mircalla

Isobel Black........Ingrid Hoffer
Kathleen Byron........Katy Weil
Harvey Hall........Franz
Alex Scott........Hermann
Roy Stewart........Joachim
Luan Peters........Gerta
Dennis Price........Dietrich
Maggie Wright........Alexa
Sheelah Wilcox........Lady in coach
Inigo Jackson........Woodman
Judy Matheson........Woodman's daughter
Kirsten Lindholm........Girl at stake
Peter Thompson........Jailer
with Roy Boyd, Maxine Casson, Vivienne Chandler, Doreen Chanter, Irene Chanter, George Claydon, John Fahey, Harry Fielder, Kenneth Gilbert, Derek Glynne-Percy, Cathy Howard, Jason James, Sebastian Graham Jones, Jackie Leapman, Janet Lynn, Annette Roberts, Bill Sawyer, Peter Stephens and Garth Watkins

Selected Credits

Directed by John Hough
Screenplay by Tudor Gates
Based on characters created by J Sheridan Le Fanu
Produced by Harry Fine/Michael Style
Music Composed by Harry Robinson
Musical Supervisor Philip Martell
Director of Photography Dick Bush BSC
Camera Operator Dudley Lovell
Second Unit/Special Effects Photography Jack Mills BSC
Editor Spencer Reeve
Art Director Roy Stannard
Sound Recordist Ron Barron
Sound Camera Operator Stan Samworth
Sound Editor Bill Trent
Dubbing Mixer Ken Barker
Production Manager Tom Sachs
Chief Makeup George Blackler
Makeup Assistant John Webber
Hairdressing Pearl Tipaldi

Wardrobe Rosemary Burrows
Continuity Gladys Goldsmith
Dialogue Coach Ruth Lodge
Casting Director Jimmy Liggat
Special Effects Bert Luxford
Construction Manager Arthur Banks
Assistant Director Patrick Clayton

87 minutes Eastmancolor
Produced March 22, 1971/
Released October 17, 1971
Rank/Universal (USA)

VAMPIRE CIRCUS

Cast

Adrienne Corri........Gypsy woman
Thorley Walters........Burgermeister
Anthony Corlan........Emil
John Moulder-Brown........Anton
Laurence Payne........Mueller
Richard Owens........Kersh
Lynne Frederick........Dora
Elizabeth Seal........Gerta
Robin Hunter........Hauser
Domini Blythe........Anna
Robert Tayman........Count Mitterhouse
John Brown........Schilt
Mary Wimbush........Elvira
Christina Paul........Rosa
Robin Sachs........Heinrich
Lalla Ward........Helga
Skip Martin........Michael
Dave Prowse........Strongman
Roderick Shaw........Jon
Barnaby Shaw........Gustav
Milovan and Serena........The Webbers
Jane Derby........Jenny Schilt
Sybilla Kay........Mrs Schilt
Dorothy Frere........Grandma Schilt
Sean Hewitt........First soldier
Giles Fibbs........Sexton
Jason James........Foreman
Arnold Locke........Old villager
with Anna Bentinck, Nina Francis, Drina Pavlovic, Jenny Twigge and Bradforts-Amaros from Billy Smarts Circus

Selected Credits

Directed by Robert Young
Screenplay by Judson Kinberg
Produced by Wilbur Stark
Music Composed by David Whitaker
Musical Supervisor Philip Martell
Director of Photography Moray Grant BSC
Camera Operator Walter Byatt
Editor Peter Musgrave
Art Director Scott MacGregor
Assistant Art Director Don Picton

Sound Recordist Claude Hitchcock
Sound Camera Operator Laurie Reed
Sound Editor Roy Hyde
Dubbing Mixer Ken Barker
Production Manager Tom Sachs
Makeup Jill Carpenter
Hairdressing Ann McFadyen
Wardrobe Supervisor Brian Owen-Smith
Continuity June Randall
Casting Director James Liggat
Special Effects Les Bowie
Construction Manager Arthur Banks
Animal Adviser Mary Chipperfield
Production Supervisor Roy Skeggs
Assistant Director Derek Whitehurst

87 minutes Eastmancolor
Produced August 9, 1971/
Released April 30, 1972
Rank/20th Century Fox (US)

DRACULA AD 1972

Cast
Christopher Lee................................Count Dracula
Peter Cushing......................Professor Van Helsing
Stephanie Beacham................Jessica Van Helsing
Christopher Neame......................Johnny Alucard
Michael Coles.............................Inspector Murray
Marsha Hunt..Gaynor
Caroline Munro..Laura
Janet Key..Anna
William Ellis..................................Joe Mitchum
Philip Miller...Bob
Michael Kitchen..Greg
David Andrews........................Detective sergeant
Lally Rowyers..Matron
Constance Luttrell..........................Mrs Donnelly
Michael Daly...Charles
Arturo Morris...............................Police sergeant
Jo Richardson..............................Crying matron
Penny Brahms....................................Hippie girl
Brian John Smith................................Hippie boy
Stoneground......................................Rock group
with Jane Anthony, John Franklyn-Robbins and Christopher Morris

Selected Credits
Directed by Alan Gibson
Screenplay by Don Houghton
Produced by Josephine Douglas
Music Composed by Michael Vickers
Musical Supervisor Philip Martell
Songs: "Alligator Man" by Sal Valentino; "You Better Come Through" by Tim Barnes
Director of Photography Dick Bush BSC
Camera Operator Bernie Ford
Editor James Needs
Production Designer Don Mingaye
Assistant Art Director Ron Benton

Sound Recordist Claude Hitchcock
Sound Editor Roy Baker
Recording Director A W Lumkin
Dubbing Mixer Bill Rowe
Production Manager Ron Jackson
Makeup Jill Carpenter
Hairdressing Barbara Ritchie
Wardrobe Supervisor Rosemary Burrows
Continuity Doreen Dearnaley
Casting Director James Liggat
Special Effects Les Bowie
Construction Manager Bill Greene
Production Supervisor Roy Skeggs
Assistant Director Robert Lynn

97 minutes Eastmancolor
Produced September 27, 1971/
Released September 28, 1972
Columbia-Warner/Warner Bros. (US)

CAPTAIN KRONOS—VAMPIRE HUNTER

Cast

Horst Janson....Kronos
John Carson....Dr Marcus
Shane Briant....Paul Durward
Caroline Munro....Carla
John Cater....Grost
Lois Daine....Sarah Durward
Ian Hendry....Kerro
Wanda Ventham....Lady Durward
William Hobbs....Hagen
Brian Tully....George Sorell
Robert James....Pointer
Perry Soblosky....Barlow
Paul Greenwood....Giles
Lisa Gollings....Vanda Sorell
John Hollis....Barman
Susanna East....Isabella Sorell
Stafford Gordon....Barton Sorell
Elisabeth Dear....Ann Sorell
Joanna Ross....Mira
Neil Seiler....Priest
Olga Anthony....Lilian
Gigi Gurpinar....Blind girl
Peter Davidson....Big man
Terence Sewards....Tom
Trevor Lawrence....Deke
Jacqui Cook....Barmaid
Penny Price....Whore
with B H Barry, Michael Buchanan, Linda Cunningham, Steve James, Ian McKay, Barry Smith, Caroline Villiers and Roger Williams

Selected Credits

Directed/Written by Brian Clemens
Produced by Albert Fennell/Brian Clemens
Music Composed by Laurie Johnson
Musical Supervisor Philip Martell
Director of Photography Ian Wilson

Camera Operator Godfrey Godar
Editor James Needs
Production Designer Robert Jones
Assistant Art Director Kenneth McCallum Tait
Recording Director A W Lumkin
Sound Recordist Jim Willis
Sound Editor Peter Lennard
Dubbing Mixer Bill Rowe
Production Manager Richard Dalton
Makeup Jim Evans
Hairdressing Barbara Ritchie
Wardrobe Supervisor Dulcie Midwinter
Continuity June Randall
Casting Director James Liggat
Fight Arranger William Hobbs
Production Supervisor Roy Skeggs
Assistant Director David Tringham

91 minutes Eastmancolor
Produced April 10, 1972/
Released April 7, 1974
Bruton-EMI/Paramomt (US)

THE SATANIC RITES OF DRACULA
(US: Count Dracula and His Vampire Bride)

Cast
Christopher Lee............................Count Dracula
Peter Cushing...................................Van Helsing
Michael Coles............................Inspector Murray
William Franklyn..................................Torrence
Freddie Jones............................Professor Keeley
Joanna Lumley..Jessica
Richard Vernon.....................................Mathews
Barbara Yu Ling..................................Chin Yang
Patrick Barr.................................Lord Carradine
Richard Mathews.......................................Porter
Lockwood West..................................Freeborne
Valerie Van Ost...Jane
Maurice O'Connell..................................Hanson
Peter Adair..Doctor
Maggie Fitzgerald/Pauline Peart/Mia Martin/
Finnuala O'Shannon......................Vampire girls
John Harvey..............................Commissionaire
with Marc Zuber, Paul Weston and Ian Dewar

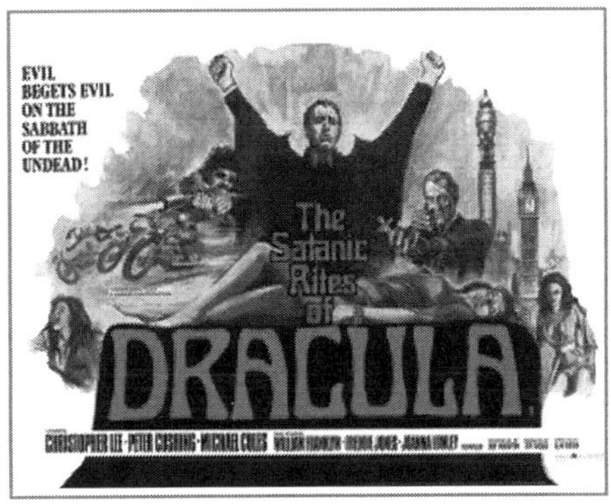

Selected Credits
Directed by Alan Gibson
Screenplay by Don Houghton
Produced by Roy Skeggs
Associate Producer Don Houghton
Music Composed by John Cacavas
Musical Supervisor Philip Martell
Director of Photography Brian Probyn
Camera Operator Chic Anstiss
Editor Chris Barnes
Art Director Lionel Couch
Assistant Art Director Don Picton
Sound Recordist Claude Hitchcock
Sound Editor Terry Poulton
Dubbing Mixer Dennis Whitlock
Production Manager Ron Jackson
Makeup George Blackler
Hairdresser Maude Onslow
Wardrobe Supervisor Rebecca Breed
Continuity Elizabeth Wilcox
Casting Director James Liggat
Special Effects Les Bowie
Construction Manager Ken Softley
Stills Cameraman Ronnie Pilgrim
Production Secretary Sally Pardo
Assistant Director Derek Whitehurst

87 minutes Technicolor
Produced November 13, 1972/
Released January 13, 1974
Columbia-Warner/Dynamite! Entertainment (US)

THE LEGEND OF THE 7 GOLDEN VAMPIRES
(US: The Seven Brothers Meet Dracula)

Cast

Peter Cushing....................Professor Van Helsing
David Chiang..Hsi Ching
Julie Ege..Vanessa Buren
Robin Stewart......................Leyland Van Helsing
Shih Szu..Mai Kwei
John Forbes-Robertson............................Dracula
Robert Hanna................................British consul
Chan Shen..Kah
James Ma..Hsi Ta
Liu Chia Yung..Hsi Kwei
Feng Ko An..Hsi Sung
Chen Tieng Loong.....................................Hsi San
Wong Han Chan..................................Leung Hon
with Liu Hoy Ling, Wai Lo and Te Hsiang Teng

Selected Credits

Directed by Roy Ward Baker
Screenplay by Don Houghton
Produced by Don Houghton/Vee King Shaw
Music Composed by James Bernard
Musical Supervisor Philip Martell
Directors of Photography John Wilcox BSC/ Roy Ford
Camera Operator Roy Ford
Focus Puller Keith Jones
Editor Chris Barnes
Assistant Editor Larry Richardson
Art Director Johnson Tsau
Sound Recordist Les Hammond
Sound Editor Frank Golding
Boom Operator Tommy Staples
Sound Maintenance Dan Grimmel
Production Manager Chua Lam
Makeup Wu Hsu Ching
Hairdresser Peng Yen Lien
Costumes Liu Chi-Yu
Continuity Renee Glynne
Props Master Li Wu
Special Effects Les Bowie
Martial arts sequences staged by Tang Chia/ Liu Chia Liang
Assistant to Producer Christopher Carreras
Production Secretary Jean Walter
Unit Manager Shen Chung
Floor Manager Peng Cheng
Assistant Director Erh Feng

89 minutes Technicolor/Panavision
Produced October 22, 1973/
Released October 6, 1974
Columbia-Warner/Dynamite! Entertainment (US)

Bibliography

Anonymous
Paris views new films and theatres
The New York Times, 15 January 1933
Today's Cinema, 29 July 1957
The Brides of Dracula Pressbook
Universal-International Pictures, 1960

Bartholomew, David
Review of Vampire Circus
Cinefantastique, Summer 1973

Borst, Ronald V
Horror of Dracula: An Analysis of the Hammer FIlm Classic
Photon #27, 1974

Dehn, Paul
The Daily Chronicle, 23 May 1958

Del Vecchio, Carl
I Met David Peel
Little Shoppe of Horrors #12

Dyer, Peter John
Films and Filming, July 1958

Frank, Alan
Interview with Michael Carreras
Little Shoppe of Horrors #4

Glut, Don
Interview with Christopher Lee
Monsters of the Movies #2

Hall, Mordaunt
Nosferatu the Vampire
The New York Times, 4 June 1929

Hibbin, Nina
The Daily Worker, 23 May 1958

Hinds, Anthony
Little Shoppe of Horrors #10/11

Irvin, Sam
Bizarre #3, 1974

Jeavons, Clyde
Monthly Film Bulletin, September 1972

Johnson, Tom/Miller, Mark A
The Christopher Lee Filmography
McFarland & Company, Jefferson, 2009

Kinsey, Wayne
Hammer Films: The Bray Studios Years
Reynolds & Hearn, London, 2002

Klemensen, Richard
Interview with Michael Carreras
Little Shoppe of Horrors #4

Knight, Arthur/Alpert, Hollis
Playboy's Sex in Cinema 2
Playboy Press, Chicago, 1972

Lee, Christopher
Tall, Dark and Gruesome
Weidenfeld & Nicolson, London, 1997
The Christopher Lee Club Bulletin, April-May 1968
The Christopher Lee Club Bulletin, October-November 1969
Lipskin, Larry
The Hollywood Reporter, September 1963
Lumley, Joanna
Stare Back and Smile
Viking, New York, 1989
Luxford, Albert J/Owen, Gareth
Albert J Luxford, the Gimmick Man
McFarland & Company, Jefferson, 2002
Martinez, Oscar
Interview with Andree Melly
Little Shoppe of Horrors #14
McNally, Raymond T/Florescu, Radu
In Search of Dracula: A True History of Dracula and Vampire Legends
Galahad Books, New York, 1972
Meikle, Denis
A History of Horrors: The Rise and Fall of the House of Hammer (Revised Edition)
Scarecrow Press Inc, Lanham, 2008
Miller, Mark A
Christopher Lee and Peter Cushing and Horror Cinema
McFarland & Company, Jefferson, 1994
Owen, Dean
The Brides of Dracula
Monarch, New York, 1960
Parfitt, Gary
Interview with Roy Ward Baker
Little Shoppe of Horrors #4
Pirie, David
A Heritage of Horror: The English Gothic Cinema 1946-1972
Gordon Fraser, London, 1973
Pitt, Ingrid
Life's a Scream: the Autobioigraphy of Ingrid Pitt
William Heinemann, London, 1999
Pryor, Thomas M
U-I plots movie about a vampire
The New York Times, 3 February 1953
Ryan, Alan (ed)
The Penguin Book of Vampire Stories
Penguin, New York, 1987
Sangster, Jimmy
Do You Want It Good or Tuesday?
Midnight Marquee Press, Baltimore, 1997
Inside Hammer: Behind the Scenes at the Legendary Film Studio
Reynolds & Hearn, London, 2001
Sothcott, Jonathan
Little Shoppe of Horrors #14
Stensgaard, Yutte
The Hammer Vampire Film Music Collection, liner notes
GDI Records, 2001
Taylor, Al
Interview with Barbara Shelley
Little Shoppe of Horrors #7

Weiler, A H
Horror of Dracula with Oxford Accent
The New York Times, 29 May 1958
wikipedia.com
imdbpro.com

www.hemlockbooks.co.uk

Hemlock Books is an independent publisher specialising in genre-related film titles, with particular emphasis on horror, mystery and the macabre.